Special issue

Crisis to Catastrophe:

Lineages of the Global New Right

Edited by

Leah Feldman and Aamir R. Mufti

boundary 2

an international journal

of literature and culture

Volume 50, Number 1

February 2023

Duke University Press

boundary 2

boundary 2
an international journal of literature and culture

Founding Editors   Robert Kroetsch and William V. Spanos

Editor   Paul A. Bové
Victoria Glavin, Assistant to the Editor

Assistant Editor   Casey A. Williams

Contents

Introduction: The Returns of Fascism

Leah Feldman and Aamir R. Mufti

This project first began to be conceived in the months after Donald Trump's victory in 2016, and this introduction was written the year following his removal from office, in 2022. In the interim, we, the coeditors, found ourselves increasingly immersed in the development of the so-called alt-right and white nationalism more broadly. We quickly realized that we were seeing the emergence of an assemblage of individuals, movements, ideas, memes, and motifs that was worldwide in its reach, scope, and significance. American white nationalists and self-described national socialists were showing up in neo-Nazi videos in Greece, writers belonging to the Nouvelle Droite in France were receiving standing ovations at conferences of white nationalists in the United States, and an idea like "the great replacement" was clearly able to travel from a fourteenth-century castle near the Pyrenees in France to Christchurch, New Zealand, and to Pittsburgh, El Paso, and Buffalo in the United States.

As we continued our expansive research into contemporary forms of the far right, we also, not surprisingly, began to delve more and more

boundary 2 50:1 (2023) DOI 10.1215/01903659-10192081 ©2023 by Duke University Press

into the literary, political, theoretical, and philosophical archives of Euro-American fascisms of an earlier era. As our research and teaching acquired this new direction, and as we began to realize the enormity of the political, social, and cultural transformations underway, we also confronted with some dismay the seeming indifference of our profession to the catastrophes unfolding in the world around us, reflected in a whole series of evasive and self-destructive tendencies, many of them mutually contradictory—"post-critique" sentimentalism, big-data-obsessed digital humanities, a renewed hyperspecialization, and "new formalism," to name just a handful. We began to recognize that the New Right's attack on critical humanities scholarship (which extends beyond its crusade against critical race theory and queer theory) has accompanied a longer institutional turn toward defunding and eventually eliminating humanist study as the failing (degenerate) arm of the ascending corporate university brand. These aligned shifts within our profession and beyond expose how a late capitalist veneration of an all-knowing market serves to conceal the forms of patriarchal white supremacy that continue to shape our political and social world. Paul Bové takes on this crisis of the academic literary profession directly in his contribution, but this special issue as a whole is the contributors' collective response to this situation both in the profession and in the wider world.

Since the emergence of the Trump coalition in 2015, *fascism* returned to the political vocabulary of the times suddenly and without much intellectual preparation. As events hurtled us forward—or was it backward?—toward some indiscernible catastrophe, many seemed to grasp spontaneously at this relic in the hope that it might deliver an understanding of the present and how we got here, or at the very least give us a stability of orientation as we tried to survive this unsettling and dangerous historical process. But this return of an old concept immediately raised the possibility that this hoary specter from and of another time could easily lead to intellectual paralysis and political ineffectiveness, leaving us permanently lamenting the return of the 1930s in the 2020s. (The meme-makers of the white nationalist Right have a mocking name for this ubiquitous feature of center-left culture—"the current year.") The fact that this concept has entered the political landscape does not guarantee its analytical effectiveness, but it does mean that this efficacy (or lack thereof) is itself a genuine and viable object of analysis. The group effort here is not concerned with developing a global definition of fascism, a concept to encompass a wide range of far-right politics around the world or even just in the Euro-American world. But some things it ought to be possible to say. Between the "fascist maximum" of a radical and militarized state and what Robert Paxton (2005: 206) calls the "elusive 'fascist minimum'" lies a broad landscape of ideas, individuals, movements, political parties, and even state forms. The rush to identify the fascist nature of the Trump phenomenon has sometimes produced facile results—the spectacle of his political rallies being seen through the lens of Nuremberg, for instance, and even through Walter Benjamin's notion of the aestheticization of politics. But in various actions and statements before and after his ascent to the presidency, and in various elements of his movement, aspects of the classic fascism complex have been clearly discernible: both authoritarian and (in Max Weber's sense) "charismatic" leadership of the movement, the followers' cultlike veneration of the person of the leader, the populist identification with "the people" against variously defined elites—Trump as the "blue collar billionaire"—the presence of a frankly white nationalist element—anti-Black, anti-immigrant, and anti-Semitic—within the base of the GOP's electoral coalition, to list merely the most obvious ones.

But what has also begun to be clear over the course of the last six years is that far-right and white nationalist culture in Europe and the United States now not only takes organized political form but also extends across vast areas of culture and society, forms of extension and dissemination made possible by the ecologies of the new media landscape and the growing precariousness of more and more lives lived in the wealthiest zones of global capitalism. From social media forums such as 4chan, 8chan, Stormfront, Reddit, Gab, and the Russian messaging service Telegram to textual and graphic science fiction in all its online variety, an enormous cacophony now characterizes the culture of the far right. Until very recently, far-right content was also available with complete impunity on more mainline platforms like Facebook and YouTube and still often manages to evade their algorithmic restrictions. (And outside the Global North, nationalisms and fascisms of the most violent sort—far-right Hindu nationalism, for instance—still seem to have near complete impunity on these global platforms.) Ideologically, this space is some sort of soup-kitchen slop of anti-liberalism, anti-modernism, white supremacy, Southern nationalism, neo-Nazism, anti-Semitism, "social nationalism," Holocaust "revisionism," white nationalism, white "advocacy," white "identitarianism," "race-realism," anti-feminism, "anti-poz" homophobia, heterosexual and homosexual "manosphere" misogyny, traditionalism, varieties of mysticism, "alt-right" hipsterism, "Orthodox nationalism," and Nordic paganism, to name just some of the more prominent tendencies. In addition to these ideological contents, however, questions of style and form are equally important in understanding this cultural space—irony, parody, satire, and a generalized self-conscious assertion of "joyfulness" and jouissance are among the preeminent stylistic tendencies in this space in which varieties of racism, anti-Semitism, misogyny, homophobia, and xenophobia can be freely expressed in mocking repudiation of the pieties of what is derided as "woke" liberal political correctness and multiculturalism.

The ongoing debates about the applicability of the concept of fascism to our historical moment must not only take all these aspects of the contemporary reality into account but also address the retooling of nativist, settler colonial, and blood and soil narratives of white supremacy. This special issue is meant as a small contribution in this direction and proposes to put on a firmer *conceptual* as well as *historical* footing the possibility of understanding the present political and social crisis as the "return" of the far right as a political culture across the Euro-American world—the United States, Western Europe, Russia—but also in India under the rule of Narendra Modi and the Bharatiya Janata Party (BJP). Wherever possible, we are also interested in examining the links between these regional spaces, links that are organizational, ideational, historical, or socioeconomic, or combinations of several of these. In many cases, from the (now defunct) Traditionalist Worker Party or the Proud Boys in the United States to Génération Identitaire in France, Skandza Forum in the Nordic countries, Jobbik in Hungary, Golden Dawn in Greece, and neo-Eurasianism in Russia, these far-right groupings increasingly see themselves as not merely fraternal organizations but rather as local elements of an assemblage of "white" advocacy across the world, even if the racial concept is often concealed within explicitly territorial, linguistic, or cultural imaginaries. But this growing sensibility and experience of "a worldwide white nation," as the late French neofascist thinker Guillaume Faye (2012) put it in front of an American audience in 2012, is at least in tension with the ubiquitous political and social imaginary of the "ethnostate," which revives the term coined by Wilmot Robertson (1992) in his book of that name. Some of Faye's most influential work is an attempt to defuse this tension and bridge this contradiction. This much ought to be clear: this political and cultural space marks distinct and powerful tendencies in contemporary society that have survived Trump's loss in the 2020 election, and the struggle against them is just beginning. In what ways can an antifascist Left be created and mobilized against this diffuse movement and social imaginary, which (for now at least) eschews institutional state politics, preferring the symbology of tribal and occult rites, conspiracies about high finance and the deep state, the social possibilities of the commune, and the organicism of ethno-nationalism as the ideological foundations of its alternative to the liberal international order? The possibility of an organized and popular Left that is adequate to this historical task at different levels of society remains, we fear, very much an open question.

Many of the analyses of fascism that come to us from the early decades of the twentieth century—for instance, those by Emmanuel Levinas, Georges Bataille, Arthur Rosenberg, Theodor Adorno and Max Horkheimer, Wilhelm Reich, Hannah Arendt, and even Erich Auerbach, to name only some of the most well-known cases—perform various balancing acts between historical explanations and what we might call transhistorical ones, such as psychological (and psychosexual), ethical, or civilizational-spiritual accounts. Against the brutal contextualism and "vulgar" economic determinism of the official Comintern position—"Fascism is the power of finance capital itself"—these early observers of fascism offer deeper indictments of the historical development of the Western bourgeois world over the *longue durée* and its collapse into barbarism in the twentieth century.

But, of course, no analysis of fascisms as historical formations can bypass the question of their relation to the crises of capitalism, a broad question which can itself be reconfigured into a number of more circumscribed ones. With regard to our contemporary moment and to the attempt to reanimate the concept of fascism for analyses of present-day politics, this means at the very least a reconsideration of neoliberalism as a set of economic theories and policy positions and the structural arrangements that have emerged from the interaction of the theories (and theorists) with policy around the world over the last several decades (see Mirowski 2002; Mirowski and Plehwe 2009; Slobodian 2018). It hardly needs pointing out that the two biggest moments in the history of the far right over the last century coincide exactly with the two biggest crises of world capitalism in the same time period, namely, the Great Depression and the Great Recession (the latter taking the form of an outright depression in some regions and countries). Trump's protectionist expostulations during his first campaign and some of the policy decisions that followed during his term in office, such as the abandonment of the Trans-Pacific Partnership (TTP) and the "cold" trade war with China and even the European Union, led some commentators, including such fervent Trumpistas as Patrick Buchanan, to declare too early the end of neoliberal "free trade" and "Washington Consensus" globalism. In this ideological inversion, the GOP, whose base now consists of the white nationalist Right in the country, appears as the party of the (white) working class, whereas the party of the center-left, namely, the Democrats, appears as the party of "special interests" and neoliberal globalization.

The truth of course is quite otherwise, namely, that a host of major policies of the Trump administration and his party in Congress—the relentless (if mostly failed) attacks on Obamacare, the multipronged attack on (primary, secondary, and tertiary) public education, the massive transfer of wealth to the super wealthy through the signature tax bill, and perhaps most catastrophically of all, the chaotic outsourcing of the pandemic response to the private sector, reducing states, cities, and even hospitals in the same city to ruthless competition with each other for the most basic medical supplies, to name just a few of the most disastrous policies—are instances of neoliberal consolidation par excellence in their brutally unrelenting worship of market-centered politics. Against all the talk of antiglobalism and disdain for multilateralism, it would be more accurate to speak of alternative forms of globalization, less multilateral, certainly, but all the more committed to neoliberal arrangements of economies and states. The successful packaging of perhaps the most ostentatiously corrupt crony capitalist and huckster in America as a man of the people bent on clearing out "the swamp" at the nexus of business and politics is a remarkable historical event that needs to be understood in deep sociological, semiotic, and psychological terms, and Donald Pease here offers us a path to such an understanding in his contribution. And Trump's uncanny ability to mobilize a crowd to attack the Capitol and send senators and representatives of both parties scurrying for their physical safety makes crystal clear that he remains at the head of the right-wing mob. Only a fool or a charlatan would now deny that fascism is a mass presence in this country, even if it is not as yet a mass movement.

Much of the post-2016 literature on fascism has taken up the logic of definition and diagnosis, counterposing a schematic ordering of populist and authoritarian movements against the possibility of their creative capacities of reinvention (see Burley 2017; Griffin 2018; Reid Ross 2017; Snyder 2017). Thus, while fascism appears immediate and present in a series of spectacular events—from the Charlottesville rally and riot, resulting in the murder of the young antifascist Heather Heyer, to the massacres perpetrated by white nationalists—it also, at the same time, remains peripheral, unorganized, ever-flailing, and failing. This is hardly a historical novelty, because ascendant fascist movements typically fabricate their mass power precisely from this structural position of peripherality and precariousness in relation to the state apparatus—from their "heterogeneity" to the market and the state, as Bataille ([1934] 1979) already argued in the 1930s. Up to and even including the moment of the seizure of state power, they appear as exogenous to the state apparatus, taking power from the outside through a crisis of party representation, growing militarization, and, more generally, a process of economic, political, and social destabilization (see Belew 2018; Poulantzas [1970] 1979: 331–35). In our present historical conjuncture this enabling peripherality is expressed in the narrative of "white" societies' (and especially their men's) victimization under the sign of "the great replacement."

Among the recurring motifs of a great deal of the culture of the contemporary far right are cataclysm and catastrophe. The "ecopocalyptic" visions elaborated by writers of the far right in France since 1968, from Jean Raspail in *Camp of the Saints* (1973) to Guillaume Faye in *Archeofuturism* (1999) and *Convergence of Catastrophes* (2004), have available to them the work of the older avant-garde of fascio-modernism, including the Italians Julius Evola and Filippo Marinetti, and its veneration of war and a violent hypermodernity. And in the United States, the influence on the contemporary Right of such early twentieth-century proponents of eugenics and environmentalism as Lothrop Stoddard and Madison Grant is wide and palpable—and of course these two had also influenced the official raciology of the Third Reich through the work of Alfred Rosenberg. John Tanton, founding figure of the anti-immigrant and ecological movements in this country, was the publisher who brought Raspail's novel to English-speaking audiences and helped establish it in its present unassailable position in the literary canon of the white nationalist Right. The right-wing apocalyptic imaginary has a quality of "accelerationism" to it, the notion that the only way out of the morass of capitalism and liberalism is a speeding up of their destructive tendencies. As Benjamin Noys (2014: 98, 108) writes, accelerationism "is not merely a historical curiosity, but an aesthetic and political attitude that continues to exert a gravitational pull on the present. . . . The political vagaries of these aesthetic forms of accelerationism do not fall on the tired tropes of fascism and 'totalitarianism,' but rather on this difficult and tense imbrication with the dynamics of capitalism." Alexander Dugin's philosophical crusade in Russia against the post-Soviet incursion of Satanic Western capitalism and liberalism, while traditionalist rather than modernist in its impulses and ideological contents, also carries the imprint of accelerationism in the traces of the constitutional crisis of 1993 and Boris Yeltsin and Yegor Gaidar's violent shock therapy reforms. Leah Feldman's contribution turns to this conjuncture in Russia and its ideological contours.

A transnational approach to reading the contemporary rise of a new right, especially in the United States and Europe, can in part be framed by two historical nodes—1968 and 1989—both crucial moments in the hegemonic institutionalization of neoliberal socioeconomic and political ideas and practices. The historiography of the intellectual scene in France after May 1968 often does not give sufficient attention to the fact that the period saw the emergence of a vibrant intellectual right as well, not just the Left, as Olivia Harrison lays out in some detail here. These new right-wing formations often saw themselves as ideologically distinct from the mid-century Right, from Catholic monarchism, for instance, and some of their thinkers, above all Alain de Benoist, were influential more than two decades later in post-Soviet Russia in the 1990s. The French New Right saw itself as a response to what it considered the "Marxist revolution" of 1968 (see Faye 2012). But it quickly became aligned with the National Front in its focus on postcolonial immigration and, with the collapse of the Soviet Union and the disappearance of its satellite states in Eastern Europe, turned its attention to what it correctly saw as the stunning expansion to hegemonic status worldwide of US-led neoliberalism, which its thinkers condemned for its reducing of a rich tapestry of human populations to an undifferentiated mass of producers and consumers.

In turn, the fall of the Soviet Union led to a distinct process of the rise of the New Right in its former zone—former communists morphing into right-wing nationalists in the midst of the application of neoliberal shock therapy to entire populations as a matter of routine policy. The aggravation of the class struggle that accompanied these violent economic transformations contributed to the rise of anti-liberal ethno-nationalisms in the post-Soviet world, often armed with "post-secularist" critiques of Western liberalism and secularism. To a significant extent this development of the Right alongside the Left from the late 1960s on was an international development, with resurgent neoreactionary movements and parties emerging to respond to the political, social, and cultural protest movements of the previous decade, in some cases leading to the overthrow of democratically elected progressive governments in military coups d'état more or less supported by the Western powers—Chile and Pakistan immediately come to mind.

Russia and the former Soviet states have particularly come to be associated with a resurgence of authoritarianism, which has only accelerated with Putin's invasions of Ukraine in 2014 and 2022. However, despite these renewed encroachments, transformations of the right-wing and nationalist sort across post-Communist Eastern Europe have been accompanied by unexpected geopolitical realignments. For instance, despite the living memory of the Soviet invasion of Budapest in 1956 and Putin's recent invasion of Ukraine, which has only enlivened the already persistent presence of anti-Russian sentiment in Hungary's political culture, Hungary's resurgent nationalist Right displays a marked political warming toward Russia. Viktor Orban's celebration of "illiberal democracy" is politically aligned with Putin's internal vision for Russia and his geopolitical vision of an alternative political and social axis to the forces of Western liberalism and globalism. Hungary in fact has emerged as a global beacon for white nationalists—many Americans have chosen to move there—and Arktos, the main English-language translator and publisher of the works of the European and Russian right, including those by De Benoist, Faye, and Dugin, was founded there in the second decade of this century. It briefly even drew to its senior staff a representative of the "neo-Aryan" tendency in the monarchist Iranian diaspora. The dissemination of these materials to the Anglophone reading public has played no small role in disseminating the social imaginary of "the worldwide white nation" to white nationalists in the Anglo-Saxon world. The three figures mentioned above are routinely cited by such individuals in the US alt-right as Richard Spencer, Matthew Heimbach, Jared Taylor, and Matthew Raphael Johnson as major influences.

The question for us is not whether or not Donald J. Trump, Vladimir Putin, or Narendra Modi (or even Steve Bannon, Stephen Miller, Alexander Dugin, Alain de Benoist, or any one of a host of other more macabre acolytes) *is* a fascist but whether and to what extent fascist tendencies in US culture and society have emerged and coalesced around Trump's 2016 campaign, then his presidency, and now his conspiracy-driven grievance crusade, and whether and to what extent these social forces are in a position to redefine aspects of social relations—race and gender relations, for instance—and of culture. What answers we find to such questions, which are the domain of the critical humanities, will also help us understand whether and to what extent these social and political forces are capable of again seizing control of the presidency or of elements of the state despite the liberal-constitutional regime of "checks and balances," which has been put under severe pressure repeatedly since 2017, although it also has clearly survived that onslaught. Fascism may not be *in power* in the United States, or in any European country, but at the very least it has been *empowered* by a whole series of political developments, including Brexit, the Trump phenomenon, Putin's invasion, the reelection of Orban, and the near-election of Le Pen. Equally remarkable and disturbingly closer to home is the apparently seamless appropriation by the far right of aspects of the contemporary humanities—ideas linked to postcolonial critique, cultural studies, queer studies, and minority rights discourse: immigrants and their children are routinely spoken of as a colonial occupation force; whites are viewed as a marginalized minority in their own homelands; queerness is envisioned through violent ritual performances of white masculinity; and, recently, whites have even come to be referred to as stateless, peoples without a state that they can call their own. It is a fundamental task of the critical humanities in these times to understand these acts of appropriation of their ideas and formulate adequate responses to them.

As we confront this new social, cultural, and political landscape, it becomes dismally apparent that the humanities in the academy have been too often oblivious to these social, cultural, and political forces in recent years—including the appropriation of parts of their own discourse by white nationalists. Clearly, some of the most vaunted new trends in the literary profession—world literature, big-data-driven literary history, or postcritique, for instance—aim to depoliticize the practice of criticism and scholarship in their distinct ways, often explicitly so. Seeking to build a broad critical-intellectual approach to the crisis of the present moment, this special issue of *boundary 2* takes up the call outlined by Edward Said for a worldly orientation for criticism as an intellectual practice and form of writing, which he elaborated as an agile, alert, and skeptical orientation of thought in the world, seeking to expose the hierarchies of Culture and Value, on the one hand, and, on the other, the false comforts of critical-ideational systems, political or theoretical positions worked out fully in advance, merely awaiting their "application" to this or that context or body of material.

This special issue calls for such a worldly orientation to criticism as it considers the reemergence of New Right political cultures in several parts of the world. Donald Pease demarcates and analyzes the workings of the constituent power of the Trump coalition and its near complete takeover of the Republican Party. The Trumpist New Right, he argues, marks a return to a variant of liberalism initiated by American settler colonists' expansionist politics. Attending to Birtherism, the Charlottesville protests, and the January 6th uprising, Pease argues that Trump levied his attack on liberal-democratic institutions and principles by lending the insurrectionists presidential-institutional support. Leah Feldman discusses the rise of Alexander Dugin's (2000) Eurasianist "fourth" political theory and traces lines of influence and continuity between Dugin and such movements as the French Nouvelle Droite, Hungarian Jobbik, and the US Traditionalist Workers Party. She argues that these New Right movements have generated a white supremacist neo-traditionalist politics in response to the global political and economic shifts following the collapse of the Soviet Union. She concludes by analyzing how the emergence of a conservative vanguard and its vision of neo-imperial messianism and authoritarian "neo-trad" multipolarity have shaped discourse around the war in Ukraine. Olivia Harrison turns to the post-1968 moment to expose the emergence of a fantasy of white minority status and white nativism within the French New Right as an attempt to recuperate a "reverse decolonial" politics in defense of a white nativist vision of France, revealing white supremacy's foundations in the invention of race in the colonial laboratory. The pandemic's occasioning of authoritarian state expansion further turns this issue's focus to ecofascist visions of the end of times. Through a comparative reading of ecofascist literature alongside Bong Joon-ho's South Korean thriller *Parasite*, April Anson and Anindita Banerjee attend to ecofascist literary imaginaries that are at once global and virally settler colonial, highlighting the continuities between climate catastrophe and paranoias of demographic extinction that scale at the level of the everyday and proximate.

Aamir R. Mufti draws our attention to contemporary India and the rise to near hegemony not just of the ruling party but of what he calls Hindutva power, which works through both the transformation of the exercise of sovereign power and the inculcation of a distinct habitus in more and more sectors of society. This Hindu supremacist and nationalist habitus marks a far-reaching transformation not only of democratic political culture but of religious belief and practice as well. But despite their sense of inevitability, he argues, these developments are part of a scene of contestation and the staging of pro-democracy and antifascist dissent. Finally, tracing a historical arc to the epistemological shift at the end of the Cold War and emergence of new technologies of rule within the university, Paul Bové exposes a corrosive shift in humanities scholarship amid a growing technocratic corporatization in the profession beginning in the late 1970s, which has displaced criticism for high theory-driven narratives that conceive of themselves as derived from literary study but as independent of and indeed prior to literature. This turn away from criticism was accompanied by the popularization of new jargons and subfields and "studies" from digital humanities to world literature, that is, technocratic orders tied to mainstream institutions that aimed to provide career possibilities at a moment when the state investment in the literary humanities began to wane with the end of the Cold War.

Exposing some of the ways in which the violence of neoliberal capitalism has been absorbed by our own institutions and profession in this moment of fascist returns, like the corporatized remaking of an entrepreneurial humanities, this special issue offers a reminder of the necessity to return to criticism and to the possibilities of understanding the human through poetry and literature. By drawing our collective attention to the globalization of a New Right political culture, it seeks to call us to a skeptical and worldly criticism and pedagogy against some of the most powerful tendencies in the profession as well as the wider world.

References

Bataille, Georges. (1934) 1979. "The Psychological Structure of Fascism." *New German Critique*, no. 16: 64–87.

Belew, Kathleen. 2018. *Bring the War Home: The White Power Movement and Paramilitary America*. Cambridge, MA: Harvard University Press.

Burley, Shane. 2017. *Fascism Today: What It Is and How to End It*. Chico, CA: AK Press.

Dugin, Alexander. 2000. *Osnovy Geopolitiki*. Moscow: Arktogeia.

Faye, Guillaume. (1999) 2010. *Archeofuturism: European Visions of the Post-catastrophic Age*. Translated by Sergio Knipe. London: Arktos.

Faye, Guillaume. 2012. "Europeans and Americans: Brothers in Arms." American Renaissance Conference. YouTube video, 0:55:41. https://www.youtube.com/watch?v=pYc-IEFVU2E.

Griffin, Rodger. 2018. *Fascism: Key Concepts in Political Theory*. Cambridge: Polity.

Mirowski, Philip. 2002. *Machine Dreams: Economics Becomes a Cyborg Science*. Cambridge: Cambridge University Press.

Mirowski, Philip, and Dieter Plehwe. 2009. *The Road from Mont Pèlerin: The Making of the Neoliberal Thought Collective*. Cambridge, MA: Harvard University Press.

Noys, Benjamin. 2014. *Malign Velocities: Accelerationism and Capitalism*. London: Zero.

Paxton, Roger. 2005. *The Anatomy of Fascism*. New York: Vintage.

Poulantzas, Nicos. (1970) 1979. *Fascism and Dictatorship: The Third International and the Problem of Fascism*. Translated by Judith White. London: Verso.

Raspail, Jean. (1973) 2013. *Camp of the Saints*. Petoskey, MI: Social Contract Press.

Reid Ross, Alexander. 2017. *Against the Fascist Creep*. Chicago: AK Press.

Robertson, Wilmot. 1992. *The Ethnostate*. Cape Canaveral, FL: Howard Allen Enterprises.

Slobodian, Quinn. 2018. *Globalists: The End of Empire and the Birth of Neoliberalism*. Cambridge, MA: Harvard University Press.

Snyder, Timothy. 2017. *On Tyranny: Twenty Lessons from the Twentieth Century*. New York: Tim Duggan.

Preemptive Impunity: The Constituent Power of Trump's Make America Great Again Movement

Donald E. Pease

Introduction: Trump's Revivification of Settler Colonist Conquest Culture

For close to a quarter century, members of the foreign policy community throughout the transatlantic world embraced Francis Fukuyama's thesis in *The End of Ideology and the Last Man* that with the dissolution of the Soviet Union and the dissemination across the planet of the triumphant US model of liberal democracy, humankind had arrived at the end point of its ideological evolution. Fukuyama (1992) said it was the exhaustion of a systematic, viable alternative that sealed the comprehensive victory of US-style liberal democracy. Yet voters who cast ballots in electoral insurrections that mushroomed across European countries in 2016 and 2017 threw this consensus into crisis when they stood united in their revolt against this model of global governance (Zielonka 2018; Holmes and Krastev 2020). Milestone events included the 2016 UK vote to secede from the EU, the drastic increase of support for France's National Front, the insurgence of

boundary 2 50:1 (2023)   DOI 10.1215/01903659-10192102   ©2023 by Duke University Press

the anti-establishment Five Star Movement in Italy and the ANO party in the Czech Republic, the decision by leaders of right-center parties in the Netherlands and Austria to embrace the policies of the Far Right to secure victories in the March 2017 Dutch and the October 2017 Austrian parliamentary elections, the mutation of Hungarian prime minister Viktor Orbán's campaign platform into the template of governance for Poland's Law and Justice Party, and the elevation of the reactionary Alternative für Deutschland into the Bundestag.[1]

Political commentators have customarily sorted the 2016 US election of Donald J. Trump into this series.[2] However, if we situate Trump's election wholly within the context of these European revolts against the hegemony of the US model of liberal democracy, we risk losing sight of Trump's anomalous relationship to liberal democratic institutions and principles as well as the liberal international order founded on them.[3] Trump differs from other political figures in this series because he is at once the elected head of the world's most powerful liberal democracy and the self-declared leader of an insurrectionary movement whose members are intent on subverting the foundational principles of US liberal democracy and dismantling its core institutions.

During his term in office, Trump introduced difficult to reverse changes in representations of the United States and its historic role in the world. Unlike nearly all his predecessors in the Oval Office, Trump refused to

1. In *The Light That Failed: Why the West Is Losing the Fight for Democracy*, professor of law Stephen Holmes and political theorist Ivan Krastev have argued that Europeans who refused to emulate the United States' model of liberal democracy did so because they no longer needed to regard liberal democracy as the only acceptable method of organizing collective life. Across nations in post–Cold War Europe, liberal democratic norms and institutions did not protect the rights of minoritized populations oppressed by the state; they functioned instead as an ideological state apparatus under the control of political and media elites.

2. For representative examples of this trend, see Judis 2016; Müller 2016. Both Judis and Müller define liberal democracy as a structure of governance that values popular sovereignty and majority rule but that aims to avoid the emergence of the "tyranny of the majority" through institutions—an independent judiciary, a free press, regulatory agencies—commissioned to guarantee the protection and fundamental rights of minorities.

3. Several notable figures in the foreign policy community consider Trump's actions in the national and international arenas as a two-tiered strategy designed to decouple US hegemony from the liberal norms and institutions that formerly legitimated US global dominance nationally and internationally, and to inaugurate what the MIT political theorist Barry Posen (2018) has described as a grand strategy of "illiberal hegemony."

identify American democracy as historically unique, morally superior, or ideologically exceptional. Trump considered the obligation to maintain the nation's reputation as the world's exemplary liberal democracy an impediment to the United States' assertion of economic and military dominance. He replaced Fukuyama's ideological valuations with strictly economic criteria to determine the winner and loser of a geopolitical contest. Regarded from Trump's perspective, winning entailed the rejection of any moral or ideological responsibilities that might interfere with getting the better of a potential adversary. In a ruthlessly competitive world, Trump believed that only a loser would choose to be tethered to moral constraints (Holmes and Krastev 2020). With the postwar economies of Japan and Germany as case in point, Trump complained that the United States had no business rehabilitating enemies that it had decisively conquered in World War II into competitors in international trade. Why, Trump wondered, should the United States Americanize nations it intended to dominate militarily and economically?

And yet, as the political theorists Jan-Werner Müller (2016) and John B. Judis (2016) have sagely observed, no matter how much Trump may have wanted to decouple the US populace from long-standing liberal principles and institutions, neither he nor the participants in the Make America Great Again movement are antagonistic to American democracy as such. Building on Judis's and Müller's observations, Fareed Zakaria (1997, 2016) diagnosed the Trump movement's antipathies as the symptomatic disposition of a globally ascendant political formation that he calls "illiberal democracy" whose participants pose a special danger to the norms and institutions of American liberal democracy. In her 2017 monograph, *Undoing the Demos*, Wendy Brown (2017: 208) indicated the dire consequences of this emergent political formation when she warned that if American liberal democracy were ever to be fully supplanted by this illiberal alternative, a foundational "platform of critique" and "source of radical democratic inspiration and aspiration" would disappear altogether from US political culture. While in office, Donald Trump nonetheless based his mode of governance on the supposition that America's return to global dominance necessitated severance from the liberal principles and institutions that Zakaria and Brown believe foundational to US national identity.

For at least the last seventy-seven years of United States history, the liberal strand of American democracy seemed so deeply interwoven in its political fabric that it could not be pulled apart without doing irreparable damage to the nation. How are we to understand the Americanness of a populist movement notorious for its attacks on equal rights, civil liberties, constitutionalism, and basic norms of tolerance and inclusion? How and why have freedom and legitimized social hierarchies and exclusions become fused in Trump's America? What causative factors can explain the emergence within twenty-first-century US political culture of Trump's Make America Great Again movement (Brown, Gordon, and Pensky 2018)? Across the post–World War II era, weren't US citizens instructed to expect this sort of intolerant and uncivil behavior from the illiberal totalitarian Other against whose mode of fascist governance US liberal democracy was set in a relation of insuperable enmity? In their efforts to respond to such questions, prominent historians, political commentators, and theorists have correlated Trump's rise to political power in terms of his transmogrification of a large segment of the American populace into the nation's fascist totalitarian Other (Snyder 2021). While Trump's illiberal pronouncements and actions do indeed bear a resemblance to the political behavior of European fascists, the Americanness of Trump's conquest disposition might be better understood as his resurrection of an archaic variant of liberalism practiced by American settler colonists (Robinson 2017; Rana 2010).

Accounts of the nation's origins premised on Alexis de Tocqueville's exceptionalist assumptions pass along a historical narrative that describes American democracy as based on the political ideals of individual liberty, equality, rule of law, and consent, emanating from Enlightenment centers in Europe to the nation's founders and onto the rest of the globe. According to de Tocqueville (2000), Americans were shielded from the inegalitarian difficulties plaguing Europe, and its earliest leaders essentially solved the problems posed by feudalism and class conflict. However, as a matter of historical fact, the nation emerged from revolt and warfare, and the historical agents responsible for the nation's emergence were Anglo-American settler colonists whose freedom practices were incompatible with European Enlightenment ideals of liberty and equality. Anglo-American settler colonialism complicates colonialism understood as a relationship to a distant ruling authority in that Anglo-American settlers did not simply extract wealth and return to the metropole (Rana 2010; Veracini 2021). Anglo-American settler colonists displaced Indigenes and replaced them on the land they expropriated.

In *Johnson v. McIntosh*, Chief Justice John Marshall ruled that when American settlers won independence from England, they acquired through this victory exclusive right to extinguish American Indian entitlement to occupancy and retroactively disallowed Native Americans the condition of ownership that the court defined as an exclusively Euro-American faculty that did not preexist the right of discovery. Echoing John Locke, Justice Marshall described American Indians' uncultivated relationship to land as proof there was no inherent right to property and that only the appropriation of land through labor provided the rights of ownership. Since Marshall the constitutional justifications for American liberal individualism have been that rights are given substance by property, and made private in acts of appropriation settled through entitled ownership, which in turn is the basis for the self-determination of possessive individuals (Bruyneel 2021; Young 2018; Wolfe 2016).

The settlement of America involved the expropriation of land, a campaign of genocidal violence against the land's inhabitants, the exploitation of the labor power of slaves forcibly uprooted from Africa, and a successful revolution against a European imperial power. Establishment histories and popular fictions of the nation's beginnings routinely disaggregate American settler colonists' successful overthrow of British tyranny from their freedom practices of enslavement and American Indian killing (Anker 2022). Such popular accounts invariably refuse to acknowledge that the precondition for the settler colonist understanding of American liberty was "both the expansion of slavery and the expropriation of indigenous groups" (Rana 2010: 22). In his 2010 monograph *The Two Faces of American Freedom*, the historian of law Aziz Rana redressed this lapse by excavating the military, economic, and legal apparatuses interconnecting American settlers' notions of individual personhood, self-rule, free trade, private property, and other core values of American liberal democracy with the practices of Indigenous dispossession, enslavement, economic exploitation, environmental devastation— what Rana calls the "second face of American freedom"—responsible for their development.

Acts of nation-making violence constitute the infrastructure for the "settler liberal" notions of freedom underpinning American liberal democracy. For more than three centuries settler colonialism set the ideological and structural parameters for collective life and provided the basic governing framework for American life (Rana 2010). American conceptualizations of freedom as founded on the rejection of state tyranny, self-governance, rule of law, and uncoerced labor were intricately dependent on settler colonists' violent expropriation of Native land, subjugation of American Indian populations, law-making frontier violence, indentured servitude, and slave labor. In *The Two Faces of American Freedom*, Rana explains that throughout US history the right to individual liberty and the emancipation from tyranny were inextricably tied to the right to dispossess, the freedom to exploit, and the power to oppress.[4] Aspirations for economic independence and democratic self-rule were deeply enmeshed in assumptions about settler imperial power and the need for external rule and control over Indigenous and dependent communities, and these assumptions in turn rested on a project of continual expansion and the formation of an imperial settler state.

Rather than an unevolved historical trace, settler colonialism might be understood as a precondition for the emergence of both Trump's unemancipatory democratic movement as well as the principles and institutions of liberal democracy to which Trumpists are inalterably opposed (Young 2018; Bruyneel 2021). Trump was speaking as the avatar of a twenty-first-century settler conqueror when he expressed the intention to liberate himself from any and all obligations, responsibilities, or commitments that might hobble his drive to "keep winning" (Anderson 2017). Trump discovered that it was his particular fondness for this persona that enabled him so gladly to countenance the interdependence of American civilization and the acts of barbarism that achieved it (Young 2018).

Trump models the subversively archaic disposition of settler colonists who exercised the rights of conquest and ostentatiously displayed the freedom practices of exploitation and extractive and predatory capitalism (Herzfeld 2021). With this settler conquest disposition as retrotopian warrant, participants in Trump's movement take delight in connecting their individual and collectively shared experiences of freedom to preexisting social hierarchies (Bauman 2017); they correlate self-reliance to anti-Black violence, conjoin economic prosperity to environmental destruction, and construe self-possession as the freedom to dispossess others.

However, before Trump's settler conquest disposition could be credibly taken to represent the nation's interests, he needed a significant portion of the American electorate to acclaim his transgression of liberal norms and activities as representatively American. To achieve this objective, Trump had to overcome formidable obstacles within the domestic sphere that can be formulated as interrelated questions. If liberal democracy constituted for the majority of Americans the hegemonic iteration of American democracy, why should a markedly large group of US citizens accede to the decoupling of American democracy from the liberal principles and institutions to which it seemed inextricably linked? What enabled Trump to advocate with appar-

---

4. In her 2022 monograph *Ugly Freedoms*, Elizabeth Anker (2022) argues that settler colonists construed these "ugly" freedom practices as prerequisite to the achievement of democratic self-government and economic prosperity.

ent impunity the demolition of liberal institutions and principles? Why were the legislative and judicial branches of the US government unable to protect these institutions and norms from Trump's efforts to dismantle them? How was Trump able to turn extremist organizations like the Ku Klux Klan, neo-Nazis, and white nationalist militias into quasi-legitimate actors in American political discourse? How could he serve simultaneously as the president of the world's most powerful liberal democracy and leader of an insurrectionary movement?

In an effort to address these questions, I have divided the remarks that follow into sections that engage five distinct but related conjunctural moments in the trajectory of Trump's movement. I intend to clarify the criteria for the selection of these inflection points and their interrelationship as the exposition unfolds.

Birtherism: A Lie Too Big to Be Untrue

The origins of the Make America Great Again movement can be traced back to CNBC newscaster Rick Santelli's borrowing the venerated name of a colonial era Tea Party insurrection against British tyranny to dignify the February 19, 2009, rant he directed at Barack Obama's stimulus package on the floor of the Chicago stock exchange (Baker 2015). The next day Republican Congressman Dick Arney, former speaker of the House Newt Gingrich, the Koch brothers, and fifty representatives of sundry factions of the Republican Party held a conference call to share ideas on how to turn Santelli's four-minute harangue into the verbal call to arms of a grassroots insurrectionary movement.

To capitalize on the generalized domestic insecurity that emerged in the wake of the 2007–08 global financial crisis, the symbolic engineers of this as yet nonexistent movement focused on Obama's efforts to change the provisos of the social contract pertaining to health care as the alarum that would conscript new recruits to the Tea Party. President Obama aspired to change health care policies at a conjunctural moment when the US body politic had undergone a frightening depletion of its vital energies, and the American middle class was experiencing the foreclosure of its customary forms of life. White men who felt dethroned by the offshoring of union factory jobs, the nationalization of the auto industry, the disappearance of affordable housing, the shrinkage of pension funds and retirement benefits, sensed a correlation between America's declining status in the world of nations, the diminution of their economic well-being, and the loss of white male entitlement (Brown, Gordon, and Pensky 2018; Kelleter 2020). To stoke the vindictive white rancor at the core of the Tea Party movement, Arney described Obamacare as the continuation by economic means of the terrorist attack on the homeland on September 11, 2001 (Pease 2010).

Rather than becoming signatories to the first Black president's social contract, members of the Tea Party movement collaborated over social media outlets, talk-radio call-ins, Facebook postings, and Internet chat rooms in the construction of a collectively authored conspiracy narrative that situated Obamacare within a framework designed to translate aspects of Bush's War on Terror into the Tea Party's antagonism to Obamacare (Pease 2009; Ackerman 2021). This quasi-epic fiction portrayed President Obama as a Kenya-born Black Muslim terrorist who had obtained a forged US birth certificate to usurp the office of president, take over control of the nation's political and economic institutions, commandeer the financial ruin of the United States, and forcibly detain the Americans who resisted his tyranny in concentration camps (Smith and Tau 2011).

As the so-called Birtherist narrative circulated across alt-right communication networks it underwent revisions that shaped and were reshaped by the desires, grievances, fears, and political demands of a growing aggregate of its cocreators. Americans who contributed to this political fiction articulated their mistrust of President Obama's Americanness to liberal elitism, job loss, members of minoritized groups jumping the queue, and an array of related issues that Obama's presidency was made to signify. Birthers transferred the composite of their mistrust onto lurid speculations concerning the authenticity of President Obama's birth certificate. The fear and the terror that a Black Muslim terrorist had penetrated white American citizens' most intimate levels of social belonging to get elected president comprised the affective vectors motivating Birtherism's collectively authored fantasies (Remnick 2011).

On June 25, 2009, the Nigerian American right-wing political commentator L. E. Ikenga published an essay titled "Obama, the African Colonial" that added a reverse colonization plot to this affectively charged concoction. Depicting President Obama as Muslim Africa's revenge for Bush's War on Terror, Ikenga (2009) wrote that "despite what CNN and the rest are telling you, Barack Obama is nothing more than an old school African Colonial who is on his way to turning this country into one of the developing nations that you learn about on the *National Geographic Channel*." Rush Limbaugh opened his June 26, 2009, talk-radio show with a transmissible tweet rendition of Ikenga's argument, which forewarned listeners that "[Obama] wants to turn this into a Third World country. . . . The only way to try to do this is to just attack the private sector and deplete it of its resources, of its money, of its capital, which is exactly what he is doing." Limbaugh intensified the consternation of call-ins who wanted to know more when he added, "We've elected somebody who is more African in his roots than he is American, loves his father who is a Marxist, and is behaving like an African colonial despot" (Willis 2010).

Andrew C. McCarthy, the federal attorney who led the terrorism prosecution of Sheikh Omar Abdul-Rahman before becoming a contributing editor at the *National Review*, grafted a Black Muslim conspiracy theory to the Birtherist frame narrative in his 2010 monograph, *The Grand Jihad: How Islam and the Left Sabotage America*. As "proof" of the "grand jihad" referenced in the title, McCarthy described Barack Obama's repeal of the ban on openly gay service members and his endorsement of same-sex marriage as indisputable evidence of his collusion with leaders of international Islamic movements to impose a secular leftist adaptation of Islamic Sharia law on US citizens.

Birtherism may be a political fabrication, but it is a fiction that possesses the performative power, what Slavoj Žižek (2009b) calls the symbolic efficiency, to shape and occasionally generate events in the political field. What matters to the participants in the collective authorship of Birtherist fictions is the way these narratives are organized in response to enframing anxieties over imagined and real threats to the survival of their American way of life. Was the election of Barack Obama a species of historical vengeance for American settler colonists' ethnic cleansing of Indigenous Native peoples and enslavement of American Africans? Was Obama going to construct concentration camps for white Americans modeled on the slave plantations and American Indian relocation centers of their settler-colonist forebears? These questions could not be answered by facts because they inscribed Obama within an order made in the image of the questioners' real fears (Pease 2010).

Following Žižek (2009a), I would argue that far from offering an escape, the political fictions that Birthers traffic in actively generate an alternative social reality as an escape from a traumatic actuality. The collectively authored Birtherist narrative circulating across alt-right media platforms has what they once believed an impossible matter of fact at its foundation. The intractable factuality of Barack Obama's election as the first African American president designated that part of their practical reality that the producers and consumers of Birtherist conspiracy narratives could not accommodate without relinquishing belief in the ongoing viability of white regulatory control of the nation. Birtherism enabled participants in the production, consumption, and circulation of this interactive fiction to shape their reality practically so as to control what could not be incorporated within it. Only the restoration to power of white superintendence of Black lives could nullify the spectacle of a Black man being in charge of the Tea Party's America.

With this interactive political fiction as backdrop, Donald Trump's presidential campaign officially began on March 23, 2011, when he asked the cohosts and audience of *The View*, a popular daytime television talk show, "Why doesn't he show his birth certificate? There's something on that birth certificate that he doesn't like" (Krieg 2016). In posing variations of this question on numerous occasions and in different settings, Trump presented himself as a conduit for the circulation of a preexisting narrative whose value he signally enhanced by impressing the Trump brand (Mazzarella 2019). At the time Trump asked this question he had not formally announced his candidacy for the presidency, he had not taken part in either the production or the consumption of Birther narratives, he had not offered an alternative vision of America, and he had not yet come up with the idea of integrating segments of the Tea Party and other political, religious, economic, and social factions into the Make American Great Again movement. However, the moment Trump transferred this "Big Lie" from the precincts of disreputable alt-right communication networks to the center of the presidential race, he seized control of a vast voting bloc consisting primarily of white nationalists in the Tea Party and other extreme factions on the Far Right who regarded Obama as "more African in his roots than he is American." By taking public ownership of this preexisting, collectively authored political fiction, he also claimed proprietary rights to the surplus productivity of the fantasies that Birtherism coalesced.

Before Trump's takeover, the Tea Party was a leaderless, reactionary fringe group lacking strong ties to the Republican Party whose members were best known for the tricorn hats, Gadsen flags, and other colonial era regalia they kitted out when staging protests of Obama's African colonial despotism. Speaking and acting from the subject position of aggrieved white entitlement already opened by the Tea Party's fierce antagonism to Obama's policies, Trump transformed the Tea Partiers' heterogeneous, inconsistent, counterinsurgent, politically reactionary motives and purposes into the agentic, insurgent, white settler nationalism of the Make America Great Again movement. When Trump asked the question, he summoned into virtual existence the political movement to which he conferred ontological reality in the hundreds of rallies he has held since he officially announced his candidacy for the office of president on June 15, 2015.

Trump won the loyalty of this voting bloc because he did what no reputable Republican candidate for president would have risked doing. By questioning the validity of President Obama's birth certificate, Trump unashamedly conjured in the historical present a constellation of nonsynchronous scenes—of a white man compelling an African American to show his freedom papers, of a white poll worker demanding an African American voter's proof of citizenship, of white immigration officers stopping an African for interrogation at the nation's border—from the intractably nonprogressive facets of United States history that Trump's question synchronized.

Trump's question confronted the first Black president of the United States with the demand that he show incontrovertible evidence of his certification as a "natural-born" American citizen. At the same time that Trump's called for empirical proof of his birth certificate's validity, he assumed a bellicose attitude eager to decertify any document purporting to legitimate Obama's presidency (Serwer 2020). Obama did in fact release the long-form version of his birth certificate on April 27, 2011 (Pfeiffer 2011). It verified that he was born August 4, 1961, in Kapi'olani Maternity and Gynecological Hospital, Honolulu, Hawai'i. That certificate of live birth would have sufficed in a court of law. But Trump's question had not brought the president before a judge; it hauled him into a people's court composed of white settler nationalists from the nation's past and present. The day after Obama published the document, Jason Miller, a spokesman for Trump's campaign, described President Obama's exhibition of his birth certificate as a response to Trump's demand to see his papers. "Having successfully obtained President Obama's birth certificate when others could not, Mr. Trump believes that President Obama was born in the United States," Miller said (Helsel 2016). Miller's statements notwithstanding, Trump continued to express Birther uncertainties for years after, and to this day has never declared his unqualified belief that Barack Obama is a birthright citizen of the United States. Not a month after President Obama displayed his long-form birth certificate, on CNN, Trump told Wolf Blitzer that "a lot of people do not think it was an authentic certificate" (Krieg 2016).

Trump's citation of what "a lot of people" find dubious about Obama's birth certificate explains why he never found believable, *incontrovertible* proof of the authenticity of Obama's certificate. Trump had staged his inquest into the circumstances of President Obama's birth as the basis for a twenty-first-century colonial encounter. Trump understood that the ingrained beliefs on which Birtherism is based cannot be falsified because they are entangled in the deep-rooted conviction held by nineteenth century settler colonists and a broad swath of his contemporary supporters that no African American can possess the identity credentials required to become a legitimate candidate for the office of president (Serwer 2020).

During his presidential campaign Obama had correlated the moment Martin Luther King Jr. called the "fierce urgency of now" with his campaign's rallying cry "Yes, we can!" Participants in Obama's grassroots movement encouraged voters to believe their ballots could redeem the nation's "original sin" of slavery (Coates 2012). They cast the 2008 presidential election as a redemptive turning point that would empower twenty-first-century Americans to actualize an American dream that had previously been deferred to an unattainable future. Trump's questioning opened a space of dubiety between the matter of historical fact that Obama was elected president of the United States of America and the legitimacy of the birth certificate documenting his right to be that person. The serial uncertainties Trump associated with the authenticity of Obama's birth certificate instigated doubts that empirical certification procedures could not fully and finally invalidate. There is no certification that can decisively put an end to the legion of Birther doubts saturating the gap between Obama's presidency and its certification. Without a certifiably legitimate response to Birthers' skepticism, Trump's questioning all but reinstated the qualifier "deferred" to the dream that Obama's election victory actualized. When he situated America's telos in its white settler slave-power past, Trump cast Americans' election of the first Black president as a historical anomaly rather than an irreversible step forward into the nation's "post-racial future." Trump's repeated enactment of this settler-colonist transaction did not simply contravene Obama's redemptive vision of America; it overturned its historic efficacy by inciting a temporal rollback to an America wherein a hetero-patriarchal, white, Anglo-Saxon, Protestant settler-colonist disposition claimed preemptive rule over the nation's past—and future (Mamdami 2015; Lewis 2017; Young 2018; Byrd et al. 2018).

Settler colonialism is not a bygone historical era or a mode of historical eventfulness whose significance was eliminated with the overthrow of British rule. It is a transhistorical condition of eventfulness that remains formative while also changing over time (Gregory 2004; Byrd et al. 2018; Bruyneel 2021). The series of different yet politically intertwined scenes of subjugation that Trump's question elevated into representation comprised separate historical enactments of America's settler-colonial division of humanity. Although they took place as distinctly different historical events, these incidents are nevertheless imbricated within the ongoing iterative eventfulness of the disposition of settler colonialism that Birtherism continues. These enfolded processes constitute American settler colonialism as a structural yet sequential event (Bruyneel 2021; Veracini 2021; Robinson 2017; Byrd et al. 2018; Kim 2022). Trump reperformed this structural event at the moment he took up the position of *the* American settler to confront President Obama with the question about the legal certifiability of his birth certificate.

In extracting his interrogatory stance from the collectively authored Birther narrative, Trump activated scenarios of decertification that otherwise lay dormant within Birtherism's virtual archive. Trump's iterative questionings did not merely render Obama's decertification imaginable; they activated a retroactive procedure of denaturalization that added the quality of natal alienation to Obama's body at the instant of his birth. From the moment he articulated this inquest that threatened to dispossess the first Black president of his right of citizenship, Trump modeled and authorized the conquest mentality of a prototypically American settler colonist. Trump's usage of Birtherism to question the certification of Obama's presidency turned the collective responsible for the production of this discursive resource into the latter-day settler nationalists that he mutated into a legitimate political constituency.

That Trump had not merely quickened these vindictive specters but had done so with pride-filled impunity warrants the recognition that the institutions of American liberal democracy could do nothing to prevent their recurrence (Chomsky 2016; Patel 2017). Trump has made it a policy not to put himself in a position where he can be assigned culpability for a potentially criminal action or enterprise. Trump never professes to speak solely for himself. He reportedly starts each day by collating, curating, and distilling his followers' tweets, blogs, and other messaging into executive tweets that at once discern and purport to give expression to the constituent power of the Make America Great Again movement (Johnson 2016). In his engagement with these twenty-first-century settlers, Trump includes the possibility of insurrection against the normative constituted order as a potentiating motive for their aggregation. Although he aligned this people's movement to his purposes, Trump nonetheless claims to depend on their constituent right to revolution as the warrant for his impunity.

In the rallies that followed his announcement to campaign for the presidency, Trump depicted the United States as a settler conquest nation in which winning was a permanent ontological condition. Trump believed it axiomatic that America's standing as a conquest culture endowed its nation-making violence with the temporal authority to impede modes of historicization that would replace or overthrow it. He viewed the winning or victory culture of his movement as akin to a settler colonist settlement in that it was always threatened by terrorists from within and without. Trump associated this disposition with American settlers' rights of revolutionary conquest and instructed rally-goers to refuse to feel either personal guilt or collective shame for their forebears' having routed foes whose unwillingness to accept defeat was inherited by their twenty-first-century descendants. Trump never regarded as admirable the resistance of Indigenous peoples or rebellious slaves or the British loyalists the settlers defeated. However, he wholeheartedly identified with the settler conquest disposition of Andrew Jackson, the US president who overthrew a British imperial army in the War of 1812, who carried out American Indian removal policies, and who put down slave rebellions.

At press conferences and during stump speeches, Trump took pleasure in exemplifying the ethos and bearing of President Jackson.[5] He urged members of the Make America Great Again movement to personify Jacksonian colonial conquest mentality in confrontations with radical Muslim terrorists, feminists, members of Black Lives Matter, Antifa, undocumented immigrants, and to protect the Republic against other twenty-first-century versions of enemies who did not know how to stay vanquished. Trump also directed settler-nationalist bellicosities against an ensemble of domestic antagonists whose campaigns for social justice, equal political and civil rights, and reparations for historical wrongs threatened to deprive the Real Americans in his movement of their birthright privileges of supervisory control of the nation.

Trump's people structure their belief in Trump's affectively real facts on their need to disbelieve in the truth of the progressive liberal narrative that has relegated them to the trash bin of history. US historian Greg Grandin speculates that when Trump was deliberating over effective slogans for his presidential campaign, he decided that the promise to build a wall at the nation's southern border would ignite a collective reawakening of America's settler-colonist frontier mentality. It was on the frontier that American settler

---

5. Walter Russell Mead (2017) has articulated the foreign policy implications of Trump's identification with the settler-conqueror president Andrew Jackson. For an account of what presidential advisor Bannon made of Mead's claims, see Glasser 2018.

colonists arrived at their inegalitarian and white nationalist understanding of America insofar as it entailed "putting down people of color, and then continuing to define their liberty as what set them apart from the people of color they put down" (Grandin 2019). The demand that Trump "Build that wall!" along the US-Mexico border stands as a stark reminder that American settlers' representative freedom practices involved unregulated acts of extra-legal nation-making violence aimed at racially marked "savages" within as well as on the other side of the nation's border (Grandin 2019; Anker 2022).

The Make America Great Again movement is not about citizens of the United States, and its members do not primarily identify as Republicans. Trump's American people consider themselves the wellspring of nation-making power out of which the United States emerged and believe in their bones that the bedrock America they inhabit constitutes the sacred homeland of true nativist belonging. America's elect, the people Trump leads, do not describe themselves as citizens of the United States but as Real Americans. The Trump movement has always been about the reconstruction of the settler-colonist division of humanity through the construction of an internal border distinguishing who belongs and who doesn't; who counts and who shouldn't; who can wield power and who must be subject to it. It is they, and not the liberal elite, who are the Americans who set the rules and model the behavior to which immigrants who wish to become citizens of the United States must conform and who are ever ready to take up arms against every threat, foreign and domestic, to the American Way of Life (Gingrich 1984; O'Neill 2020).

Shortly after he announced his intention to run for the presidency, Trump's future speechwriter and national security adviser Michael Anton (2016a) authored a series of polemical manifestos under the pseudonym Publius Decius Mus that lent academic respectability to aspects of Trump's campaign that his critics dismissed as laughable ineptitude. With Birtherism as the background concept shaping his argument, Anton took pains to falsify two of the foundational tenets in the credo of American liberal democracy. "'Diversity' is not 'our strength,'" Anton (2016b) remarks of the first of these precepts. "It's a source of weakness, tension and disunion." Anton (2016b) offered a more elaborate rationale to shed doubt on the historical accuracy of the second of these foundational beliefs: "America is not a 'nation of immigrants'; we are originally a nation of settlers, who later chose to admit immigrants, and later still not to, and who may justly open or close our doors solely at our own discretion, without deference to forced pieties." As warrant for his rejection of the aspirational ideal of welcoming the foreign-born, Anton (2016a) writes, "The ceaseless importation of Third

World foreigners with no tradition of, taste for, or experience in liberty . . . provide [Democrats] ringers to form a permanent electoral majority."

Like Anton, Trump differentiates immigrants from the past and present white settler nationalists who revile them. Members of Trump's movement do not regard themselves as part of a nation of immigrants. American settler colonists differ from immigrants in that, unlike the latter, settlers were intent on eliminating preexisting societies rather than becoming part of them (Behdad 2005; Pease 2008; Mamdami 2015). In Trump's reckoning, an immigrant is a person who is permanently out of place. It bears repeating that Trump did not confine the classification "immigrant" to persons recently admitted entry to US territories; he extended the condition of being out of place within United States territory to all people of color no matter whether their place of birth was Africa, Latin America, South America, Asia, the so-called Middle East, or the United States of America (Dunbar-Ortiz 2021). To advance his effort to designate all people of color immigrants, Trump used a version of the legal fiction Orlando Patterson calls "natal alienation" to expand Birtherism's provenance. Chief Justice Roger Taney fabricated this fiction in the *Dred Scott v. Sandford* case to explain why African Americans, no matter whether born in Africa or the United States, could never acquire the condition of national belonging (Patterson 1982; V. Brown 2009).

Political commentators have successfully exposed the tissue of lies, distortions, and half-truths that Birtherism braids together. However, whether Birtherism is factually true matters less than the congeries of historically factual white supremacist scenarios it scatters across the contemporary political landscape. Trump's supporters behave according to the emotional logics saturating what Brian Massumi (2015b) describes as a "politics of affect" that enmeshes emotions and cognition in an inextricable knot.[6] His followers' attachments to Trump's affectively factual fictions are stronger than the objective facts his critics present to expose them.

---

6. Critics who restrict their focus to cognitive mistakes relative to economic interest fail to recognize how emotional attachments have overridden what should have been seen as economic self-interest on the part of Trump's working-class and lower-income voters. Lauren Berlant (2011: 23) has shrewdly remarked that "all [affective] attachments are optimistic. When we talk about an object of desire, we are really talking about a cluster of promises we want someone or something to make to us and make possible for us. This cluster of promises could seem embedded in a person, a thing, an institution, a text, a norm, a bunch of cells, smells, a good idea—whatever." Thomas Frank (2004) offers an important corrective to this perspective in *What's The Matter with Kansas? How Conservatives Won the Heart of America*.

What Trump's opponents and critics refuse to recognize or even acknowledge is the ineluctable fact that Trump's question generated a materially real twenty-first-century event that drew on the settler-colonist repertoire of scenarios, themes, settings, antagonists, and protagonists enmeshed within the Birtherist narrative. This Birtherist fiction cast Donald Trump as a twenty-first-century leader of American settlers involved in a colonial struggle with an African Muslim undocumented immigrant who had usurped the sovereign power of the presidency to conduct a domestic war on terror against American citizens. Trump had in effect announced his candidacy for office by subordinating the first African American president to the sovereign power of the collective movement that Trump's question personified.

By confronting Obama with this question about the legality of his birth certificate, Trump took up a subject position that turned President Barack Obama into the condensed signifier for an assemblage of political, economic, and social actors and activities to which Trump's movement set itself in a relationship of insuperable antagonism (Laclau 2005; Mouffe 2005). When repeated at Trump rallies, the question facilitated the consolidation of settler power from the very highest level of leadership to the most granular structure of feeling to which this power owes its social, cultural, and political longevity. Interpreted from the perspective of Birtherism's true believers, Donald Trump's question recovered sovereign nativist control of the United States of America at the precise moment he forced the nation's first Black president to show proof of legal belonging.

If Trump did not want the long-form birth certificate, what bureaucratic procedures did Trump and his political constituency want to set into operation when they questioned the official certification of President Obama's birth? Among other matters, Trump wanted to know what process of authorization in a white nation made it possible for the son of an African immigrant from Kenya to be verified as the president of the most powerful country on earth. More specifically, Trump's question wanted answers as to how and why all the safeguards installed in the bureaucratic infrastructures that organize the American political system in ways that would have and should have made impossible the certification of the son of a Kenya-born African as president failed to accomplish that purpose.

Over and above all else, Trump's questioning conveyed the demand to know why state-authorized bureaucratic processes responsible for specifying the details surrounding Obama's birth had not already done the work of decertification. Bureaucratic decertification procedures rely on the nation's sedimented history of settler lawfare, settler-colonist warfare, US settler imperialism, and ongoing settler-colonial capitalist predation that instituted the American system of governmentality at its founding and continue to sustain it (Coulthard 2014; Kim 2022). Trump's ongoing inquest could cite the pre–Civil War legal fiction of natal alienation and radical kinlessness as ample legal precedent for prohibiting African Americans from ever belonging to the nation as free citizens; if necessary, it could requisition the property laws that were fashioned by the judicial branch of the post–Civil War expansionist state to grant westward moving white settlers' preemptive ownership of any Indigenous land they homesteaded and the right to construe whiteness itself as a status property tangentially related to inegalitarian property rights (Frederickson 1982; Harris 1993; Lipsitz 1995; Rana 2010; Issar 2021; Nichols 2018).

When situated within the context of his insurrectionist movement, Trump's casting doubt on the validity of Barack Obama's birth certificate can be viewed as serving a set of interconnected psychosocial purposes.[7] This fantasy did indeed gratify the antagonistic disposition of a movement whose members took obscene enjoyment in Trump asking a question that harbored the potential penalties of the loss of US citizenship, detention, deportation, and the possible capital punishment of America's first Black president.[8] However, given its calculable effectiveness within the US socio-symbolic order, Birtherism might be better understood as a long-term political stratagem designed to take advantage of preexisting decertification procedures within the bureaucratic infrastructure of the American political system.

In its standing as a question asked on behalf of the American descendants of settler colonists, Trump's interrogatory tapped into whiteness as the default operative ideology of what political theorist Charles W. Mills calls the "racial contract." According to Mills the United States of America was, like other British settler-colonist nations, built on the self-evident assumption of white supremacy. As such, it installed one set of rules that applied to white persons and another to nonwhite subpersons. This system of dual governance utilized expropriation, slavery, colonization, and cultural deracination as interrelated modes of domination. White American settlers based the legalization of slavery on the religious belief that it benefited uncivilized

---

7. Slavoj Žižek's (2009a: 43–56) analysis of fantasy has supplied the interpretive framework for my understanding of the role fantasy plays in the Trump's populist movement.

8. In *White Nation: Fantasies of White Supremacy in a Multicultural Society*, Ghassan Hage (1998) describes the way that white nationalists inhabit, experience, and conceive of their nation and of themselves as a fantasy in which they imagine themselves enacting the state's will.

nonwhite people; they justified seizing the land and resources of nonwhite people by claiming that only white men possess the moral capacities pre-requisite to owning property. Race regulates the American social contract by dividing the contractual parties into two asymmetrical, noncomparable groups: the persons who comprise the party to whom the social contract assigns its rights and liberties are white, unmarked citizens; the subpersons who lack complete contractual identification with the rights and liberties of white US citizens are racially marked (Mills 1999; Pateman and Mills 2007).

As the qualifiers marked and unmarked suggest, Mills apprehends white supremacism as a pre-political disposition deeply rooted in American history that continues into the present as the unmarked, because foun-dationally presupposed, conveyor of US culture's normativity. Functioning as a multilayered, interlocking infrastructural network that relays taken-for-granted, mostly preconscious beliefs and attitudes concerning racial, eth-nic, political, social, and economic inequalities, white supremacism works in tandem with global, racial, and settler-colonial modes of capitalism, patriar-chy, sexism, and heterosexism and multiple racialized matrices of domina-tion and exclusion that together support unequal labor, housing, and finan-cial markets. Racist nativism regulates the relationships between the United States and other nations by the denial of entry to specific ethnic, racial, or national groups; nativist racism legitimates the hierarchical distribution of civic entitlement to specific groups of immigrants and their descendants after entry has occurred (Frederickson 1982; Harris 1993; Behdad 2005; Pease 2008; Bandar 2018; Louie and Viladrich 2021).

Mills wrote *The Racial Contract* to expose this white supremacist infrastructure of the American system to critical contestation rather than social reproduction. Because of the benefits and entitlements inherent in the racial contract, however, Trump and members of his movement are ada-mantly opposed to any alteration of its foundational assumptions. Through-out his 2016 presidential campaign, Trump treated Birtherism as a repara-tion of the breach of the racial contract resulting from the election of the first Black president (Remnick 2016). While the manifest content of Birtherism may be a "Big Lie," that lie reveals the otherwise latent truth that settler-colonist white nativism is so deeply rooted in the foundations of the Ameri-can juridico-political system that it cannot be extricated without throwing the entire system into disrepair (Elkins and Pederson 2005; Simpson 2014).[9]

9. Alex Trimble Young (2018) has argued that the Second Amendment of the Constitu-tion "explicitly recognizes settler colonists' right to share in the state's monopoly of the

Trump's people did not need to cite Charles Mills to warrant their belief that the election of Barack Obama meant that a subperson who lacked the full contractual rights and liberties of white US citizens was now in charge of enforcing the US social contract. They considered the asymmetrical, dual governance assumptions of the racial contract indistinguishable from the Americanness of their way of life. As I will explain at the conclusion to these remarks, in their effort to disallow the transfer of presidential power to Joseph R. Biden, the members of Trump's movement turned Birtherism into the de jure authorization for their efforts to decertify the votes of any and all African Americans who filled out a ballot in the 2020 presidential election (Remnick 2011; Serwer 2020; Kagan 2021).

An Unauthorized Transfer of Constituent Power: President Donald J. Trump's Preemptive Impunity

The Inauguration Day ritual of a peaceful transfer of power presupposes a modicum of continuity between the incoming presidential administration and the preceding regime. This ritual is also supposed to safeguard what the *New York Times* Editorial Board (2021) describes as the foundational premise of a democratic republic: "A republic works only when the losers of elections accept the results and the legitimacy of their opponents." Although it went virtually unnoticed at the time, Trump had made clear why he could neither offer such an assurance nor undertake a peaceful transfer of power in the scenario he added to his official inauguration ceremony on January 20, 2017. The unauthorized enactment Trump surreptitiously included in this public rite of passage worked like what psychoanalysts refer to as a deferred action in that it would take a subsequent event, in this case the January 6 insurrection at the US Capitol, to make legible the irreversible subversion this surplus action potentiated.[10]

---

legitimate use of violence." This right exemplifies a conception of sovereignty specific to settler colonists. In "Necropolitics," Achille Mbembe explains how this understanding of sovereign power prevailed in spaces like the settler-colonial frontier, which he describes as anomalous spaces that are lacking a juridical order governed and "enforced by the extreme violence of the state and that have not yet created a human world" (quoted in Young 2018). On the frontier, American settlers, acting independently of the state, nevertheless put their power to kill any nonwhite aliens who obstructed them to work as they accomplished the expansionist aims of the imperial state.

10. In the following account of the January 20 alternative investiture and Trump's usage of the Phoenix, Arizona, constituent assembly, I draw on portions of the essay "Trump: Populist Usurper President" (see Pease 2018).

A presidential inauguration offers a classic example of what French sociologist Pierre Bourdieu calls a ceremony of symbolic investiture in that this ritual in the civic liturgy provides procedures, symbols, and speech acts the public requires to witness and work through the potentially disruptive effects that might ensue when a US president undergoes replacement by a political opponent. Bourdieu (2000: 243) defines an investiture ceremony as a ritual that establishes the difference between a public office and an officeholder as the precondition for a public to witness an ordinary mortal person "partake of the sempiternity and immortality of the public office they temporarily incarnate."

In his canonical description of the transformative effect of a rite of symbolic investiture on the body of the officeholder, Bourdieu alludes to Ernst Kantorowicz's ([1957] 1985) notion of the "King's Two Bodies" that distinguishes the mortal body of the officeholder and the sublime body utterly devoid of natural defects that is inherent in the office: "As representatives they (the officeholders) partake of the eternity and ubiquity of the office which they help to make exist as permanent, omnipresent, and transcendent, and which they temporarily incarnate, giving it voice through their mouths and representing it in their bodies, converted into symbols and emblems to rally round" (Bourdieu 2000: 244). No duly elected officeholder can coincide with the second or immortal body of the Office of the President. However, in "The King's Two Bodies: Lincoln, Wilson, Nixon, and Presidential Sacrifice," the political theorist Michael Paul Rogin (1987: 82) explained how three of Trump's precursors in the White House aspired to replace the "the Body natural . . . subject to all infirmities" with "the Body politic . . . utterly devoid of natural Defects and imbecilities." President Trump differed from previous occupants of the Oval Office in that at the time of the official oath-taking he remained doubly interpellated to two separate, conflicting personae. He was fastened to the Office of the President of the United States on the one hand, and on the other, he identified as the leader of an extra-constitutional movement.

Noting the irremediable incompatibility between Trump's behavior and the bodily practices and behavioral dispositions inscribed in the office, Trump's detractors have denounced him as an impostor possessing neither the comportment nor the temperament nor the know-how prerequisite to occupy the office (Shrum 2017). Rather than conforming his behavior to the mores and customs of the Office of the President, Trump occupied it as the refusal to embody or personify the norms and mandates of the presidency. Befittingly, Trump's unpresidential deportment communicated a different meaning to members of his movement, who considered it an apt expression of their leader's usurpation of the office (Beinart 2018; Kay 2017).

Bourdieu's account of a felicitous investiture ceremony affords a particularly generative vantage point to explain how the scenario Trump added to the January 20, 2017, altered the import and efficacy of the inauguration ceremony. Bourdieu (2000: 243) does not provide an explicit account of an unsuccessful investiture ceremony, but he does explain how an elected official's difficulty in bodily taking up the symbolic function of a public office can precipitate an investiture crisis that is "always present in inaugural moments." This is the case "because the appropriation of the function by the nominee is also the appropriation of the nominee by the function: the nominee enters into the function only if he agrees to be possessed bodily by it, as is asked in the rite of investiture" (244). In the following description of the expected disposition of the person undergoing the ritual, Bourdieu also provides criteria to understand why Trump's January 20, 2017, inauguration ceremony might not have yielded the expected result: "He must be personally invested in his investiture, that is, engage his devotion, his belief, his body, give them as pledges, and manifest, in all his conduct and speech—this is the function of the ritual words of recognition—his faith in the office and in the group which awards it and which confers this great assurance only on the condition that it is fully assured in return" (243). With the precision of a canonist, Bourdieu remarks that a public investiture ritual quite literally secures and legally protects the person undergoing this solemn ceremony against the accusation that the event has validated "the delirious fiction of the impostor . . . or the arbitrary imposition of the usurper" (242). With this observation, Bourdieu implies that if the person going through the ceremony is not "personally invested" in or has not bodily taken up the official symbols and emblems of the office, the investiture ceremony could misfire in the sense that it might not succeed in turning a candidate answerable to the accusation of being an impostor or usurper into, in the case of Donald J. Trump, the president of the United States of America (Soros 2017; Tabachnik 2019).

Bourdieu (2000: 244) goes on to state that an investiture crisis might transpire at an inaugural event should an elected official either refuse or fail to be "bodily taken up by the symbolic function of the office."[11] Trump

---

11. Although I put it to a quite different usage, my understanding of how a crisis in symbolic investiture can affect elected officials draws on Eric Santner's (1996) elaboration of this notion in *My Own Private Germany: Daniel Paul Schreber's Secret History of Modernity*.

brought about an investiture crisis when he delivered an inaugural address just after taking the presidential oath—"I do solemnly swear . . . that I will faithfully execute the office of President of the United States, and will to the best of my ability, preserve, protect and defend the Constitution of the United States"—that made clear that he had no intention to perform either of the functions he had just solemnly sworn faithfully to execute (Wittes and Jurecic 2017).

> Today's ceremony, however, has very special meaning. Because today we are not merely transferring power from one administration to another, or from one party to another—but we are transferring power from Washington, DC and giving it back to you, the American People. For too long the people have borne the cost. Washington flourished—but the people did not share in its wealth. . . . That all changes—starting right here, and right now, because this moment is your moment: it belongs to you. It belongs to everyone gathered here today and everyone watching across America. This is your day. This is your celebration. And this, the United States of America, is your country. . . . What truly matters is not which party controls our government, but whether our government is controlled by the people. January 20th, 2017, will be remembered as the day the people became the rulers of this nation again. The forgotten men and women of our country will be forgotten no longer. Everyone is listening to you now. You came by the tens of millions to become part of a historic movement, the likes of which the world has never seen before. (Trump 2017a)[12]

As discussed above, the primary purpose of the inauguration ceremony was for Trump, the newly sworn president, to invest himself in and getting bodily taken up by the symbols, emblems, and other accoutrements surrounding the ritual of a peaceful transfer of power that Democrats and Republicans alike have celebrated for more than a century as what make the United States an exemplary liberal democracy. The inauguration of the forty-fifth president of the United States was supposed to be the sole investiture ceremony that took place on January 20, 2017. However, to underscore the "very special meaning" of this event, Trump's speech writers, Ste-

---

12. Benjamin Willes and Quinta Jureci argue that the Inauguration ceremony might not have accomplished the transformation of Trump into president because he is constitutionally unable to take an oath (Jurecic and Willes 2017).

phen Bannon and Stephen Miller, placed this ritual into contestation with an alternative investiture ceremony staged for the insurrectionary movement Trump continues to lead.

Trump did not run as a normal presidential candidate; he ran as the operative will and embodied voice of a movement whose members felt that they had been set aside by twenty-first-century realities. They wanted Trump to usurp the office of the president and use it to transgress constitutional statutes and rules and transform the coordinates of the national polity. In keeping with these aspirations, moments after taking the solemn oath to "execute the responsibilities of his office and to protect and defend the constitution," President Trump performed an activity that the Constitution did not authorize, and that discontinued the long-standing tradition of a peaceful transfer of power.

Rather than appropriating and being appropriated by the symbolic function of receiving, bodily taking up, and personifying the peaceful transfer of power, Trump invested himself in a contrary activity that precipitated a self-division to which the ambiguous referent of the pronoun "we" in this passage calls attention: "Because today we are not merely transferring power from one administration to another, or from one party to another—but we are transferring power from Washington, DC and giving it back to you, the American People." The "we" that is "not merely transferring power from one administration to another, or from one party to another" is significantly different from the "we" that is "transferring power from Washington, DC and giving it back to you, the American People." The "we" involved in the relay of power within Washington, DC, institutions and structures (presidential administrations, political parties) is a placeholder in a series of preexisting socio-symbolic networks of political actants and self-executing activities. But the "we" who arrogates the authority to give this sovereign power "back to you, the American People" is at once the effect and the delegated cause of the activities inherent in this transferential process. By way of the recursive process animating this alternative investiture, the presidential "we" appropriating the power to give back to the American people already will have been appropriated by the American people's sovereign power to actuate this transaction.

What is more significant to this transaction, when Trump shifts the referent of "you, the American People," from "everyone" to "the forgotten men and women . . . who came by the tens of millions" to join the Make America Great Again movement, it becomes apparent that the American people to whom "we" transfers the sovereign power vested in the Office of the President are not identical with all Americans. This slippage reveals that Trump intends the members of the Make America Great Again movement as at once his primary addressees, the ultimate source of sovereign power, and the co-enactors of this unauthorized investiture ceremony that would make them "rulers of this nation again."

Now it is customary for newly elected presidents to formally recognize "We the People" as the final authorizing conduit of their sovereign power to govern. At presidential inauguration ceremonies, the phrase "We the People" has traditionally performed the strictly rhetorical function of endowing newly elected presidents with the people's imprimatur for the policies and agendas they laid out during their campaigns. When, at a key moment in his 2013 inaugural address, Barack Obama (2013) said, "We, the people, still believe that our obligations as Americans are not just to ourselves, but to all posterity," he spoke as if the American people had already authorized the Climate Action Plan that he would not announce until June 25, 2013. The people Trump institutes through this supernumerary ceremony differ from "We the People" Obama represents, in that Trump's "forgotten" Americans exist within United States constitutional democracy as a constituent power that exceeds any legitimate power to rule and transcends the grasp of already constituted law.

The January 20, 2017, inauguration ceremony was supposed to establish an irreversible distinction between Trump the leader of a movement and President Trump by hailing the latter figure as representative leader of all the people of the United States. However, his inaugural address makes it clear that President Trump remained primarily invested in the symbols and regalia of the Make America Great Again movement on whose extra-constitutional authority he has usurped the office of president. Trump indicated the magnitude of the political transformation he intended this rogue investiture ceremony to realize, when, consequent to his act of giving power back to "you, the American People," he turned the members of the Make American Great Again movement into the quite literal referent for and first-person collective agency retroactively empowered to enunciate the otherwise strictly rhetorical phrase "We the People."

The mystery in this supernumerary investiture ceremony pertains to the source of the sovereign power to rule that Trump gave back to the people. This alternative investiture ceremony effectively displaced the central ritual involving the symbolic function of the peaceful transfer of power from one administration to the next with this unauthorized transfer. This extralegal investiture ceremony would not be completed until an event took place months later in Charlottesville, Virginia, that required the American people to whom he transferred this power on January 20 take part in a separate inauguration that would retroactively invest Trump with their power to rule the nation.

Nothing about this transfer of power should be considered peaceful. Trump was not handing on power the Obama administration had peacefully passed along to the Trump administration. The American people to whom Trump has given back power were inalterably opposed to Obama's policies. Since they never recognized President Obama as the legally elected bearer of their collective agency, they could not have regarded the sovereign power Trump handed back to them as having emanated from President Obama's administration. The American people who made a virtual appearance in this investiture ceremony instead granted Trump the extralegal sovereign power to perform this hostile takeover of the 2017 inauguration ceremony.

In performing this supplemental ceremony that restored his move-ment to the status of the nation's rulers, Trump had, for the time it took to perform it, impersonated the presidential "we" and assumed the Office of the President as the embodiment of the movement's sovereign will. Although the scenario Trump added to the official inauguration ceremony may have appeared merely symbolic at the time, the historically material effects of this unauthorized hand over became evident after his 2020 elec-toral defeat when President Trump adamantly refused to participate in the peaceful transfer of power to his successor in the office. It would take the intervening four years to realize, in retrospect, that Trump's superfluous ritual had also changed the 2017 presidential inauguration ceremony into the setting for the installment of a deferred-action coup d'état, a de facto usurpation of power by the head of an insurrectionary movement that would invade the Capitol building rather than hand it back to the political establish-ment in Washington, DC.

The 2017 inauguration ceremony did accomplish the self-executing task of "merely transferring power from one administration to another" that legally recognized Donald J. Trump as the forty-fifth president of the United States of America. However, this outlaw investiture ceremony vested in President Trump the unofficial authority to rule the nation as the expres-sive voice of his white nationalist movement's will: "What truly matters is not which party controls our government, but whether our government is controlled by the people. January 20th, 2017, will be remembered as the day the people became the rulers of this nation again."

The American people through whose will Trump acquired the power to govern the nation differed from Obama's "We, the people" in that they wanted no part of the political order governed by the Washington, DC, establishment. This insurrectionary movement claimed the "revolutionary" power to dismantle the free press, colonize public lands, undermine voters' rights legislation, and wreak havoc on other venerated institutions of American liberal democracy (Todd and Zito 2018). Scholars in constitutional law have described previous examples of the American people's revolutionary assertion of the right to rule as enactments of constituent power. According to these scholars, the American Revolution changed the meaning and practice of popular sovereignty in the West, "transforming the people from a source of power defensively appealed to in constitutional crises . . . to an agent capable of ongoing, collective self-government and, when necessary, radical constitutional reform" (J. Frank 2010: 10). Linking it to the right to revolution, the founders who drew up the US Constitution presupposed the constituent power of "We the People" as the sovereign agency that was responsible for its authorship (Partlett 2017). As constitution-making, the American people's constituent power could not be subject to the rules and laws in "the existing constitution and implies in practice its legal abrogation" (957).

Over the nation's two-hundred-fifty-year history, remarkably diverse movements on the right and the left have claimed the sovereign authority of "We the People" to validate their revolutionary demands. During his 2008 presidential campaign, Barack Obama spoke with the constituent power of his grassroots movement when he repudiated President George W. Bush's curtailment of Americans' constitutional rights. Occupy Wall Street, Black Lives Matter, and the #MeToo movements emerged during the Obama-Biden administration. As did the Tea Party movement.[13] In his 2016 campaign Donald Trump galvanized the constituent power of the Make America Great Again movement when he promised to repeal and replace the "unconstitutional rule" of Obamacare.

13. Jason Frank (2010: 5) offers this succinct account of these heterogeneous usages:

> Remarkably diverse movements and policies, reforms, and reactions have invoked the sovereign authority of the people. The people have been used to justify popular revolution against colonial authorities and to found a constitutional order premised on 'excluding the people in their collective capacity'; to embolden the states and to empower the union; to authorize vigilantism and to affirm the rule of law; to create a broad populist front against Gilded Age economic exploitation and to perpetuate some of the nation's worst racial atrocities; to increase the power of the presidency and to return power to the grassroots.

Its core members consider Make America Great Again an insurrectionary movement (Mogelson 2021). And Trump's declaration—"That all changes—starting right here, and right now, because this moment is your moment"—instantiated a classic example of what the political theorist Jason Frank calls a "constituent moment." At such moments, Frank explains, the people are enacted as an extralegal constituent power higher than the constituted order but not formally mandated from within that order. Frank (2010: 8) defines a constituent moment as what takes place when an impostor or usurper or other unauthorized agent "seizes the mantle of authorization" and claims to speak in the name of the people to open up new places (in this case, the investiture ceremony Trump added to his 2017 inauguration) for the accomplishment of "the people's aspirations." It is through the achievement of such a "felicitous infelicity," Frank explains, that the American people's sovereign power effectively demonstrates its capacity to alter the conditions and contexts through which the people's voice gets heard and recognized as politically efficacious (8). Trump's investiture ceremony imbued a "very special meaning" in the Inauguration when it positioned the recipient ("you, the American People") of this transfer of power as what authorized Donald Trump's taking up the Office of the President. On January 20, 2017, Donald J. Trump was formally inaugurated as president, but he accepted sovereign power as the head of an insurrectionary populist movement.

Rather than accomplishing the felicitous transformation of Donald J. Trump into the Second Body inhering in the office of the US president, this extralegal investiture ceremony precipitated an ongoing investiture crisis. The crisis effected the disjuncture of the president of all the American people, who was expected to conform his policies and actions to the rules and laws embedded in the institutions of American liberal democracy, from Donald J. Trump, the de facto usurper-agent of a populist movement whose members demanded that he overturn American liberal democracy's hegemonic rule. During his four years in office, President Trump occupied the rift in between them so as to turn the personae of president and usurper into each other's foil. When doing official state business, Trump formally acceded to the rules and norms of existing institutions of government; in speaking as and for the Make America Great Again movement's sovereign power, he exceeded and transgressed extant rules and laws.

Trump did not govern as a president whose actions and policies were authorized by the guardians of the sacred epistemes of US liberal democracy. Trump based the authority of the policies, actions, and decisions he made as president on the sovereign power from the future anterior of the Make America Great Again movement. As it turns out, Trump's Inauguration Day assertion that "January 20th, 2017, will be remembered as the day the people became the rulers of this nation again" was not merely an instance of Trump the campaigner playing to his movement's grandiose fantasy. With this declaration as authorization, Trump announced his post-inauguration plan to repurpose the sites on which he staged his campaign rallies as assemblages of We the People's power. In so doing Trump designated the members of his movement as at once his Real addressees and as the "We the People" source of the sovereign power enunciating itself though his presidential speech acts.[14]

When he was inaugurated president, Obama disbanded the grass-roots movement animating his presidential campaign and invested himself wholly in the Office of the President. Unlike Obama, Trump's repurposing of the sites at which he formerly held campaign rallies into "We the People" constituent assemblies elevated popular sovereignty's authorizing entity, the People, into larger-than-life visibility. The constituent assemblies into which Trump rallies mutated supplied the condition of self-presencing for the American people whose constituent power Trump claimed to embody and express (J. Frank 2021). Trump's radical claim is that he better represents the will of these Real American than do partisan members of the US Congress and Senate or the justices of the Supreme Court. At each of the assembly-rallies Trump held during his four years in office, his supporters vociferously acclaimed President Trump's power to nullify, suspend, ignore, and on occasion change the rules of the liberal democratic order.

President Trump rarely appealed to liberal watchwords when he wanted to defend, justify, or even represent his executive decisions. Whenever members of the House or Senate impugned his policies, Trump traveled to one or another of these assemblies where the Real American People claimed a power higher than the constituted authorities to exercise the constituent power to preemptively endow their leader with a "legitimacy

---

14. Jacques Derrida (1986: 10) has famously analyzed this retroactive temporality within the context of the Declaration of Independence. "We the people," as he explains their emplacement within the paradoxical logic of a representative democracy, "do not exist as an entity; it does not exist, before this declaration, not as such. If it gives birth to itself, as free and independent subject as possible signer, this can only hold in the act of the signature. The signature invents the signer. The signer can only authorize him- or herself, to sign once he or she has come to the end . . . if one can say this, of his or her signature, in a sort of fabulous retroactivity."

so profound that his rule-breaking had the effect of rule-making" (O'Neill 2020). These "We the People" assemblies did not grant him immunity *within* the law. The provenance of the assembly's constituent power exceeded the authority of constituted law and preemptively exempted him from punishment for his rule-breaking. Trump reveled in the power his constituency granted him to transgress with impunity the laws, rules, and norms of American liberal democracy. This preemptive impunity made Trump seem unanswerable to the discipline of his party, the impeachment powers of the House and Senate, the punishment of the courts, or the impugning of the liberal media. It sabotaged as well attempts by journalists and pundits to use fact-checking to disqualify his public pronouncements.

The fact that they based the grant of preemptive impunity on their extra-constitutional sovereign power did not impede the members of these "We the People" assemblies from efforts to gain political control of legislatures in states across the country. They also used social media to organize street protests, to circulate threats to "primary" elected Republican officials in Washington, DC, and to perpetrate related forms of symbolic and actual aggression on anyone who failed to recognize the higher authority of their constituent power. In retrospect it is difficult not to see that these populist assemblies were training grounds for the protesters who gathered outside the state capitols in Georgia, Michigan, Arizona, Wisconsin, and other "battleground states," chanting "Stop the Steal!" and issuing demands that their state governors, judges, and members of the House of Representatives and US Senate take action to reverse the punitive results of the 2020 election (Gabriel and Saul 2021).

President Trump carried out the transfer of power back to "you, the American People" in an actually existing historic action on February 18, 2017, when he traveled from Washington, DC, to hold the first of these "We the People" assemblies in Melbourne, Florida. Midway through the Florida meeting an anonymous member of the assembly acknowledged the people's part in receiving this transfer of power when he stepped up to the podium and said, "Mr. President, thank you sir. We the people, our movement is the reason why our President of the United States is standing here in front of us today" (Trump 2017f). At this assembly and the close to two hundred rally-assemblies that followed, Trump purported to enact the sovereign power of the people on whose authority and as whose voice he governed.

Because Trump had not yet faced any major challenge in Washington, DC, he wanted the Florida assembly's acclaim rather than its preemptive authority. Trump could do without a rally-assembly's surplus constituent power as long as Attorney General Jeff Sessions (and later William Barr), Senate Majority Leader Mitch McConnell, and House Minority Leader Kevin McCarthy agreed to interpret existing rules, norms, and constitutional statutes from a point of view that did not pose a threat to Trump's aberrant governmentality. The first constituent assembly Trump convoked to acquire preemptive impunity took place in Phoenix, Arizona, on August 22, 2017, ten days after the presidential statements he issued about events that took place in Charlottesville generated a controversy that led the entire Washington, DC, political establishment to distance themselves.

Charlottesville-Phoenix:
The Unauthorized Authority of White Supremacism

Donald Trump may be the first president who aroused in a significant bloc of the American electorate the collective desire to unseat him even before he took up the office of president(Remnick 2016; McManus 2018). Victorious in the Electoral College, Trump received three million fewer votes in the 2016 election than Hillary Clinton. From the moment the election results became official, pundits and political opponents deliberated over the most effective stratagems for his removal (Fallows 2016; Winecoff 2016; Toobin 2018; Levits 2021).

The danger Trump's election posed for American liberal democracy required that his term in office be accompanied by the open-ended threat of impeachment that functioned as a liberal democratic surplus to compensate for the perceived democratic deficit that resulted from Trump's election. By promising to mend the constitutional statutes and governmental rules that Trump took delight in violating, the specter of Trump's impeachment exerted a paradoxically reparative influence that made additional punitive measures seem unnecessary. The ongoingness of the threat of impeachment attested to the fear that Trump's presidency exceeded the jurisdiction of American liberal democracy—as did the constituent power of the populist movement that facilitated this excess. Ironically, the unceasing threat of impeachment solidified Trump's condition of preemptive impunity by proleptically rectifying whatever damage he might do to American liberal democracy.

During the first two hundred days of Trump's tenure as president, political commentators joined talk show hosts and late-night comics in casting as clownishly incompetent the failure of Trump and his appointees to understand the established rules and carry out the duties traditionally associated with their offices as the premise for an ongoing situation comedy.[15] Individually and collectively these commentators needed to believe that the election installed a bright line segregating the serious responsibilities of the governing president from Trump the campaigner's reckless political tactics. This belief rendered them unwilling to countenance the notion, save through the psychic defense of satire, that Trump embodied the intentionality of an alternative America that he could "make great again" only by transgressing the norms, breaking the rules, and dismantling the institutions of American liberal democracy. Inasmuch as these comedians appealed to the rules and norms he transgressed, the political satires directed at Trump and members of his administration exerted a quasi-emendatory influence on the institutions he damaged (Hennefield 2017; McClennan 2017; Levitz 2021). However, after these comedians and pundits witnessed the events unfold on August 11–12, 2017, in Charlottesville, Virginia, their satiric accommodations of Trump's presidency devolved into an encompassing situation tragedy that threatened the entire socio-symbolic order with "utter, abject unraveling" (Berlant 2011: 6).[16]

The Unite the Right protest bore a family resemblance to a Trump rally but without the leader's presence. Richard Spencer and Jason Kessler organized the demonstration to protest the removal of a statue of Confederate general Robert E. Lee from Charlottesville's historic courthouse district, and the demonstrators drew on the emblems and costumes of white supremacism to buttress their protestations. At this mass protest, neo-Nazis chanting "Blood and soil!" and "Jews will not replace us!" combined forces with white nationalists and polo-shirted members of the Ku Klux Klan waving Confederate flags while shouting "White lives matter." Weapon-carrying members of paramilitary white nationalist movements provided both groups armed protection. Counter-protesting organizations included the National Council of Churches, Democratic Socialists of America, Revolutionary Communist Party, Redneck Revolt, the Industrial Workers of the World, Antifa, Black Lives Matter, and Anti-Racist Action. Some counter-protesters came armed. On August 12, James Alex Fields Jr., a self-identified white

15. The effectiveness of satire as resistance to Trump has been argued eloquently by Sophie A. McClennan (2017). Nancy Loudon Gonzalez (2016) uses Bakhtin's understanding of the social utility of carnival to offer a contrary perspective on Trump's presidency. She specifically employs Bakhtin's paradigm of carnival culture to analyze the antiestablishment attitudes that defined Trump's presidential campaign from the start.
16. Lauren Berlant (2011: 6) defines "situation tragedy" as a moment when "the subject's world becomes fragile beyond repair, one gesture away from losing all access to sustaining its fantasies."

supremacist, rammed his car into a group of counter-protesters, killing Heather Heyer and injuring thirty-five other people (Wamsley 2017).

What went on in in Charlottesville made starkly evident the crisis in the nation's self-representation as an exemplary liberal democracy that Trump's white supremacist people's movement prompted. After such events, US presidents are typically expected to speak with the moral authority of the nation's conscience and offer a coherent representation of the ethical values uniting all Americans. However, the statement Donald Trump issued at his private golf club in Bedminster, New Jersey, on August 12, 2017, was glaringly lacking in the needed provision of moral clarity. Trump's press statement began with a forthright condemnation that seemed clearly directed at the participants in the Unite the Right protest: "We condemn in the strongest, possible terms this egregious display of hatred, bigotry and violence." Rather than concluding this condemnatory sentence after "violence," however, Trump (2017d) added the phrase "on many sides." This rider did not restrict the intended recipients of this censure to the Ku Klux Klansmen, neo-Nazis, and sundry additional cohorts of white supremacists participating in the Unite the Right protest but distributed Trump's denunciation to as yet unidentified counter-protesting persons and groups.

Apparently in response to the demand for moral clarity, Trump published a second statement on August 13, which he addressed to "anyone who acted criminally in this weekend's racist violence you will be held fully accountable. Justice will be delivered. . . . Racism is evil. And those who cause violence in its name are criminals and thugs, including the KKK, neo-Nazis, white supremacists and other hate groups that are repugnant to everything we hold dear as Americans" (Trump 2017d). The next day Trump once again said he found fault "on many sides." In a news conference at Trump Tower on August 15, President Trump insisted that there were "many fine people . . . on both sides" (Sitrin 2017).

The anarchic frontier violence that took place across the Charlottesville historic district had shadowed the nation from its settler-colonist inception into the present. Moreover, the "egregiously" racist events that took place Charlottesville were not substantively different from the white supremacist demonstrations that sprang up during Barack Obama's presidency and that pundits hurled into the nation's forgettable past. But Donald Trump did not consign Charlottesville to that past. Indeed, during his campaign for the presidency, Trump enjoined the forgotten white Americans in his movement to reenact in the present the lurid, racist scenarios from the nation's settler colonist past (Mitropoulos 2016; Pease 2020).

Marked by multiple, heterogeneous, often violent political antago-
nisms, Charlottesville made the contemporary political order appear to be
a restoration of settler warfare. Which is to say that the events taking place
in Charlottesville displayed political actors and activities who represented
the limit to the applicability of American liberal democracy's basic norms of
plurality, inclusivity, and tolerance. Arbiters of American liberal democracy
customarily have applied the disqualifying descriptor "extremist" to these
organizations. The hate-filled violence and bigotry these "extremist" gangs
promoted had to be ousted from the precincts of legitimate political rivalries
to safeguard the liberal norms of inclusivity and tolerance that were believed
to be protective of the human rights of all members of a liberal democracy.

However, since a substantial segment of the protesters who took part
in the demonstration were also members of the Make America Great Again
movement, President Trump could not broadcast a blanket condemnation
of the Unite the Right demonstration without numbering some "very fine
people" in his core political constituency among the condemned. Moreover,
President Trump could not banish these extremist groups from his movement without conforming to the liberal democratic norms that members of
his movement were united in opposing. Organizers of Trump rallies and
constituent assemblies did not routinely exclude members of these extremist groups. Indeed, every Trump rally, every Make America Great Again
assembly, and every America First demonstration possessed the *potential* to become a version of the Charlottesville event. How could President
Trump impose strict speech and behavior regulations on a white supremacist protest without jeopardizing the political viability of his movement?
Trump's response to this question was at once unprecedented and certain
to instigate moral panic.

Trump's critics represented the individuals and groups assembled
in Charlottesville, with the notable exception of the counter-protesters, as
"extremist" political actors unworthy of legitimate political standing within
American liberal democracy. Trump strenuously condemned what he
described as criminal acts of racist violence perpetrated by "criminals and
thugs" but did not apply the exclusionary rule to white supremacist organizations. Tellingly, Trump replaced the qualifier "extremist" with "egregious"
to distinguish members of these organizations who resorted to physical violence from those who did not. This distinction enabled Trump to recognize
the political legitimacy of *all* the actors and activities at the Unite the Right
demonstration. None of his condemnatory statements explicitly excluded
members of the KKK or neo-Nazis or white nationalist militias from mem-

bership in the Make America Great Again movement, nor did he denounce them as "domestic terrorists."

Rather than describing Charlottesville as having been overtaken by discredited political organizations, he represented the scene as structured in a primary antagonism setting those protesting the removal of the statue in an adversarial relationship with counter-protesters alongside sporadic, individualized agonisms of varying degrees of violence. Most importantly, Trump's indiscriminate assignment of the culpatory trait "egregious display of hatred and bigotry" to Antifa and Rednecks against Fascism as well as to neo-Nazis and members of the Ku Klux Klan suggested that the injurious animosities that Ku Klux Klansmen and neo-Nazis directed against Black, Jewish, and other minoritized populations were morally equivalent to the campaign of brute force that Rednecks against Fascism members of Antifa mounted to protect these groups.

Trump's condemnation of the *egregious* display of white supremacist and white nationalist violence in the KKK and paramilitary organizations tacitly endorsed nonegregious, unmarked whiteness as the operative ideology and prevailing norm of US politics. He could condemn particular instantiations of white supremacist violence because whiteness did not need to assume this restricted expression to sustain its status as the normative condition of the American political system. What apologists of American liberal democracy cannot acknowledge and must foreclose from recognition is that white supremacism functions as the unmarked normative presupposition regulating liberal democratic productions of inclusivity and diversity (Harris 1993; Lipsitz 1995; Rodríguez 2020; Louie and Viladrich 2021; Issar 2021; Wiegman 1999). After Trump recognized ordinary, nonviolent white supremacy as a legitimate political stance embraced by some "very fine people . . . on both sides" of this political antagonism, white supremacism underwent a radical shift in its positionality from that of a particular ideology to the structuring matrix for the entire field of political contestation.

The pronouncements about the Ku Klux Klan and neo-Nazis in the three statements about Charlottesville that President Trump put out between August 12 and August 15 undermined the moral consensus that had united political factions on the right and left for more than eighty years (D. Clark 2017). Trump's failure to recognize any justiciable difference between neo-Nazis and Ku Klux Klansmen disgorging hate speech and those who opposed them provoked outrage across the political spectrum. The indignation was not restricted to news reporters, pundits, and political opponents. Republican colleagues whom Trump had come to trust were uncharacteristically forthright in their criticism. "We must be clear," Speaker of the House Paul Ryan cautioned. "White supremacy is repulsive. This bigotry is counter to all this country stands for. There can be no moral ambiguity." To which nostrum Senate Majority Leader Mitch McConnell added, "There are no good neo-Nazis" (Gambino 2017). In a widely circulated tweet, Mitt Romney, the 2012 Republican candidate for president, offered a useful disambiguation of Trump's offensive phrase "many sides": "One side is racist, bigoted, Nazi. The other opposes racism and bigotry. Morally different universes" (Balz 2017). Nancy Pelosi and other leaders in the Democratic Party alluded to the remarks of Trump's Republican colleagues when they contemplated bringing impeachment procedures against him (L. Clark 2017; Siegel 2017).

Charlottesville opened a paradoxical space within the US political order wherein advocates of liberal democracy were required to mirror the exclusionary practices of their authoritarian and illiberal Other to sustain America's integrity as a pluralistic democratic order. The political establishment's exclusionary and intolerant response to the Unite the Right protest at Charlottesville revealed what might be described as American liberal democracy's illiberal underside. After Trump's press conference on Charlottesville, apologists for American liberal democracy could only maintain the norms and principles of liberal democracy by forswearing the Unite the Right protesters. However, their procedure of condemnation perforce violated liberal norms of tolerance and inclusivity. Upon entering this paradoxical space, Trump transgressed this procedure. His transgression assumed the form of rendering the principles of inclusivity and tolerance applicable to persons and groups that proponents of liberal democracy had declared "extremist," hence illegitimate, political actors and organizations. Rather than shoring up the foundational liberal democratic norms of diversity and plurality, however, Trump's deployment of these acts of inclusion worked to undermine American liberal democracy from within. Throughout his tenure in office, President Trump governed the US political order by occupying this site of inherent transgression as the vantage from which he aspired to disconnect American democracy from quintessentially liberal principles and norms. More significantly, he represented the constituent power of the Make America Great Again movement as the authorizing power for this aspiration.

Because Trump's diktats on Charlottesville contradicted the consensus reached by representatives across the political spectrum, the guardians of liberal democracy were eager to construe what they found inappropriate in Trump's response to Charlottesville as the pretext for bringing Trump and his insurrectionary movement before the disciplinary authority of the liberal democratic consensus. Trump's adviser and speech writer, Stephen Bannon, who had a hand in crafting the president's August 12 press statement, said Trump's August 15 press conference was the "defining moment" in his presidency because he had taken sides with "his people" against the "braying mob of reporters" and the entire "liberal establishment they represented" (Swan 2017).

As we have seen, prior to Charlottesville the Make America Great Again movement's extra-constitutional authorizing power endowed President Trump's transgressive behavior with preemptive impunity. Trump's responses to the Charlottesville protest rally made publicly evident the self-division that had remained dormant since the Inauguration. During his initial seven months in office, Trump was able to obscure his primary commitment to an illiberal, white supremacist, populist movement by following the procedural rules of liberal democracy: he submitted policies to the House and Senate for approval, negotiated with senators and members of the House to secure passage of key pieces of legislation, appealed Supreme Court rulings on executive decisions. However, the statements Trump felt compelled to make about Charlottesville exposed the disparity between the president and the head of a white nationalist movement. At this moment of danger both Trump and the American people to whom he had handed the power to rule of the country were exposed to the punitive powers of liberal democracy. Charlottesville had rendered Trump's contradictory identifications spectacularly evident, and his political opponents were now eager to use constitutionally authorized powers to initiate impeachment hearings to remove President Trump from office and to disassemble the Make America Great Again movement.

Trump knew that his statements about Charlottesville would remain subject to nearly unanimous denunciation as long as liberal norms offered the sole criteria for their adjudication. Rather than continuing to subject his statements to liberal democracy's impeachment powers, Trump decided to call on the higher authority of the Real Americans in his movement. So, he arranged a rally/constituent assembly meeting for August 22, 2017, in the Phoenix, Arizona, Convention Center. Neo-Nazis, white supremacists, and paramilitary organizations might have seemed out of place in Charlottesville, Virginia, but Phoenix is in Maricopa County, Arizona, the location of the notorious tent-city jail that its designer, Sheriff Joe Arpaio, described as a "concentration camp" for undocumented immigrants. Sheriff Joe's detention center had received accolades from the full gamut of ultra-right paramilitary and white supremacist groups, including neo-Nazis and members of the Ku Klux Klan (Finnegan 2009; Oppenheim 2017). Despite the fact that Arpaio's illegal detention of persons suspected of being undocumented immigrants resulted in his July 2017 conviction for criminal contempt, Trump never missed an opportunity to extol Sheriff Joe's extralegal rounding up and incarceration of undocumented immigrants as exemplary stratagems for defending US borders.

The Washington, DC, political establishment and the mainstream media had already concluded that Trump's Charlottesville pronouncements rendered him signally unqualified to hold the office of president. However, when he traveled to the people's assembly in Phoenix, Arizona, Trump made clear his intention to recognize the higher authority of the Real American people to decide on the ethical and political status of his statements about Charlottesville. Earlier I mentioned that the investiture ceremony Trump added to his inauguration could not achieve completion until the American people to whom he gave back the power to rule retroactively used that power to make Trump the embodiment of their will. The alternative inauguration ceremony that took place at Phoenix on August 22 effectively "resolved" Trump's investiture crisis by enabling him to demonstrate quite publicly his primary investment in accomplishing the will of the people to whom he had transferred sovereign power on January 20. Upon taking part in this ceremony, the people assembled in the Phoenix Convention Center thereby revealed themselves as the mysterious source of the power he gave back to this constituency on Inauguration Day.

At his January 20 inauguration, Trump had conjured the Real American people in their absence. The American people who traveled to Phoenix on August 22 became reflexively aware of themselves as the people whose enactments could decide the future of Trump's presidency—and the Make America Great Again movement. At Phoenix, Trump was retroactively empowered to deliver his pronouncements about Charlottesville by the people to whom he had given back this power at his official inaugural ceremony and from whom he now needed authorization to continue to exercise the American people's power to rule the nation.

The event that this assemblage co-enacted with Trump at Phoenix on August 22 thereby actualized Trump's inauguration as the Make America Great Again Movement's usurper-president. This inauguration ceremony was divided into three scenarios. The initial scenario began when the Phoenix assemblage mutated into a continuation of the Charlottesville Unite the Right demonstration, but with the protest headed by President Trump himself this time and directed against the liberal elite media's condemnation of President Trump's statements about Charlottesville. Trump fomented this transfiguration when he repeated the Charlottesville statements that he had originally enunciated as president but delivered in Phoenix as the voice of this We the People assembly's outrage at the mainstream media's response.

Members of the news media who flocked to the Convention Center brought cameras to record what they expected would be Trump's self-incriminating affirmation of his earlier statements within a setting that would expose his supporters in Phoenix as morally discreditable members of the extreme Right. The press wanted to turn the event into an instructive exposé of the extremist and illiberal behaviors that must be excluded from American liberal democracy to remedy the defects Trump added to it.

Trump did not behave as expected. He neither apologized for the equivocations in his earlier pronouncements nor clarified what he meant to say nor offered a revision of his three earlier official statements. In place of these expected scenarios, Trump opened his remarks about Charlottesville with a belligerent encore of his August 12 response to the Unite the Right protest. In place of speaking as the president, however, he spoke as the collective voice of the Phoenix assembly: "And tonight, this entire arena stands united in forceful condemnation of the thugs who perpetrate hatred and violence."

The mainstream media had rebuked Trump for the *moral* equivalence he adduced between racists and antiracists. When Trump assumed the assembled people's voice of moral indignation, he did so to draw a *political* equivalence between the liberal media's unanimously intolerant response to his statements about Charlottesville and the "hatred and violence" they condemned. He then identified the reporters from CNN, the *New York Times,* and the *Washington Post* covering the event as the proximate referents for the "thugs who perpetrate hatred and violence."

Trump did not propound this equivalence as a form of self-defense. He denigrated the perspective from which the mainstream press was prepared to cover the Phoenix meeting as itself indistinguishable from the bigotry exhibited on "many sides" at Charlottesville. To let the "dishonest media" feel the specular effects of the assembly's outrage at the perspective the press had imposed, Trump enjoined his addressees to cast their antagonistic gaze at the reporters' cameras. As they returned the press's gaze, the people dispossessed the press of the power to represent the event from the press's point of view: "But the very dishonest media, those people right up there with all the cameras (BOOING). . . . So the—and I mean truly dishonest people in the media and the fake media, they make up stories . . . I'm telling you folks, look, look, I know these people probably better than anybody" (Trump 2017c). As Trump shouted into this throng he became bodily interfused with their reciprocating vociferations and spoke as the force of their coalesced voices (Freud 1928). Throughout their inter-locutory transactions with Trump, the participants in this event collectively acted out the nullification of the liberal principles informing the press per-spective and took delight in the strike-down they cocreated with Trump. They questioned the liberal media's ability to represent, interpret, or explain the movement's values; they did not recognize the media as credible arbi-ters of Trump's political, cultural, or moral authority; and they regarded as hypocritical the liberal media's claims of neutrality and objective report-ing. With each shout of disapproval, this assembly authorized what Trump said through their deauthorization of the press's impugning and the politi-cal establishment's calls for impeachment. They joined Trump in taking obscene transgressive enjoyment, what Jacques Lacan calls *"jouissance,"* in the press corps's growing vexation at this *coup de force* exempting him from punitive measures (Glynos and Stavrakakis 2008; Jutel 2017).

After orchestrating this antagonistic response to the liberal media's perspective, Trump proceeded to the portion of the inauguration ceremony in which he asked the Phoenix constituent assembly to decide on the apt-ness of his Charlottesville pronouncements. This second scenario in the people's inauguration ceremony began with a speech-event that made leg-ible the self-doubling that Trump's investiture crisis precipitated. Rather than repeating the morally offensive statements as the US president who said them, however, Trump, as if standing beside that person (in what I am tempted to describe as an out-of-Second-Body experience), delivered verbatim recitations of the contested passages from all three of the presi-dent's declarations about Charlottesville as if these speech acts were origi-nally uttered by someone other than himself: "So here is my first statement when I heard about Charlottesville. So here's what I said, really fast, here's what I said on Saturday: 'We're closely following the terrible events unfold-ing in Charlottesville, Virginia'—this is me speaking. 'We condemn in the strongest, possible terms this egregious display of hatred, bigotry and vio-lence.' That's me speaking on Saturday" (Trump 2017c). Trump's virtuoso double-voiced performance effected an asymmetrical presentation of the two personae he felt compelled to take up when he first heard about Char-lottesville: The persona who said, "We condemn in the strongest, possible terms this egregious display of hatred, bigotry and violence" is the figure who was inaugurated on January 20, 2017, and who was summoned on August 12 by the moral responsibility and solemn obligations attendant to the Office of the President to condemn the violently hateful activities unfolding in Charlottesville. However, the persons who said, "That's me speaking on Saturday. Right after the event," is the usurper-president (the president that is not one) who cannot identify with the official statements of the president without the loss of identification with the people assembled in the Phoenix Convention Center. The latter figure cannot successfully usurp the Office of the President until the segment of American people before whom Trump is now reciting these official presidential announcements in the Phoenix Convention Center spontaneously acclaim his power to divest these utterances of their connection to the obligations and responsibilities inherent in the Office of the President and retroactively infuse these utterances with the people's sovereign acclamatory power.

The indexical phrases "So here is my first statement" and "So here's what I said, really fast, here's what I said on Saturday" interject a disparity between the presidential "We" that enunciated the sentences "We're closely following the terrible events unfolding in Charlottesville, Virginia" and "We condemn in the strongest, possible terms this egregious display of hatred, bigotry and violence" and the person who is citing these phrases in the here and now. When he appends the deictic tags "this is me speaking" and "that's me speaking" to the preceding sentences, Trump divests the "I" addressing the Phoenix assemblage viva voce from the presidential "me" that "I" was obliged to impersonate when "I" delivered "this" pro forma presidential statement of concern ("We're closely following the terrible events unfolding in Charlottesville, Virginia") and "that" pro forma presidential condemnation ("We condemn in the strongest, possible terms this egregious display of hatred, bigotry and violence"). The "I" that emerges fully divested of officious presidential obligations is wholly invested in the people who are acclaiming these words as felicitous expressions of their will. This newly emanated "I" who gives expression to the sovereign enunciative instantiation of the people's power is the usurper-president whom the people's acclamatory sovereign voice now inaugurates.

Throughout this opening scene Trump divided the audience of this virtuoso performance into primary interlocutor-addressees and secondary witness-addressees. The primary addressees were comprised of the Phoenix interlocutors whom Trump recognized as the extra-constitutional sovereign voice endowed with the people's constituent power to decide on two questions: (1) whether his official condemnations of the Charlottesville big-otry conformed to the proprieties vested in the Office of the President; and (2) whether the liberal mainstream media and the political establishment should have been satisfied with these official condemnations. The primary addressee-interlocutors would also include the participants in the Unite the Right protest at Charlottesville, who were the initial targets of his pro forma presidential condemnations as well as all the members of the Make America Great Again movement whose voices Trump and the members of the Phoenix assembly conjointly channel. The secondary witness-addressees include the press recording this spectacle and the sundry local, national, and international audiences taking in, with varying degrees of apprehension, Trump's usage of liberal formalities as vehicles for substantively illiberal and white supremacist populist disruptions.

In the third scene of this contraband inauguration ceremony, Trump disclosed that the official statements he made as president could not acquire the status of felicitous or legitimate speech acts as he initially said them because they were accompanied by an ongoing and simultaneous impeachment from members of the press and the political establishment who found them infelicitous responses to what took place in Charlottesville: "So I'm condemning [sic] the strongest, possible terms, 'egregious display,' 'hatred, bigotry and violence.' OK, I think I can't do much better, right? OK. But they didn't want to put this on. They had it on initially, but then one day he talked (ph)—he didn't say it fast enough. He didn't do it on time. Why did it take a day? He must be a racist. It took a day (BOOING)" (Trump 2017c). Now it should be noted that the speaker enunciating the utterance "So I'm condemning the strongest, possible terms, 'egregious display,' 'hatred, bigotry and violence'" is different from either the figure of the president or the substance of what "that's me speaking on Saturday" previously said about Charlottesville when impersonating the office of president. The figure who repeats these lines viva voce before the segment of the American people whose retroactive sovereign will he purports to incarnate is Donald Trump the usurper-president. He required the people's retroactive approbation because every one of the speech acts Trump uttered as "this is me speaking" while impersonating the president underwent ongoing and simultaneous impeachment ("he didn't say it fast enough. He didn't do it on time. Why did it take a day? He must be a racist. It took a day") as he uttered them and necessitated the anterior supplement of the American people's constituent power to retroactively appropriate these utterances as expressions of their will and thereby grant him preemptive impunity for enunciating them.

Notice, however, that the phrases "egregious display" and "hatred, bigotry and violence," which Trump initially pronounced as president, have now become newly potentiated. Since the press who formerly criticized the efficacy of these phrases are also present in the Convention Center, these phrases become freshly activated as sovereign speech acts uttered by the "I" who has appropriated the president's phrases here and now to denounce the press's ongoing injurious "bigotry." However, the "I" who now utters these phrases to express the will of a people united in unambiguous condemnation of the press's "egregious display [of] hatred, bigotry and violence" is no longer impersonating the president. This I, who is invested in speaking and being spoken by the people's outraged indignation at the liberal elite, is the enunciative agency of their newly inaugurated usurper-president.

At his January 20, 2017, inauguration, Trump hailed the people in his movement as a nation-making force that exceeded the authority of the constituted order. However, insofar as the people to whom he gave back this power assumed a merely virtual presence, this power stayed latent in the Washington, DC, alternative investiture ceremony. The people who assembled in Phoenix on August 22 actuated this power by effecting two indissolubly related outcomes. The Phoenix people "resolved" Trump's investiture crisis; they did so by inaugurating Trump as a leader vested in primarily serving as the expressive agency of their nation-making power. The supererogatory inauguration ceremony Trump cocreated with the Phoenix assembly thereby imparted to him the Make America Great Again movement's sovereign power to usurp the presidency and occupy that office as their vox populi. Upon being bodily taken up by the people's acclamatory voice, Trump, who previously had uttered the statements about Charlottesville in his office as the US president, now spoke them as the incarnation of the voice of the Make America Great Again movement. Trump therewith and thereafter dedicated the power and authority of that office to the work of enacting the sovereign will of the Make America Great Again people.

The inauguration ceremony the Make American Great Again movement enacted at Phoenix achieved the interrelated objectives of potentiating the sovereign power Trump had given back to the Real American people at his inauguration ceremony, authorizing Trump's Charlottesville statements as the expression of the Forgotten American People's will, decoupling the movement from the jurisdiction of American liberal democracy, and inaugurating Trump as usurper-president of the Make America Great Again movement. They demonstrated the efficacy of this power by rejecting the judgment of the press, overruling the House's charges of impeachment, and deauthorizing the Senate's power to remove him from office. The People's preemptive powers, which accompanied the president like a djinni throughout the remaining three years, three months, and fifteen days of his tenure as president, found its extralegal constituent powers confronted with a potentially lethal threat on November 5, 2020, when President Trump sounded the alarm that at polling stations throughout the United States large-scale and centrally organized electoral fraud had happened, was happening, and that, without an intervention, Joseph R. Biden. Jr. would illegally be declared president-elect of the United States. "If you count the legal votes, I easily win. If you count the illegal votes, they can try to steal the election from us" (Trump 2020).

Time in the Après-Coup

Numerous commentators have cogently analyzed the historical, political, and psychosocial significance of the January 6 insurrection and the part Trump's Save America rally at the Ellipse played in inciting it. However, in keeping with the restricted focus of the trajectory of these remarks I want, by way of conclusion, to explain briefly the part Birtherism played in Trump's effort to persuade Vice President Pence to refuse to certify the Electoral College votes that made official Joseph R. Biden Jr.'s election as the forty-sixth president of the United States.

When Trump asserted, "If you count the legal votes, I easily win. If you count the illegal votes, they can try to steal the election from us," he put into place the preconditions for the production of what Brian Massumi (2015a) calls an "affective fact." For Trump's supporters, the threatened reality of the state of affairs referenced in the alarum "If you count the illegal votes, they can try to steal the election from us" felt so superlatively real that it translated into a certainty about the election even in the absence of actual grounding for it in observable facts. The threat conveyed in the warning "If you count the legal votes, I easily win. If you count the illegal votes, they can try to steal the election from us" overlays its own conditional determination on the objective situation through the mechanism of alarm that makes the threatening and the objective coexist. If the threat does not materialize, it still always would have if it could have. This would have been voter fraud if it could have been. Rather than referential truth value, Trump's alert possessed performative threat value (Massumi 2015a). The measure of its factuality pertained to the immediacy of response to the threat it triggered. More than any correspondence with the semantic content of observable facts, it was the performed commensurability of the alert to the action it triggered—the inception of a series of actions that culminated in the January 6 insurrection—that qualified the alarum's accuracy.[17]

Following their reception of this alarmingly affecting factual matter, the Birthers in Trump's movement revised their understanding of Trump's decertification of the citizenship rights of the first African American president to entail the disenfranchisement of every African American voter. In response they extended Birtherism's provenance to encompass all African Americans, who, by virtue of their African heritage, lacked the identity credentials required to make them legitimate voters in an American election. Viewed from a Birther's perspective, the votes of African American and "always already" illegal immigrants could not be counted as equal to those of Trump's electorate without "diluting" or "polluting" the ballots of white voters. It is because he received an even greater number of votes than he had in 2016 that Trump says he won the 2020 election by a landslide (Chalfant and Samuels 2020).

Trump based this claim on Birtherism's aspiration to invalidate the votes of millions of Americans on the basis of race and heritage. For the Americans who remade themselves in the image of Trump's settler-nationalist alternative to liberal democracy, only Make America Great Again votes count. In Trump's America to be white is to perform Americanness. As Cheryl Harris (1993) has explained, whiteness alone endows an individual with the dispossessive power of birthright citizenship to exclude or render natural the condition of forced noncitizenship. Black people and migrants cannot belong to the America over whom the *Real* American People have the birthright to sole ownership; it follows that they cannot vote in the country to which they do not belong. Trumpists who went to polling stations to decertify legally cast Black votes on November 8, 2020, were exercising the power of whiteness to Make America Great Again. By this logic, the disenfranchisement of Black voters is a nation-making event.

However, Trump's contestation of election results was not based simply on Birtherism's aspirational ideals. It was built on the infrastructure of an entrenched culture of minority rule buttressed by an insurrectionary populist movement whose members considered the 2020 election results a theft of *their* country. Trump based his claim that the election was stolen on the fact that Republican state legislatures in the swing states he won in 2016

17. See Massumi 2015a. For splendid analyses of the affective attachments and bonds of affiliation among Trump's supporters, see Anderson 2017; and Peters and Protevi 2017.

had purged voter rolls, passed "use it or lose it" right to vote laws, authorized retroactive signature checks, reduced or eliminated ballot boxes and drive-in registration sites, and enacted other voter suppression legislation that supposedly should have made it impossible for him to lose the 2020 election (Serwer 2020).

Trump supporters who participated in the communication of Trump's affective facts trafficked in lurid spectacles of trucks dumping votes numbering in the millions cast by dead (in the civil and literal sense) Black people and other aliens. This illegal vote-counting invariably took place under the shield of darkness and occurred only within the rat-infested, unsupervised polling stations in cities with sizable African American populations—specifically Atlanta, Detroit, Milwaukee, and Philadelphia—within the battleground states that Trump lost. To right this wrong, Trump's legal team asked various courts to invalidate millions of Black and undocumented immigrant votes and extend his term in office. When the courts did not arrive at that verdict, Trump enjoined the paramilitary wing of his movement to act upon the event prefigured in the alternative investiture ceremony he had added to his official inauguration.

On January 20, 2017, Trump the Usurper, whose 2016 election resulted from a nonviolent insurrectionary movement, stated that he was "transferring [sovereign] power from Washington, DC, and giving it back to you, the American People" (Trump 2017a; Deans 2018). In a December 2, 2020, YouTube video President Trump initiated a much more grandiose version of the Unite the Right demonstration that had taken place at Charlottesville by urging members of the Make America Great Again movement from across the United States to gather in full movement regalia in Washington, DC, on January 6, 2022, the day the joint session of Congress was to officially certify Joseph R. Biden Jr. as the forty-sixth president. On January 6, the "American People" to whom he had transferred this power on January 20, 2017, traveled to Washington, DC, as an insurrectionary movement that would use whatever force necessary to preempt the president-elect from taking back this power (O'Toole 2020).

• • • •

"Stop the coup!" might have been—and in some quarters was—taken as a realistic call to action during the early morning hours of November 9, 2016. Now, however, in the wake of Trump's hostile takeover of the Republican Party, revivification of settler-colonist agents and events, sabotaging of the US administrative state apparatus, hollowing out of key institutions of the liberal international order, shattering bedrock principles of the US political system (equality under the law; impartial and Independent courts and tribunals; separation of church and state; the protection of basic liberties of speech, assembly, religion, and property; checks on the power of each branch of government), insurrectionary pillaging of the Capitol, what remains of the Trump event feels somehow more *real* than the reality of Biden's presidency (Pease 2021). Without a planetary reckoning with the settler-imperial specters of American liberal democracy, time in the après-coup will belong to its revenants.

References

Ackerman, Spencer. 2021. *Reign of Terror: How the 9/11 Era Destabilized America and Produced Trump.* New York: Viking.

Ahmed, Sara. 2004. "Affective Economies." *Social Text* 22, no. 2: 117–39.

Anderson, Ben. 2017. "'We Will Win Again. We Will Win a Lot': The Affective Styles of Donald Trump." *Society and Space,* February 28. https://www.societyand space.org/articles/we-will-win-again-we-will-win-a-lot-the-affective-styles -of-donald-trump.

Anker, Elizabeth R. 2022. *Ugly Freedoms.* Durham, NC: Duke University Press.

Anton, Michael (Publius Decius Mus). 2016a. "The Flight 93 Election." *Claremont Review of Books,* September 5. https://www.claremont.org/crb/basicpage /the-flight-93-election/.

Anton, Michael (Publius Decius Mus). 2016b. "Toward a Sensible, Coherent Trumpism." *Unz Review,* March 10. https://www.unz.com/article/toward-a -sensible-coherent-trumpism/.

Baker, Kevin. 2015. "The Incredible True Story of the Tea Party's Rise to Power." *TakePart,* October 30. http://www.takepart.com/feature/2015/10/30/tea-party -history.

Balz, Dan, 2017. "After Charlottesville, Republicans Remain Stymied over What to Do about Trump." *Washington Post,* August 19. https://www.washingtonpost .com/politics/after-charlottesville-republicans-remain-stymied-over-what-to -do-about-trump/2017/08/19/.

Bandar, Brenda. 2018. *Colonial Lives of Property: Law, Land, and Racial Regimes of Ownership.* Durham, NC: Duke University Press.

Bauman, Zygmunt. 2017. *Retrotopia.* Cambridge: Polity.

Behdad, Ali. 2005. *A Forgetful Nation: On Immigration and Cultural Identity in the United States* Durham, NC: Duke University Press.

Beinart, Peter. 2018. "Why Trump Supporters Believe He Is Not Corrupt." *Atlantic,* August 22. https://www.theatlantic.com/ideas/archive/2018/08/what-trumps -supporters-think-of-corruption/568147/.

Berlant, Lauren. 2011. *Cruel Optimism.* Durham, NC: Duke University Press.

Bourdieu, Pierre. 2000. *Pascalian Meditations*. Translated by Richard Nice. Palo Alto, CA: Stanford University Press.

Brown, Vincent. 2009. "Social Death and Political Life in the Study of Slavery." *American Historical Review* 114, no. 5: 1231–49.

Brown, Wendy. 2017. *Undoing the Demos: Neoliberalism's Stealth Revolution*. New York: Zone.

Brown, Wendy, Peter Gordon, and Maxim Pensky. 2018. *Authoritarianism: Three Inquiries in Critical Theory*. Chicago: University of Chicago Press.

Bruyneel, Kevin. 2021. *Settler Memory: The Disavowal of Indigeneity and the Politics of Race in the United States*. Chapel Hill: University of North Carolina Press.

Byrd, Jodi, Alyosha Goldstein, Jodi Melamed, and Chandan Reddy. 2018 "Predatory Value: Economies of Dispossession and Disturbed Relationalities." *Social Text* 36, no. 2: 1–18.

Chalfant, Morgan, and Brett Samuels. 2020 "Trump Prematurely Declares Victory, Says He'll Go to Supreme Court." *Hill*, November 4. https://thehill.com/home news/campaign/524404-trump-says-hell-go-to-supreme-court-to-stop-votes -from-being-counted.

Chomsky, Aviva. 2016. "Is Trump an Aberration? The Dark History of the 'Nation of Immigrants.'" *Salon*, September 15. https://www.salon.com/2016/09/15 /is-trump-an-aberration-the-dark-history-of-the-nation-of-immigrants_partner /ctheory.net.

Clark, Dartonurro. 2017. "Democratic, Republican Lawmakers Decry Trump's Latest Charlottesville Remarks." NBC News, August 17. https://www.nbcnews .com/politics/white-house/not-my-president-lawmakers-decry-trump-s-latest -charlottesville-remarks-n793021.

Clark, Lesley. 2017. "Democrats Drafting Articles of Impeachment against Trump." *Miami Herald,* August 17. https://www.miamiherald.com/news/nation-world /article167795437.html.

Coates, Ta-Nehisi. 2012. "Fear of a Black President." *Atlantic*, September 2012. https://www.theatlantic.com/magazine/archive/2012/09/fear-of-a-black president/309064/.

Coulthard, Glenn. 2014. *Red Skin, White Masks: Rejecting the Colonial Politics of Recognition*. Indigenous Americas. Minneapolis: University of Minnesota Press.

Deans, Effie. 2018. "Trump the Usurper." *Daily Globe*, August 16. http://www.dailyglobe .co.uk/comment/trump-the-usurper/.

Derrida, Jacques, 1986. "Declarations of Independence." Translated by Tom Keenan and Tom Pepper. *New Political Science* 15: 3–13.

Dunbar-Ortiz, Roxanne. 2021. "Not a Nation of Immigrants." *Monthly Review* 73, no. 4. https://monthlyreview.org/2021/09/01/not-a-nation-of-immigrants/.

Editorial Board. 2021. "Trump Still Says He Won. What Happens Next?" *New York*

Times, January 5. https://www.nytimes.com/2021/01/05/opinion/trump-call
-georgia.html.

Elkins, Caroline, and Susan Pedersen, eds. 2005. *Settler Colonialism in the Twentieth Century*. New York: Routledge.

Fallows, James. 2016. "After the Election: 'What a Pathetic Thing Is Decadence.'"
Atlantic, November 14.

Finnegan, William. 2009. "Sheriff Joe: Joe Arpaio Is Tough on Prisoners and Undocumented Immigrants. What about Crime?" *New Yorker*, July 20. https://www
.newyorker.com/magazine/2009/07/20/sheriff-joe.

Frank, Jason. 2010. *Constituent Moments: Enacting the People in Postrevolutionary
America*. Durham, NC: Duke University Press.

Frank, Jason. 2021. *The Democratic Sublime: On Aesthetics and Popular Assembly*. Oxford: Oxford University Press.

Frank, Thomas. 2004. *What's The Matter with Kansas? How Conservatives Won
the Heart of America*. New York: Henry Holt & Company.

Frederickson, George W. 1982. *White Supremacy: A Comparative Study of American and South African History*. Oxford: Oxford University Press.

Freud, Sigmund. 1928. *Group Psychology and the Analysis of the Ego*. Translated
by James Stratchey. London: Hogarth.

Fukuyama, Francis. 1992. *The End of History and the Last Man*. New York: Free
Press.

Gabriel, Trip, and Stephanie Saul. 2021. "Could State Legislatures Pick Electors
to Vote for Trump? Not Likely." *New York Times*, January 5. https://www.ny
times.com/article/electors-vote.html.

Gambino, Lauren. 2017. "Republicans on Charlottesville: Who's with Trump and
Who's against Him?" *Guardian*, August 16. https://www.theguardian.com
/us-news/2017/aug/16/republicans-charlottesville-trump-response-for
-against.

Gingrich, Newt, and the Republican National Committee. 1984. *Contract with America*. New York: Three Rivers.

Glasser, Susan B. 2018. "The Man Who Put Andrew Jackson in Trump's White
House." *Politico*, January 22. https://www.politico.com/magazine/story/2018
/01/22/andrew-jackson-donald-trump-216493.

Glynos, Jason, and Yannis Stavrakakis. 2008. "Lacan and Political Subjectivity:
Fantasy and Enjoyment in Psychoanalysis and Political Theory." *Subjectivity*, no. 24: 256–74.

Gonzalez, Nancy Loudon. 2016. "Carnival or Campaign? Locating Robin Hood
and the Carnivalesque in the U.S. Presidential Campaign" *Humanist*, April
19. https://thehumanist.com/magazine/may-june-2016/features/carnival-or
-campaign.

Grandin, Greg 2019. "The Myth of the Border Wall." *New York Times*, February 20.
https://www.nytimes.com/2019/02/20/opinion/trump-border-wall.html.

Gregory, Derek. 2004. *The Colonial Present*. Oxford: Blackwell.

Hage, Ghassan. 1998. *White Nation: Fantasies of White Supremacy in a Multicultural Society*. Sydney: Pluto.

Harris, Cheryl. 1993. "Whiteness as Property." *Harvard Law Review* 106, no. 8: 1707–91.

Helsel, Phil. 2016. "Campaign, Not Trump, Says He Believes Obama Was Born in U.S." *NBC News*, September 16. https://www.nbcnews.com/politics/2016-election /trump-again-refuses-say-whether-obama-was-born-u-s-n649221.

Hennefield, Maggie. 2017. "Fake News: From Satirical Truthiness to Alternative Facts." *New Politics*, February 19. http://newpol.org/content/fake-news-satirical -truthiness-alternative-facts.

Herzfeld, Michael. 2021. *Subversive Archaism: Troubling Traditionalists and the Politics of National Heritage*. Durham, NC: Duke University Press.

Holmes, Steven, and Ivan Krastev. 2020. *The Light That Failed: Why the West Is Losing the Fight for Democracy*. New York: Pegasus.

Ikenga, L. E. 2009. "Obama, the African Colonial." *American Thinker*, June 25. https:// www.americanthinker.com/articles/2009/06/obama_the_african_colonial.html.

Issar, Siddhant. 2021. "Theorising 'Racial/Colonial Primitive Accumulation': Settler Colonialism, Slavery, and Racial Capitalism." *Race & Class* 63, no. 1: 23–50.

Johnson, Jenna. 2016. "A Lot of People Are Saying How Trump Spreads Conspiracy Theories, Lies, and Innuendoes." *Washington Post*, June 13. https:// www.washingtonpost.com/politics/a-lot-of-people-are-saying-how-trump -spreads-conspiracies-and-innuendo/2016/06/13/b21e59de-317e-11e6-8ff7 -7b6c1998b7a0_story.html.

Judis, John B. 2016. *The Populist Explosion: How the Great Recession Transformed American and European Politics*. New York: Columbia Global Reports.

Jutel, Olivier. 2017. "Donald Trump's Libidinal Entanglement with Liberalism and Affective Media Power." *b2o*, October 23. https://www.boundary2.org/2017 /10/olivier-jutel-donald-trumps-libidinal-entanglement-with-liberalism-and -affective-media-power/.

Kagan, Robert. 2021. "Our Constitutional Crisis Is Already Here." *Washington Post*, September 23. https://www.washingtonpost.com/opinions/2021/09/23/robert -kagan-constitutional-crisis/.

Kantorowicz, Ernst. (1957) 1985. *The King's Two Bodies: A Study in Medieval Political Theology*. Princeton, NJ: Princeton University Press.

Kay, Katy. 2017. "Why Trump's Supporters Will Never Abandon Him." *BBC World News*, August 23. https://www.bbc.com/news/world-us-canada-41028733.

Kelleter, Frank. 2020. "Hegemoronic Vistas: The Pseudo-Gramscian Right from the Powell Memo to 'The Flight 93 Election.'" In *Trump's America: Political Culture and National Identity*, edited by Liam Kennedy, 23–78. Edinburgh: University of Edinburgh Press.

Kim, Jodi. 2022. *Settler Garrison, Debt Imperialism, and Transpacific Imaginaries*. Durham, NC: Duke University Press.

Krieg, Geoffrey. 2016. "Fourteen of Trump's Most Outrageous 'Birther' Claims—Half from after 2011." CNN, September 16. https://www.cnn.com/2016/09/09/politics /donald-trump-birther/index.html.

Laclau, Ernesto. 2005. *On Populist Reason*. London: Verso.

Levitz, Eric. 2021. "Liberal Hyperbole about Trump Was Never the Problem." *Intelligencer*, November 30. https://nymag.com/intelligencer/article/liberal-hyper bole-trump-coup.html.

Lewis, Adam. 2017. "From Standing Rock to Resistance in Context: Towards Anarchism against Settler Colonialism." *E-International Relations*, February 1. https://www.e-ir.info/2017/02/01/from-standing-rock-to-resistance-in-context -towards-anarchism-against-settler-colonialism/.

Lipsitz, George. 1995. "The Possessive Investment in Whiteness: Racialized Social Democracy and the 'White' Problem in American Studies." *American Quarterly* 47, no. 3: 369–87.

Louie, Vivian, and Anahí Viladrich. 2021. "Divide, Divert, and Conquer: Deconstructing the Presidential Framing of White Supremacy in the COVID-19 Era." MDPI, *Social Sciences* 10, no. 8: 1–20. https://ideas.repec.org/a/gam/jscscx /v10y2021i8p280-d598434.html.

Mamdami, Mahmood. 2015. "Settler Colonialism: Then and Now." *Critical Inquiry* 41, no. 3: 596–614.

Massumi, Brian. 2015a. *Ontopower: War, Powers, and the State of Perception*. Durham, NC: Duke University Press.

Massumi, Brian. 2015b. *Politics of Affect*. Cambridge: Polity.

Mazzarella, William. 2019. "Brand(ish)ing the Name; or, Why Is Trump So Enjoyable." In *Sovereignty Inc.: Three Inquiries in Politics and Enjoyment*, by William Mazzarella, Eric Santner, and Aaron Schuster, 113–61. Chicago: University of Chicago Press.

McCarthy, Andrew. 2010. *The Grand Jihad: How Islam and the Left Sabotage America*. New York: Encounter.

McClennan, Sophie A. 2017. "Hitting Trump Where It Hurts: The Satire Troops Take Up Comedy Arms against Donald Trump." *Salon*, February 11. https://www .salon.com/2017/02/11/hitting-trump-where-it-hurts-the-satire-troops-take -up-comedy-arms-against-donald-trump.

McManus, Doyle. 2018. "Why We Should 'Normalize' Trump." *Los Angeles Times*, December 21. https://www.latimes.com/opinion/op-ed/la-oe-mcmanus-trump -normalization-20161221-story.html.

Mead, Walter Russell. 2017. "The Jacksonian Revolt: American Populism and the Liberal Order." *Foreign Affairs*, March/April. https://www.foreignaffairs.com /articles/united-states/2017-01-20/jacksonian-revolt.

Mills, Charles W. 1999. *The Racial Contract*. Ithaca, NY: Cornell University Press.

Mitropoulos, Angela. 2016. "Post-factual Readings of Neoliberalism before and after Trump." *Society and Space*, December 5. http://societyandspace.org /2016/12/05/post-factual-readings-of-neoliberalism-before-and-after-trump/.

Mogelson, Luke. 2021. "Among the Insurrectionists." *New Yorker*, January 15. https:// www.newyorker.com/magazine/2021/01/25/among-the-insurrectionists.

Mouffe, Chantal. 2005. *On the Political*. London: Routledge.

Müller, Jan-Werner. 2016. *What Is Populism?* Philadelphia: University of Pennsylvania Press.

Nichols, Robert. 2018. "Theft Is Property! The Recursive Logic of Dispossession." *Political Theory* 46, no. 1: 3–28.

Obama, Barack. 2013. "Inaugural Address by President Barack Obama." Briefing Room, White House [archived], January 21. https://obamawhitehouse.archives .gov/the-press-office/2013/01/21/inaugural-address-president-barack-obama.

O'Neill, Joseph. 2020. "Real Americans." *New York Review*, August 15. https://www .nybooks.com/articles/2019/08/15/jill-lepore-suketu-mehta-real-americans/.

Oppenheim, Maya. 2017. "Neo-Nazis and White Supremacists Applaud Donald Trump's Response to Deadly Violence in Virginia." *Independent*, August 13. http://www.independent.co.uk/news/worldamericas/neo-nazis-white-supre macists-celebrate-trump-response-virginia-charlottesville-a7890786.html.

O'Toole, Fintan. 2020. "At 2.23 am, the US President Launched an Attempted Coup." *Irish Times*, November 4. https://www.irishtimes.com/news/world/us /fintan-o-toole-at-2-23am-the-us-president-launched-an-attempted-coup -1.4400134.

Partlett, William. 2017. "The American Tradition of Constituent Power." *International Journal of Constitutional Law* 15, no. 4: 955–87.

Patel, Leigh. 2017. "Trump and Settler Colonialism." *California Law Review*, May 8. https://www.californialawreview.orgsettler-colonialism-white-supremacy -covid-19/.

Pateman, Carole, and Charles W. Mills. 2007. *Contract and Domination*. New York: Polity.

Patterson, Orlando. 1982. *Slavery and Social Death: A Comparative Study*. Cambridge, MA: Harvard University Press.

Pease, Donald E. 2008. "Immigrant Nation/Nativist State: Remembering against an Archive of Forgetfulness." *boundary 2* 35, no. 1: 177–95.

Pease, Donald E. 2009. *The New American Exceptionalism*. Minneapolis: University of Minnesota Press.

Pease, Donald E. 2010. "States of Fantasy: Barack Obama and the Tea Party Movement." *boundary 2* 37, no. 2: 89–105.

Pease, Donald E. 2018. "Trump: Populist Usurper President." In "Democratic Cultures and Populist Imaginaries." Special issue, *REAL: Yearbook of Research in English and American Literature* 34, no. 1: 145–74.

Pease, Donald E. 2020. "Trump's Settler Colonist Fantasy: A New Era of Illiberal Hegemony?" In *Trump's America: Political Culture and National Identity*, edited by Liam Kennedy, 22–52. Edinburgh: University of Edinburgh Press.

Pease, Donald E. 2021. "The 'Après-Coup': President Trump's Transfer of Power." *Amerikastudien/American Studies* 66, no. 1: 143–53.

Peters, Christian Helge, and John Protevi. 2017. "Affective Ideology and Trump's Popularity." John Protevi's Web Site, September 28. http://www.protevi.com /john/TrumpAffect.pdf.

Pfeiffer, Dan. 2011. "President Obama's Long-Form Birth Certificate." *What's Happening* (blog) [archived]. https://obamawhitehouse.archives.gov/blog/2011 /04/27/president-obamas-long-form-birth-certificate.

Posen, Barry. 2018. "The Rise of Illiberal Hegemony: Trump's Surprising Grand Strategy." *Foreign Affairs*, March/April. https://www.foreignaffairs.com/articles /2018-2-13/rise-illiberal-hegemony.

Rana, Aziz. 2010. *The Two Faces of American Freedom*. Oxford: Oxford University Press.

Remnick, David. 2011. "Trump, Birtherism, and Race-Baiting." *New Yorker*, April 27. https://www.newyorker.com/news/news-desk/trump-birtherism-and-race-baiting.

Remnick, David. 2016. "An American Tragedy." *New Yorker*, November 9. https:// www.newyorker.com/news/news-desk/an-american-tragedy.

Robinson, Rowland Keshena. 2017. "Fascism and Anti-Fascism: A Decolonial Perspective." *Maehkōn Ahpēhtesewen* (blog), February 11. https://onkwehonwerising .wordpress.com/2017/02/11/fascism-anti-fascism-a-decolonial-perspective/.

Rodríguez, Dylan. 2020. *White Reconstruction: Domestic Warfare and the Logics of Genocide*. New York: Fordham University Press.

Rogin, Michael Paul. 1987. "The King's Two Bodies: Lincoln, Wilson, Nixon, and Presidential Sacrifice." In *Ronald Reagan, the Movie, and Other Episodes of Political Demonology*, 81–114. Berkeley: University of California Press,

Santner, Eric. 1996. *My Own Private Germany: Daniel Paul Schreber's Secret History of Modernity*. Princeton, NJ: Princeton University Press.

Serwer, Adam. 2020. "Birtherism of a Nation." *Atlantic*, May 13. https://www.the atlantic.com/ideas/archive/2020/05/birtherism-and-trump/610978/.

Shrum, Robert. 2017. "The Big Picture: The Office of the Presidency." *Public Books*, October 19. https://www.publicbooks.org/the-big-picture-the-office-of -the-presidency/.

Siegel, Josh. 2017. "Democrats Renew Calls for Trump Impeachment after His Charlottesville Response." *Washington Examiner*, August 15. https://www .washingtonexaminer.com/democrats-renew-calls-for-trump-impeachment -after-his-charlottesville-response.

Simpson, Audra. 2014. *Mohawk Interruptus: Political Life across the Borders of Settler States*. Durham, NC: Duke University Press.

Sitrin, Carly. 2017. "President Trump's Remarks Condemning Violence 'On Many Sides' in Charlottesville." *Vox*, August 12. https://www.vox.com/2017/8/12 /16138906/president-trump-remarks-condemning-violence-on-many-sides- charlottesville-rally.

Smith, Ben, and Byron Tau. 2011. "Birtherism: Where It All Began." *Politico*, April 24. https://www.politico.com/story/2011/04/birtherism-where-it-all-began-053563.

Snyder, Timothy. 2021. "The American Abyss." *New York Times Magazine*, January 9. https://www.nytimes.com/2021/01/09/magazine/trump-coup.html.

Soros, George. 2017. "Trump Is an Impostor." *BBC News*, January 19. https://www.bbc.com/news/business-38684556.

Swan, Jonathan. 2017. "What Steve Bannon Thinks about Charlottesville." *Axios*, August 16. https://www.axios.com/what-steve-bannon-thinks-about-charlottesville-1513304895-7ee2c933-e6d5-4692-bc20-c1db88afe970.html.

Tabachnik, David Edward. 2019. "Donald Trump's Populist Presidency Is the Real Coup, Not the Impeachment Inquiry." *Conversation*, October 31. https://theconversation.com/donald-trumps-populist-presidency-is-the-real-coup-not-the-impeachment-inquiry-124972.

Tocqueville, Alexis de. 2000. *Democracy in America*. Chicago: University of Chicago Press.

Todd, Brad, and Salena Zito. 2018. *The Great Revolt: Inside the Populist Coalition Reshaping American Politics*. New York: Crown Forum.

Toobin, Jeffrey. 2018. "Will the Fervor for Impeachment Start a Democratic Civil War?" *New Yorker*, May 28. https://www.newyorker.com/magazine/2018/05/28/will-the-fervor-for-impeachment-start-a-democratic-civil-war.

Trump, Donald J. 2017a. "Inaugural Address: Remarks of President Donald J. Trump—As Prepared for Delivery." White House [archived], January 20. https://www.whitehouse.gov/briefings-statements/the-inaugural-address/.

Trump, Donald J. 2017b. "President Trump News Conference." *C-SPAN*, August 15. https://www.c-span.org/video/?432633-1/president-trump-there-blame-sides-violence-charlottesville.

Trump, Donald J. 2017c. "President Trump Ranted For 77 Minutes in Phoenix. Here's What He Said." *Time*, August 23. https://time.com/4912055/donald-trump-phoenix-arizona-transcript/.

Trump, Donald J. 2017d. "President Trump Remarks on Charlottesville Violence." *C-SPAN*, August 14. https://www.c-span.org/video/?432578-1/president-trump-condemns-hate-groups-racism-evil.

Trump, Donald J. 2017e. "President Trump Signs Veterans Health Care Bill." *C-SPAN*, August 12. https://www.c-span.org/video/?432523-1/president-trump-condemns-violence-charlottesville-va.

Trump, Donald J. 2017f. "Transcript: President Donald Trump's Rally in Melbourne, Florida." *Vox*, February 18. https://www.vox.com/2017/2/18/14659952/trump-transcript-rally-melbourne-Florida.

Trump, Donald J. 2020. "Deflated Trump Says 'If You Count the LEGAL Votes I Easily Won.'" Posted by the *Sun*. YouTube video. https://www.youtube.com/watch?v=6moQNj3JaCA.

Veracini, Lorenzo. 2021. *The World Turned Inside: Settler Colonialism as a Political Idea*. London: Verso.

Wamsley, Laura. 2017. "What Went Wrong in Charlottesville? Almost Everything, Says Report." *NPR*, December 1. https://www.npr.org/sections/thetwo-way /2017/12/01/567824446/charlottesville-made-major-mistakes-in-handling -protest-review-finds.

Wiegman, Robyn. 1999. "Whiteness Studies and the Paradox of Particularity." *boundary 2* 26, no. 3: 115–50.

Willis, Oliver. 2010. "Highbrow Birtherism: Conservatives Attack Obama as an 'African Colonial.'" *Media Matters for America*, September 13. https://www .mediamatters.org/rush-limbaugh/highbrow-birtherism-conservatives-attack -obama-african-colonial.

Winecoff, Kindred. 2016. "Trump and the End of Taken-for-Grantedness: When Exception Becomes the Rule." *Duck of Minerva* (blog), December 13. http:// duckofminerva.com/2016/12/wptpn-trump-and-the-end-of-taken-for-grant edness-when-the-exception-becomes-the-rule.html.

Wittes, Benjamin, and Quinta Jurecic. 2017. "What Happens When We Don't Believe the President's Oath?" *Lawfare,* March 3. https://www.lawfareblog.com/what -happens-when-we-dont-believe-presidents-oath.

Wolfe, Eric. 2016. *Traces of History: Elementary Structures of Race.* London: Verso.

Young, Alex Trimble. 2018. "The Settler Unchained: Constituent Power and Settler Violence." *Social Text* 36, no. 2: 1–18.

Zakaria, Fareed. 1997. "The Rise of Illiberal Democracy." *Foreign Affairs* 76, no. 6: 22–43.

Zakaria, Fareed. 2016. "Illiberal Democracy in America." *Washington Post*, December 28. https://fareedzakaria.com/columns/2016/12/30/illiberal-democracy-in -america.

Zielonka, Jan. 2018. *Counter-Revolution: Liberal Europe in Retreat.* Oxford: Oxford University Press.

Žižek, Slavoj. 2009a. *First as Tragedy, Then as Farce.* New York: Verso.

Žižek, Slavoj. 2009b. *The Ticklish Subject: The Absent Center of Political Ideology.* New York: Verso.

Trad Rights: Making Eurasian Whiteness at the "End of History"

Leah Feldman

Over three decades have passed since the fall of communism, and yet the dissolution of the Soviet Union continues to haunt our present. The effects of the collapse and the extended period of state precarity in the former Soviet sphere have registered not only in the unchecked rise of neoliberal economics but in neoliberal thought forms and sociopolitical values that have led to an increasing pace of state and nonstate violence on a global scale. The Right assembles a set of affects that address this experience of state precarity. These authoritarian attachments tether desires for consumer aspirations and security to the condition of the foreclosure of political change (see Wedeen 2019). In the post-Soviet case, however, desires for security and stability are imbricated in the Right's revanchist vision of political change tethered to a political-theological project of white Eurasian statehood.

Eurasia, an ambivalent term that has served Russian and Soviet imperial territorial imaginaries—whether toward visions of a Russian-Slavic or Soviet-multiethnic state—has been defined by and was generated

boundary 2 50:1 (2023) DOI 10.1215/01903659-10192117 ©2023 by Duke University Press

through Russia and the Soviet Union's exceptional relationship to Western modernity. Eurasianism has always been global in scope—from its animation of émigré circles during the revolution, to an anticolonial internationalist spin at mid-century, to its drawing of connections across Hungarian and US New Right movements in the first two decades of the twenty-first century despite still resonant memories of Soviet tanks in Budapest in 1956 and the long Cold War. Before Putin's invasion of Ukraine, the political threat of neo-Eurasianism as a white supremacist New Right philosophy was broadly dismissed (though important exceptions include the prescient work of Mark Bassin, Charles Clover, Marlène Laruelle, Anton Shekhovtsov, Timothy Snyder, Diana Kudaibergenova, Fabrizio Fenghi, and others). However, this blind spot exposes a more pervasive avoidance of sustained coverage of the region in popular US media and intellectual culture—in part a relic of McCarthyism—met with a reticence on the part of much Slavic scholarship to broadly address the legacy of empire and race in the Soviet and post-Soviet contexts until recently.[1]

While the New Right has a longer genealogy in Europe, emerging in France in the late 1960s, the collapse of the Soviet empire and rise of neo-Eurasianism narrates a parallel story that gave rise to a New Right public intellectual culture on a global scale. While it might have been convenient to dismiss the New Right as marginal to electoral politics or ineffectual on the ground, as an ever-expanding series of violent incidents attest, such moves to view thought as a parody of action prove strikingly dangerous. The rise of the Right not only raises a series of often willful misreadings of left theory from critiques of globalization to electoral politics. More crucially, it figures the New Right intellectual as radical successor to a failed public intellectual culture—demolished by an anemic liberalism—characterized by orthodox forms of thought and a neoliberal refashioning of critique as an extension of the corporate machinery of the big state.

One prominent example is the work of Russian philosopher and political theorist Alexander Dugin. Dugin's neo-Eurasianism is a white supremacist political theory rooted in the idea of a spiritually predestined Eurasian ethnos and its native land empire. As a nativist discourse, neo-Eurasianism

1. A new direction in scholarship in the field over the last twenty years has generated an important corpus of works that attends to race and ethnicity in the region. See NYU Jordan Center (n.d.) and Jennifer Wilson and Jennifer Suchland's (2017) "#BlackOctober Reading List." On post–Soviet racism in Russia, see especially Law 2012; Sahadeo 2016, 2019; St. Julian-Varnon 2020a, 2020b.

has influenced the global rehabilitation of the neotraditionalist Right (what the Right calls Trad culture) and their territorial claims to a contiguous land empire. These include Steve Bannon's occult mystical predestination, Hungarian Jobbik's irredentist mythos of the Carpathian basin, French Nouvelle Droite "archeofuturist" messianism and Indo-Europeanism, and Turkish neo-Turanian nationalism, to name a few.[2] As a form of revanchist modernism, neotraditionalism draws on the interwar fascist classics including the writings of Carl Schmitt, Julius Evola, René Guénon, Martin Heidegger, and Ernst Jünger. However, it also shares a media landscape and consumer culture ranging from Etsy stores to vegan cooking shows and homesteading movements, inhabiting the knowledge structures of neoliberal thought and its posthumanist vision of totality. Neo-Eurasianism thus renders legible intertwining New Right political philosophies that link vigilante violence across Europe, Russia, and the United States (as well as more broadly).

Extending beyond localized national populist formations, unofficial political links between right movements across Europe are fostered by small informal working groups, militia training initiatives, literary societies, and broad anti-globalization campaigns for supranational alternatives to the European Union such as the Eurasian Economic Union, which integrated Kazakhstan, Kyrgyzstan, Armenia, Belarus, and Russia into a single market in 2014, and the World National-Conservative Movement, which holds conferences attended by several right groups, including Hungary's Jobbik, Greece's Golden Dawn, France's Nouvelle Droite, Russia's neo-Eurasianist movement, the British National Party, and the US alt-right. The growth of national renewal movements and the expansion of multipolar geopolitical alignments are interlinking processes that have contributed to the rise of a global Right since the end of the Cold War. National renaissance in the form of Putin's imperial rhetoric, Erdogan's Ottoman historical returns, and Orban's Austro-Hungarian revival have contributed to a coordinated effort to overturn US unipolarity. Trump's withdraw from the WHO and China's Belt Road Initiative further contributed to the material dimensions of this global New Right imaginary as an alternative to the liberal international

2. Dugin's popularity in Turkey resonated in the early 2000s through his appeal to combat Western globalization through the foundation of an alternative to the EU in a multipolar Russian-Turkish project (see İmanbeyli 2015; see also Emel Akçali and Mehmet Perinçek's discussion of Kemalist Eurasainism in Akçali and Perinçek 2009). On post-Soviet Kazakh ethno-nationalism and its connections to neo-Eurasianism, see Laruelle 2008. On archeofuturism, see Faye (1999) 2010. On French Indo-European Eurasianism, see Benoist 2016. On Bannon's neotraditionalism, see Teitelbaum 2020.

order. While these institutional links remain largely informal, funding channels extend transnationally through cultural and religious organizations, crowd-sourced platforms like Kickstarter and GoFundMe, and cryptocurrencies, as well as through informal consumer markets that foreground New Right lifestyle branding.[3]

Several recent accounts of the New Right in the United States have highlighted the role of autonomous communities and vigilante movements that have cohered around structures of radical, localized self-governance in the wake of state economic and infrastructural failure—framed widely from neighborhood policing to organic farming initiatives. Whether staged in a rural town settlement, or on a gaming platform or 4chan thread, these New Right movements rely on militarized tribal imaginaries and the performance of kinship structures to highlight nativist white supremacist claims to territorial sovereignty, a defense—as the Right frames it—from their "great replacement" by immigrants and people of color. As scholars of the US New Right have crucially argued, the emergence of these groups at once echoes the autonomous settlement movement of interwar Europe and its conditions of precarity as it illustrates how the US Right solidified in the hollowed tracks of former left solidarity, spurred by the collapse of workers unions in the late 1970s and the growth of white supremacist paramilitary following Vietnam and the Iran and Iraq wars (see Neel 2018; Belew 2018; Belew and Gutiérrez 2021; on anti-globalist autonomous settlement movements in Austria, Hungary, and Germany, see Zahra 2021). Examples of homesteading and the autonomous settlement include the white ethno-state commune set up by Matthew Heimbach in Paoli, Indiana, the Oath Keepers' end of times preparedness, or transnational groups such as Ringing Cedars—an eco-nationalist movement that has spread across Romania, Canada, Ireland, and the United States—all of which join nativist visions of the homeland with a disenchantment with the state and vigilante nationalism tied to kinship networks through the performance of occult rites (see also Miller-Idriss 2018). What reading New Right thought comparatively thus reveals is that nativist calls to defend a victimized white culture are not only the outgrowth of war and imperialism, or a disaffected white working class, but a white supremacist ethno-nationalist response to the waning of Soviet multina-

3. Right groups have used crowd-sourced funding to support political platforms from local campaigns on personal websites to Trump's ambitions for the border wall (see "We the People" 2018). On transnational Christian fundamentalist links, see Provost 2019. Organizations such as the World Congress of Families have advanced an internationalized Christian Right agenda.

tionalism and liberal Cold War multiculturalism that came to a head around the refugee crisis in Europe and Obama's presidency in the United States.

This article takes up neo-Eurasianism as a case study for a larger New Right political and intellectual turn that was intensified by the collapse of the Soviet empire, the end of the Cold War, and the rise of unchecked late capitalist globalization. However, the pivot point of the collapse more crucially points to a slippage in modes of reading taken up in New Right political thought, which not only span an array of academic disciplines—ethnology, geopolitics, psychology, literature—but also media platforms—vlogs, blogs, Etsy stores, festivals, and other online lifestyle branding initiatives. The fantasies of Trad rights, at once intensified by the series of infrastructural collapses hastened by the pandemic, also reveal discursive slippages between New Right critiques of institutional politics and anti-globalization discourses, which conceal its authoritarian structures of feeling and neoliberal thought forms.

For the New Right, following a political tradition of interwar fascist movements, state precarity justified the heroism of the political outsider. Georges Bataille (1979) described fascism as a bundle of affective contradictions, which drew on the force of its heterogeneity to mass mobilize power precisely from its self-proclaimed minoritarian peripheral relation to the state apparatus. This outsider fantasy of a precarious state conjures a postsecular messianism to catastrophic ends alongside genres of performative irony that render the violence of the New Right horrifyingly ordinary. This article presents a skeptical and worldly reading of this fantasy of vigilante action on the periphery of state collapse to challenge the ethnocentrism driving the New Right's political orthodoxy. In so doing it also exposes the dangers of the application of (post–)Cold War neotraditionalist thought to shaping the latest authoritarian incarnations of neoliberal capitalism. As someone who works at a US university on the racialized and gendered fantasies of Soviet imperial expansion and collapse, the sense of the inevitability of crisis that characterizes the present moment calls for more than a diagnostic of left failure. It requires upending provincial disciplinary approaches to attend to how post–Cold War late capitalism's conditions of precarity and collapse shaped the torque of New Right thought.

Gut Politics: The Authoritarian Metabolism of Trad Life

The Right calls for a return to a pure, organic, and autonomous neotraditionalist political philosophy in order to conceal its ethno-nationalist and nativist territorial claims. These "organic" political epistemologies—as the Right alleges—recall nineteenth-century land-based sovereignty claims invoked through the imagined geographies of Eurasia, Europe, and the US South. To borrow a term from W. J. T. Mitchell, recalling Edward Said's framing of the intersections between memory and geography, this *geopoetics* describes the cognitive and affective dimensions of geopolitics (Said 2002: 241).[4] Right critiques of liberal globalization thus draw on geopoetic imaginaries of Europe, Eurasia, and the US South that bundle neofascist affects into messianic imperial territorial claims. In so doing, they also rescale the state and obscure the racialized class struggle underlying their territorial imaginaries, further sidelining the work of radical Black and Brown anti-capitalist organizing against imperialism, settler colonialism, and white supremacy. This consistent denial of the role of racism in shaping the Right's contest to liberal electoral politics is central to the Right's retooling of ethno-nationalism on a global scale—from the January 6 attack's denial of the Black vote to European calls for nativism and Russian claims to white Eurasian sovereignty. These ethno-nationalist turns thus also expose colonial returns and the attendant reproduction of the structures of global racial capitalism that thinkers from W. E. B. Du Bois to Hannah Arendt, Stuart Hall, and Edward Said made the focus of their work. They remind us of the prescience of Said's critique of Orientalism as a corporate institution and Arendt's framing of the "imperial boomerang" that returned authoritarianism to the metropole (Said 1978; Arendt 1973). They recall Du Bois's warnings of "democratic despotism" amid the First World War, in which the working-class white laborer at home—driven by opportunism—continued to demand their share despite the continued exploitation of their comrades on distant shores (Du Bois 1915). And more recently they echo Hall's discussion of Thatcherism's bundling of authoritarian populism and nationalist discourse with an "imperialist undertow" as a new phase of authoritarian

---

4. Drawing on David Harvey's synthesis of the phenomenological and experiential traditions with French Marxism in order to attend to the cognitive and affective dimensions of geopolitics, W. J. T. Mitchell (2000: 173–74) explicitly uses the term *geopoetics* in his introduction to a 2000 volume of *Critical Inquiry*. He identifies the influence of Gaston Bachelard, Martin Heidegger, Henri Lefebvre, Michel de Certeau, and Michel Foucault on Harvey's *Justice, Nature, and the Geography of Difference* (vii–xv). Dirk Uffelmann (2017: 361n3) frames Dugin's geopolitical imaginary as a geosophy, indexing the occult theosophy movement, which for Uffelmann is "more specifically critical of both the binary reductionism and the essentialization and determinism inherent in the geopolitical misuse of space."

late capitalism that works to restore the power of capital while destroying the logic of welfare state redistribution (Hall 2011: 713; 1980). While ethnonationalism in the United States recuperates a Trad-right US South tied to a land-and-blood Civil War imaginary, the transnational rise of the Right across France and Russia has been more recently marked by a return to nineteenth-century land politics, which instrumentalize geography—and its strategies of cognitive and affective conjuring. These neo-imperial land imaginaries assemble supranational identitarian and patriarchal kinship networks, obscuring discussions of race and expanding local militarized governance on a global scale (see Schrader 2019).

Dugin stages neo-Eurasianism as a novel political epistemology for a post-Soviet anti-globalist moment. Dugin was himself a product of the *longue durée* Soviet collapse. He moved from anti-communist dissident, cutting his teeth in the unofficial culture of the "Moscow mystical underground" of unofficial writers, musicians, and thinkers of the 1970s and their culture of sex, drugs, Rimbaud, and Heidegger, to become a close ally of the former Soviet security apparatus, shifting with the changing winds of the post-Soviet political system.[5] As Fabrizio Fenghi (2020) compellingly argues in his study of the influence of the conservative bohemian culture of Soviet unofficial artists and intellectual circles on post-Soviet politics, Dugin's Eurasianism emerged from aesthetic experimentations with the occult (psychedelic mysticism), readings of Western critical theory, and the immersive principles of neo-avant-garde performance art. In this sense it presented a vision of alternative conservative world-building based on the common New Right topoi of crisis and catastrophe localized around the economic and political precarity of 1990s Russia. While Dugin still holds no official political position in Putin's government, his self-presentation as a hipster Rasputin figure, moving between writer's circles, street gangs, military backrooms, and the university system, has ultimately had a notable if largely virtual influence on the contemporary Right within Russia and abroad. Shaped in part by connections he made with the European New Right during a series of trips abroad in the 1990s, Dugin developed a neotraditionalist geopoetics

---

5. The Iuzhinskii circle, named for the street Iuzhinskii Pereulok where writer Iurii Mamleev held meetings, brought together a wide range of dissident writers who were critics of both mainstream nationalism and Westernizers and who gathered around a common interest in traditionalist theory. The group included Mamleev, writer Evgenii Golovin, and Muslim revolutionary social activist and intellectual Geidar Dzhemal, among others (see Laruelle 2015; Clover 2016). For a robust study of Eurasianism's origins in this bohemian countercultural atmosphere, see Fenghi 2020.

that drew on a red-brown alliance and a post–Cold War vision of multipolarity linking suprastatist territorial spheres of influence.[6] However, aesthetically Dugin's neo-Eurasianism disavowed the "worldly political spheres"
that many Russians felt were failing them amid the *bespredel* (lawlessness)
of the 1990s, and instead promoted a metaphysical vision for a mystical
Eurasianist lifestyle politics. Neo-Eurasianism emerged through the precarity of the collapse, amid the destabilizing forces of market liberalization
brought on by Yeltsin's radical market reforms and seizure of parliamentary
control in the 1990s, which led to a rapidly widening wage gap and massive unemployment beyond the Russian metropolitan centers. Expansive
rural areas across Russia, Central Asia, and the Caucasus—where Lenin
statues loom large over decaying seventies-era infrastructure—remain like
time capsules of a lost Soviet empire that continue to heavily rely on Soviet-
built urban centers.[7] The metaphysical vision of neo-Eurasianism thus formulates a powerful political alternative to the failures of late capitalism and
decentralization in the wake of a long post-Soviet collapse and sense of
political inertia that has been widely felt across the former Soviet empire.

Facing this moment of precarity, Dugin's (1997) *Foundations of Geopolitics* (*Osnovy geopolitika*) was framed in a reparative mode, beginning as
lecture notes delivered to Russia's central military academy in an appeal to a
return to some structures of the former Soviet military and security apparatus.[8]

6. Not only did Dugin meet with members of the French and Belgian New Right from 1989
to 1993, including Alain de Benoist, Robert Steuckers, and Jean Thiriart, and members of
the Spanish Thule group, but he also worked with Alexander Prokhanov to bring the European New Right back to post-Soviet Russia to meet with red-brown generals and politicians (see Shekhovtsov 2015). Charles Clover conducted extensive interviews with Dugin
and de Benoist. While de Benoist recognizes some influence on Dugin, he denies inspiration for much of Dugin's world systems theory (Clover 2016). For an extensive discussion
of linkages between the Russian, European, and US Far Right movements, see Shekhovtsov 2018; Snyder 2018: 66–109. Benjamin Teitelbaum (2020) presents a transnational (if at moments sweeping) account—part ethnography and part intellectual history—
of the influence of neotraditionalist thought on the political worldview of New Right thinkers from Steve Bannon to Alexander Dugin and Olavo de Carvalaho.
7. On the impact of neoliberal shock therapy on the former Soviet empires, see Appel and
Orenstein 2018. For an economic developmentalist account, see Aslund 2007.
8. Dugin's lectures were given at the Military Academy of the General Staff of the Armed
Forces of Russia between 1992 and 1995, and the resulting book continues to be
assigned as a textbook at the General Staff Academy and many other military universities. Many former KGB and military personnel trained by Dugin took on significant roles
in shaping the transition under Putin. Neo-Eurasianism's revival of the Cold War rivalry
with the West and irredentist claims to reestablish the former Soviet empire made his
work popular with former Communist Party officials (Clover 2016).

Central to Dugin's theory is an alternative to liberalism, in which liberalism embodies the persistent force of "secular Western modernity," whose "dictatorship" can be fought against only by reclaiming the geopolitics of neo-Eurasianism ("Interview" 2013). Dugin's involvement in Soviet unofficial intellectual circles, like Trump's claims to outsider politics, has shaped neo-Eurasianism's appeal to an alternative political and cultural scene outside of "establishment culture," despite its reliance on many of the technologies of the state apparatus.

Neo-Eurasianist (white Russian) supremacy draws its geopoetic fantasy from an interdisciplinary body of ethnolinguistic and geographical discourses of Eurasian cultural, territorial, and economic totality.[9] While not irreducible to a linguistic model, universalist linguistics played a pivotal role in shaping neotraditionalist geopoetics. Eurasianism authorizes claims to an organic ethnic and cultural authenticity, which neo-Eurasianism in turn draws on to bolster its vision territorial sovereignty based on a logic of adjacence. While Eurasianism's investment in the Orthodox Church's imperial authority made it a Bolshevik target, Eurasianist writing crucially survived in the work of émigré comparative theorists in Prague and Paris in the 1920s and 1930s. It has since become part of the foundation of North American Slavic curricula that has returned to post-Soviet thought in Russia and the United States as a framework for an alternative neotraditionalist geopoetics (see Feldman 2018). The product of dissident circles, both among émigrés in Prague and Paris in the 1920s and 1930s and in the unofficial samizdat scholarship of the 1980s, Eurasianism and neo-Eurasianism share in their peripheral relationship to the ruling party. These strategies of reading and their tethering to the heroism of the "outsider" émigré and dissident intellectual have not only shaped area studies but, I argue, more powerfully outlined the contours of a postsecular authoritarian politics. These thought forms accommodate authoritarian state agency within a late capitalist system tuned to crisis and precarity to dismantle worldly forms of thought.

Eurasianism's most famous proponents included the geographer Peter Savitsky and the linguists Nikolai Trubetzkoy and Roman Jakobson. They combined an interest in ethnolinguistic totality with an anti-Soviet call to return to Orthodoxy and the cultural unity of Eurasia as the fundamental basis of Russian culture (see Sériot 2014: 24–60; Glebov 2011). This vision of totality emerged, perhaps paradoxically, through their compara-

---

9. Dugin writes, "Neo-Eurasianism was thus enriched by new themes: traditionalism, geopolitics, Carl Schmitt, Martin Heidegger, the Conservative Revolution, structuralism, anthropology, and so on" (2014: 11).

tive, interdisciplinary praxis, which fused epistemological frameworks from geography, linguistics, non-Darwinian evolutionary biology, and economics. In 1925, Trubetzkoy (1925, 1991: 165) famously claimed,

> In this way, all of Eurasia in the aforementioned sense of the word, represents an integral geographical and anthropological whole. The presence within this whole of geographically and economically diverse features, such as forests, steppes, and mountains, and of natural geographical connections [*estestvennoi geograficheskoi sviazi*] between them makes it possible to view Eurasia as a region that is more or less self-sufficient economically. By its very nature, Eurasia is historically destined [*istoricheski prednaznachennoi*] to comprise a single state entity [*gosudarstvennogo edinstvo*].

In Trubetzkoy's account Eurasianism marks the synthesis of diverse features into a spiritually *predestined* unified supranational state, characterized by its cultural and territorial continuity. Jakobson echoes this vision of the autonomy and totality of Eurasia in his theory of a Eurasian linguistic union. He argues that languages are not only bound by shared families, inherited vocabularies, grammars, and phonetic traits but also language alliances or unions (*iazykovyi soiuz*), a term he appropriates from Trubetskoy (Jakobson 1962: 144–201).[10] Language unions describe structural similarities that do not stem from shared inherited traits but rather from a contiguous geography, as well as a shared culture and history. Jakobson understands Eurasia through its territorial continuity and linguistic structure (defined by a shared consonant palatalization and the absence of polytony).[11] While this vision of the lateral affiliation of neighboring languages and cultures not linked by a single nation-state seems squarely in the realm of linguistic history, the very notion of alliance or union for Jakobson is tied to political and military organization. He introduces language affiliation through the analogue of a government's military, political, and economic alliances. That is, like political

---

10. In his 1923 essay, "The Tower of Babel and Confusion of Tongues" ("Vavilonskaia bashnia i smeshenie iazykov"), Trubetskoy (1991: 153–54) writes, "Several languages belonging to a single geographical and cultural-historical region often exhibit similar features and this resemblance is conditioned by prolonged proximity and parallel development, rather than by common derivation."
11. Polytony describes languages in which the opposition of shifting tone and pitch distinguishes meaning. Consonant palatalization (phonetics) refers to the pronunciation of a consonant by either touching or moving the tongue away from the hard palate (roof of the mouth).

and military alliances, for Jakobson language is correlated through several systems (morphological, syntactical, phraseological), and in this way, he concludes, "language is a system of systems" (145). Crucially, the linguistic structure for Jakobson and the other Eurasianists, unlike the Saussurean model of arbitrary signification, is governed by a romantic conception of wholeness derived from specifically non-Darwinian evolutionary biological models. Jakobson draws on the biologist Lev Berg to support his formulation of the Eurasian linguistic union as a model reliant not on coincidence but rather on convergence to internal laws, and in which hereditary variations are limited by their determined direction. Following German Romantic thinkers like Alexander von Humboldt, phonological affinities mirror the ecological affinities of plants. In this way, *convergence*, as a non-Darwinian evolutionary principle, outlines a determined linguistic and cultural union within the Eurasian space.[12]

Dugin most directly accesses neo-Eurasianism through the work of the Soviet sociologist Lev Gumilev, who translated 1920s Eurasianist linguistics and its logic of predestined convergence to serve the politics of the empire builders and red-brown opposition during the collapse of the Soviet Union in the late 1980s and 1990s.[13] While for the Eurasianist linguists, linguistic groups determine organic cultural, anthropological, and political unions, Dugin instead acquires a vocabulary for post-Soviet ethnicity from Gumilev that highlights "biological belonging" (*biologicheskaia prenadlezhnost'*) rather than an identification with state or nation. The "naturalness" of ethnic groups thus ensures their *ethnogenetic* continuity across life history. For Dugin (2002), Gumilev's neo-Eurasianism also offers a "metaphysical

---

12. Non-Darwinian orthogenetic theories also inspired other political trajectories beyond the Eurasianists' convergence theory. Anarchist philosopher and geographer Peter Kropotkin's vision of mutual aid similarly critiqued the capitalist idea of the progressive role of the struggle for existence. While both strains of evolutionary race theory grew in some sense out of the disciplinary location of ethnology within geographic studies in the Russian imperial context, Kropotkin's evolutionary vision instead emphasized a mutually interdependent ecology that framed biodiversity as not reducible to the convergence of a Eurasian people. For Kropotkin's discussion of the impact of geography on the formation of race, custom, beliefs, and forms of property, see Kropotkin 1885.

13. Marlène Laruelle (2008) has produced some of the most nuanced scholarship on Eurasianism, from the 1920s linguistic movement to Gumilev's ethnogenesis, Dugin, and beyond, considering other Muslim and Turkic neo-Eurasianist supranationalist and nationalist variants. For a discussion of the influence of Gumilev on Russian politics from Yeltsin to Putin, as well as on Central Asian post-Soviet nationalism, see Bassin 2016: 209–316; Clover 2016: 77–150.

rehabilitation of Eurasia," a messianic and geopoetic fantasy shaped by the political failure of the collapse of the Soviet empire.

While not all proponents of orthogenetic evolution argued that Eurasia should serve the foundations for a totalizing state, for Dugin it facilitated the formation of a political theory based in ethnicity and territory, that is, an ethnostate that crucially conceived of itself outside of the idiom of political statism. Dugin's engagement with the concept of a Eurasian *ethnos* lends his movement credibility as it indexes a longer crisis in twentieth-century politics, from Trubetzskoy and the émigré writers' aims to establish an "organic" alternative to political institutions to Gumilev's claims to "naturalness" of ethnic groups ensuring their *ethnogenetic* continuity across life history. However, crucially for Dugin, the organicism of Eurasian totality also reinforces a singular, ultimate "Eurasian" ethnicity as "white" Russian and Orthodox Christian. He writes,

> This (Russian) nationalism should not utilize state terminology [*gosu-darstvennyi*] but rather an ethno-cultural terminology with a special emphasis on those categories such as "*narodnost*" and "Russian Orthodoxy." . . . Precisely this nationalism of a populist ethnic [*narodnicheskii, etnicheskii*], and ethno-religious type, and not "statist politics" [*gosudarstvennost'*] and not "monarchism" should be prioritized in this situation. . . . Above all, the Orthodox consciousness [*pravoslavnoe samosoznaniia*] of the nation [*natsii*] as a Church, and then next, a clear conception of the indivisibility, cohesiveness, totality and unity of the Russian [*russkii*] ethnic organism, consisting not only of living people, but also ancestors and future generations, and then finally, the concrete experience of a particular person as an independent atomic unit. (Dugin 2000: 145)

Dugin frames *ethnos* as an organic cultural form, which emphasizes an Orthodox consciousness and *territorial community* (*obschina*) over kinship ties, a theoretical shift, which also secures the territorial continuity of the former Soviet empire.[14] He rejects "politics" as a form of statism while draw-

14. Serguei Oushakine argues more broadly for the centrality of this system in the social sciences. A group of post-Soviet Siberian scientists, he argues, "rediscovered the vital force in the *organism* of the Russian ethnos. Emerging from traumas and injuries of the past, Russia's 'biopsychosocial ethnic body' was perceived as a material ('psycho-mechanical') evidence of organic culture and, simultaneously, as a primary embodiment of the teleological principle that determines directions of the nation's development" (Oushakine 2007: 175, 188–89).

ing on populist ethno-religious consciousness as an "organic" basis for the organization of neo-Eurasian ethno-nationalism.

While the organicism of Dugin's Fourth Political Theory nominally reimagines politics in cultural terms, its nationalist vision draws on a fantasy of territorial sovereignty that conceals its interventionalist aims and in so doing also retroactively whitens an image of the Soviet empire. Dugin's engagement with Schmitt's conception of territory as an articulation of political sovereignty is governed by spheres of influence and characterized by a *Völkish* sense of place. The application of Schmitt in this way relies on the very instability of his conception of territory as a political category.[15] For Dugin (2016), "Schmitt's assertion of the primacy of politics introduced qualitative, organic characteristics into legal philosophy and political science which are obviously not included in the one-dimensional schemes of 'progressives,' whether of the liberal-capitalist or Marxist-socialist persuasion. Schmitt's theory thus considered politics to be an 'organic' phenomenon 'rooted' in 'soil.'" On the one hand Schmitt's conception of the spheres of influence, *Großraum*, like Mackinder's heartland theory, offers Dugin a platform for arguing for a post–Cold War return to multipolarity (that is, of competing *Großräumen*), which would resist a hegemonic global Western world order. On the other, this understanding of supranationalist territorial sovereignty rewrites the imperial violence of annexation as a politics of absorption into a sphere of influence, or in Schmitt's terms, the Reich exercising dominance over the *Großraum*.

The Fourth Political Theory, Dugin's prescription for a new world order, rejects the idea of "modernity" and the "failed" political systems of the past—liberalism, communism, and fascism—to imagine a neotraditionalist future.[16] It thus hinges on the very terms of political crisis that this failed narrative prompts. Dugin (2011: 169) locates the seeds of the Fourth Theory specifically in Heidegger's critique of modernity and recuperation of a "metaphysical understanding of subjectness." The basis of this "existential anthropology," which applies Eurasianist linguistics to the creation of a new political subject, frames Eurasianism as an existential understanding of a people, a history of being (*Seynsgeschichte*) based on a geopolitical

---

15. Stuart Elden (2010) makes the point that Schmitt's variable conceptions of *territorial, Gebiet/ Staatsgebiet, Flächenordnung,* and *Landeshoheit,* which are often conflated in the original German and further troublingly translated as "territory" in English, account for the ambiguity in the reception of his framing of state interventionism.

16. On Dugin's embrace of the occult as a form of chaos, see Azal 2016.

model of the coordinated efforts of traditional white Slavic religious societies to build a new world order within the contiguous landmass of Eurasia.[17] Dugin elaborates, "Heidegger founded an existential understanding of people (*Dasein exiestiert völkisch*, he used to say) that is neither nationalist, nor internationalist. This point is the basis of the Fourth Political Theory" (Millerman 2015). The Fourth Theory, Dugin (2012: 34) writes, introduces "a new understanding of politics" and "a fundamental ontological structure that is developed on the basis of existential anthropology." *Dasein* for Dugin thus introduces the Eurasianist political subject, enthralled in the historical world of Eurasia, its linguistic ethno-cultural authenticity, Orthodox tradition, and geopolitical rootedness (33, 36).

The New Right's "organic" politics, rooted in territorial land empire and its structuring around spheres of influence, also situates its seemingly paradoxical claims to global capital and the remaking of an authoritarian political entrepreneur. From Donald Trump to Poland's Jarosław Kaczyński and Hungary's Viktor Orban, the grotesque authority of the "big man," whom Lauren Berlant (2017a, 2017b) memorably described as the "combover subject" citing Bakhtin's grotesque realism, secures his claims to authoritarian rule by governing from his gut. This gut politics, in turn, rehabilitates the big man as an authentic and charismatic political subject.[18] The organic politics of the authoritarian political entrepreneur draws on the neoliberal economic writings of F. A. Hayek and members of the Mont Pelerin Society, who formed a philosophy based on the illiberal political epistemology of the intelligent market as a truth generator and reimagined life through property as corporate personhood (Plehwe 2009: 6). Much of the Right's reliance on a philosophy of the omnipotent market, despite its ideological critique of neoliberal globalization, thus imagines a posthumanist political remedy for the feeble economy and corrosive liberal individualism the system created. It simultaneously expands state power by rendering the state more invisible—or precarious—replacing legal conceptions of citizenship with the laws of corporations, trading a failing and flailing political freedom with an abstract yet more relatable ideal of economic freedom consolidated through forms of state securitization. In this model, antiglobalization in the

17. The Eurasianist landmass is juxtaposed against European Atlanticist mercantilism. For more on this binary and the role of time as a geopoetic corrective, see Uffelmann 2017: 360–84.

18. As the *Führer entrepreneur* Trump is a grotesque mash-up of the early origins of the fascist leader, blending professional politician and the strategies of manhood suffrage (see also Kisilowski 2017).

form of culturally homogeneous secession rather paradoxically ensures the greater mobility of capital through restrictions on the migration of nonwhite peoples (Slobodian 2018: 2–3).[19] As Philip Mirowski (2009: 444) writes, the centrality of the market and the Schmittian "total state" engineers a system in which the *"Führer* [is] replaced by the entrepreneur, the embodiment of the will-to-power for the community, who must be permitted to act without being brought to rational account."[20] The New Right's critique of liberalism and globalization thus realizes a performance of forms of individual subjecthood that are not determined by secular law or property but instead invested in a Schmittian conception of deterritorialized property as the basis of the corporate personhood of a privatized totalitarian state. The point here is that the Trad right's "organic politics" reimagines a neoliberal conception of corporate personhood to serve its "anti-globalist" expansionist worldview.

The Right's vision of organic politics also takes aim at the secular state. In an interview with the center Zahra, an Islamic cultural organization in Paris, Dugin outlines his theory for a Muslim-Orthodox Christian alliance that would hail a return to "traditional society" ("Interview" 2013). Denouncing the "liberal dictatorship," which for Dugin is incompatible with humanist values, he calls for the creation of a "popular front of traditional people" (*front commun des gens traditionels*), that is, those who belong to "religious society" (here, Muslim and Christian). For Dugin, religion is "social, public and even political." The principle of unification, he claims is the liberal dictatorship's "common enemy of spirituality," and a shared vision of the Antichrist located in a US-led Western civilization and its apostasy. He continues,

19. The Hapsburg empire served as a model for neoliberal theory, highlighting the role of strong state power in consolidating global flows of capital as a network of multinational forms governed by "perfect capitalism," that is, a global mobility of labor, capital, and commodities (see Slobodian 2018). In Ludwig von Mises's (1941) vision of empire, governance was determined by a dominant linguistic population. He outlines the invisible, economically driven, strong state linking linguistically defined nations in his plan for an Eastern Democratic Union.

20. Mirowski (2009: 444) writes, "While Hayek probably believed that he was personally defending liberalism from Schmitt's withering critique, his own political solution ended up resembling Schmitt's 'total state' far more than he cared to admit. In an interesting development that Schmitt did not anticipate, Hayek hit upon the brilliant notion of developing the 'double truth' doctrine of neoliberalism—namely, an elite would be tutored to understand the deliciously transgressive Schmittian necessity of repressing democracy, while the masses would be regaled with ripping tales of 'rolling back the nanny state' and being set 'free to choose'—by convening a closed Leninist organization of counter-intellectuals."

> If we compare the description of the figure of the Antichrist in Christian eschatology and what one calls in the hadiths of the prophet the end of times, there is a striking similarity between one and the other. Those who refuse their spiritual identity, who prefer materiality to spirituality, who create social, political and economic orders founded on disorder and injustice. The Antichrist or Dajjal (ad-Dajjal) wants to create a global empire founded on the basest of human instincts. ("Interview" 2013)

Dugin's invocation of a common Muslim-Christian Orthodox eschatological vision is resonant with the work of interwar Italian fascist Julius Evola who similarly argued for a rejection of a decadent Western modernity. Dugin (2001) also emphasizes the importance of an anticolonial neotraditional spiritual revolution, highlighting figures such as the Iranian revolutionary Ali Shariati's "conservative-revolutionary synthesis between revolutionary Shiism, mystical Islam, socialism, and existentialism" and the work of fellow neotraditionalist Islamic modernist Geidar Dzhemal in order to foreground a narrative of Russia's postcolonial victimization by a Western global secular elite.[21] Taking up "desecularization" (Peter Berger) and Tradition (Schmitt on "decisionist power") Dugin (2012: 33) invokes the historical role of religion in shaping the politics and political subjectivity of neo-Eurasianism. In a more recent appearance on *Al Jazeera* on March 19, 2022, Dugin frames the war in Ukraine in these transcendental terms, proposing a terrifying image of an apocalyptic end of time and humanity and declaring that if Russia is not globally recognized as a sovereign superpower then it will destroy the world ("Alexander" 2022).[22] He presents the stakes of the war in Ukraine

---

21. This vision of the radical power of political Islam in Dugin's work grew out of the influence of his early mentor, Geidar Dzhemal (Heydər Camal), a fellow neotraditionalist whom he met in the 1980s. Both Dugin and Dzhemal framed a neo–Cold War battle between a revolutionary Eurasian monotheistic "party of God" and a secular, liberal "party of Satan" in the United States (see Laruelle 2016: 81–99). Both shared a metaphysical geopolitics that fiercely rejected both Soviet atheism and post-Soviet liberal secularism, Dzhemal (2013a) arguing that "the metaphysical grounds of radical monotheism should be taken as a platform to build the new political vision." Dugin indeed credited Dzhemal's influence and his collection of metaphysical theses, *Orientation North* (1980), for shaping his conception of neotraditionalism (see Dugin 1989; Dzhemal 2013b). Dzhemal and Dugin also worked together in the neo-Nazi nationalist group Pamyat, but after both were expelled, Dzhemal went on to establish the Islamic Renaissance party and the Islamic Committee of Russia in the 1990s.

22. Dugin is introduced to his Arabic-language audience as the "popular Kalashnikov-wielding author, theorist, and mastermind driving politics and political strategy [in Russia],"

as "a war of ideas," as a battle against "a liberal world order that aims to provide other nations [giving the examples of Russia, China, and India] with the Right to self-determination." His appeal to a Muslim audience with apocalyptic messianism crucially also relies on the sovereignty claims of his Trad right project of authoritarian multipolarity ("Alexander" 2022). This postsecular politics not only authorizes post-Soviet religious practice and religious orthodoxy, but also invokes the postsecular in order to lays claims to the transcendental authority of a predestined imperial totality (see Mufti 2013a, 2013b; Gourgouris 2013, 2019).

Dugin's postsecular vision of collective personhood, or *sobornost,* is a mentality that relies on a conception of *communion* (*soborovanie*), a plural consensus of theological opinions expressing unanimity, in contrast to the Catholic notion of accepting and submitting to a hierarchically ordered authority. In the early twentieth-century Eurasianist framework, self-knowledge could thus realize the essence of the community, conceived as a "collective person" (see Sériot 2014: 24).[23] However, this vision of conciliarity is deceiving since, as Dugin clarifies, the origins of political culture rely in a conciliarity borne out of the conception of the totality (*tsel'nost'*) and universality (*vseobschnost'*) of the Church authority. He writes, "We first think of the people, Russia is (first) an indivisible whole and only then can we recognize individual personality [*otedel'naia lichnost'*]. And autocracy [*samoderzhavie*] for us is special, conciliar [*sobornoe*], and ecclesiastical [*tserkovnost'*]. And so is democracy [*demokratiia*]" (Dugin 2006). Notably, Dugin's vision of autocracy is drawn from Nicholas I's imperial ideological doctrine—Orthodoxy, Autocracy, Nationality (*pravoslavie, samoderzhavie, narodnost'*)—describing the tsar's embodiment of the Russian people or *narod.* Recalling Christian and occult conceptions of collective personhood that submit a conciliar plurality to an imperial authority and replace arbitrary signification with a convergent wholeness, Dugin's theory attempts not only to reimagine an alternative to US unipolarity but more broadly to shape the semiotics of the political.

"one of Putin's key analysts," and "chief geopolitical expert for the advisory board concerning Russian national security affairs" ("Alexander" 2022). All citations are transcribed from a March 19, 2022, Arabic-language interview on *Al Jazeera* ("Alexander" 2022). I am grateful to Hoda El Shakry for assistance with the translation.
23. Eurasianism, like nineteenth-century Slavophile intellectual traditions before it, framed race through a Romanticist conception of ethno-nationalism linked to the geographical terrain of Eurasia. However, Eurasianism's attachment to the scientific conception of evolutionary theory expanded a Slavophile spiritual conception of imperial territory.

The US reception of Dugin's work perhaps offers the most curious example of the extensive influence of his Fourth Political Theory, since unlike the French Right's flirtations with Eurasianism in the work of Alain de Benoist and Guillaume Faye, the United States lies outside the broadly defined geographical and ideological purview of the ethno-cultural construct of "Eurasia." Nonetheless, Dugin has held popularity among US alt-right ideologues from Steve Bannon and Richard Spencer to the former Traditional Workers Party founders Matthew Heimbach and Matthew Raphael Johnson. Spencer's former wife, Russian-Canadian writer Nina Kouprianova, was also one of the main translators of his work into English. Richard Spencer describes a Duginist framework, which he calls "Identitarian-focused populism." He clarifies, "I do not subscribe to pure biological determinism. I believe that one's identity is a complex interplay of nature and nurture: from one's DNA to cultural and social interactions, and, of course, geography—the sense of rootedness in one's native landscape" (Spencer 2017). Neo-Eurasianist geopoetics thus offers US thinkers a vision of white supremacy that emphasizes nativism to circumvent discussions of race. Trad Youth leader Matthew Heimbach called on the Right to create a new Comintern—the Traditionalist International—building on Russian funding and institutional support. The Trad Youth (2015) website formerly read,

> While the goals of international communism are the exact opposite of Traditionalism, the effectiveness of the Communist International and communist organizing in the Western world is a model of how a Russian-backed Traditionalist movement (of which the World National-Conservative Movement WNCM takes part) could get the training and resources needed into the hands of activists to begin changing the political discourse in our homelands.

For Johnson (n.d.[a]), Orthodox culture also situates a cultural geography that forges organic political structures, the fundamentals, as he argues, of "ethnic-socialism," which aims to rebuild a sense of solidarity in the vacuum of an individualistic left. Drawing on the commune and Church— recalling cultural touchstones of Russian nationalism—Johnson (n.d.[b]) directly advocates for a return to an Orthodox political-social theology of *sobornost*, which he describes as "a mentality rather than a set of well-defined ideas, as well as a basis for social and economic organization." He writes, "What rules is the ethnos, represented at the parish, village, region or monastic level, and, in fact, is a naturally developing synthesis of all of these"; here he includes "the commune" as a model for the extended family structure. Johnson (2008) describes his movement as anarcho-nationalist, "the notion of representation, where local ethnic custom is the basis for law and inspiration." His embrace of Orthodox society and rejection of the state, of course, bear little resemblance to anarchism when imagined through a popular monarchy and governed by religious ethics and family structures. Despite Johnson's emphasis on radical locality, he also frames his return to Orthodoxy through a cultural-historical continuity between contemporary Russian and American interests rooted in the rejection of liberal mercantilism and a return to traditionalist medieval civilization centered in the Eastern Roman Empire.

Sobornost recalls a deterritorialized vision of authoritarian power that invokes the history of Russia's overland imperialism, as for Johnson the Roman imperial imaginary, as the basis for ethno-nationalist continuity. This postsecular politics, in turn, reimagines a conception of collective personhood framed around neotraditionalist white supremacist kinship networks based in a geographical, linguistic, and culturally determined conception of ethnic convergence. In this sense, personhood is not determined by a liberal conception of secular law and property but rather by a deep attachment to the shared world-building practice of the performance of kinship networks around ethnolinguistics' application to conceptions of biological racism and political-theological rites.

The Hungarian reception of Dugin's work is also striking, particularly given that the 1956 Soviet invasion of Budapest remains integral to Hungary's cultural memory. However, between 2010 and 2014, the New Right regained broad support in Hungary. Despite a broad rejection of Russian spheres of influence, in 2010 Jobbik as well as the elite paramilitary unit, the Hungarian National Front, began to receive support from private, Russian, Kremlin-backed actors after Jobbik's president Gábor Vona met with Dugin. In 2014 Orban made a deal with a Kremlin-owned Russian company to build the twelve-billion-euro Paks nuclear facility, foreshadowing further economic entanglements with the Kremlin, and perhaps a more mainstream turn further right. While Jobbik's popularity has waned in electoral politics, Orban's mobilization of anti-immigration campaigns and legislation in response to the global refugee crisis of 2015–16 pushed his government more fully into alignment with Jobbik's anti-Roma, anti-immigrant platform.

Postsecular Hungarian neotraditionalist thinker Tibor Imre Baranyi (n.d.) describes the *noble* nation as the restoration of the existential order of the primordial state, "whose symbolic earthly projection or imprint can appear as the taking possession of a concrete geographic place, specifically of the Carpathian Basin." While this noble nation reflects a traditionalist interiority, residing in the "metaphysical perfection" of the ruling elite, it lays stakes in a broader politics of nationalist irredentism and an economic and social restructuring of society according to a caste-based system comprised of an elite group of nobles, a military class of warrior knights, and an agricultural economic stratum. For Baranyi this system also crucially opposes the antitraditional aims of the French revolution and the "geoglobal society—and the contemporary adventure of the European Union inside it," an "internationalism that washes away nations," replacing "spiritual *unity*" with "material *uniformity* at the end of times." Instead, he proposes a "primordial state of supranationality" that preserves the "differentiated and organically articulated realization of all the values and qualitative characteristics" of each nation in a state of "perfect solidarity and unifying forces with those members of other nations." In this pluriversal vision of primordial sovereignty, each nation radiates from the inner qualities of the noble class. Baranyi's authoritarian, caste-based geopolitical vision thus relocates the primordial national past in the cotemporaneous center of the noble class, and in this way, nobility and the rhetoric of metaphysical perfection become the keys to a dominant Hungarian ethnos. While Baranyi, like most neotraditionalist thinkers, insists on the division between spiritual and worldly activities, placing politics squarely within the orbit of the latter, his citation of the EU and framing of caste as a determinant for political governance—even if one that draws authority from a spiritual realm—projects this metapolitical imaginary onto worldly, material debates that undermine his disavowal of neotraditionalist intervention.

Trad Right Feels and Ordinary Violence

The postsecular messianic dimension of the Trad right at once articulates a logic of imperial adjacence as it highlights the Right's claims to outsider "gut" politics, which often hinge on modalities of political disavowal. This outsider politics also seizes the mechanisms of corporate branding. Right lifestyle products extend neotraditionalist politics to enlarge both its support-base and funding sources. The Etsy fascism of New Right activist Ayla Stewart's (2019a, 2019b, 2019c) style blog *Wife with a Purpose* calls for "the restoration and preservation of traditional values #TradLife," offering life advice on coping with precarity through Christian values, elegies to the confederate flag, DIY crochet shawl trends, and links to an Etsy store of Trad arts and goods that features mid-century toys and baby clothes alongside vintage biographies of Tolstoy.[24] Stewart's blog proffers the conversion narrative of a liberal feminist turned self-made conservative social influencer: an Appalachian-born Christian mother raised in Las Vegas with a BA in German and anthropology and a masters in women's spirituality and international studies who is also, coincidentally, trained in prenatal yoga. Similarly, events such as the nationalist music festival Magyar Sziget (Hungarian Island), an alternative to the major European alternative music festival, Sziget—or "Pepsi Sziget" as it is called—draws thousands of right supporters to Hungary every year for activities from aura photography and presentations on pikes and cudgels to lectures on the interwar Right and the politics of victimhood and linguistics classes highlighting Tibetan-Uyghur-Hungarian origins (Jones 2009). In a discrete cultural marketplace, the Right draws on an anti-capitalist rhetoric through its lifestyle branding, the market again authorizing authoritarian claims to tradition with the same confidence that it branded liberal discourses of freedom in the mid-century (see Berlant 2011; Frank 1997).

Building on the Frankfurt School's critique of mass culture, the Right has been characterized by a consumer culture that is tuned to the digital age's structures of optimization, surveillance, and networking (see Weigel 2022). New Right media is perhaps distinctive in its personalization of authoritarian late capital's forms of consumer address. However, while these modes of optimization—propaganda delivered via the individual Facebook-Instagram-Twitter feed—offer a sense of intimacy, their aesthetics of ordinary violence invoke a tradition of interwar fascist Futurist aesthetics, such as French New Right thinker Guillaume Faye's ([1999] 2010: 89) "archeo-futurist" mash-up of Julius Evola's occult mysticism and Marinetti's violent aesthetics of velocity in his call to unite authoritarian traditionalist societies of the world. In shaping an arc from Cold War multiculturalism to neoliberal color blindness following the collapse of the Soviet empire, the New Right also emphasizes its outsider or countercultural politics through the intimate genre of the inside joke (indeed, sometimes, as in the case of Faye, drawing explicitly on a tradition of modernist irony).[25] In this way, humor plays

---

24. Stewart (2019b, 2019c) writes, "Shout out to my sweet 12-year-old who has the cutest space in his bedroom. #Rockwell art, #Jesus, yo-yos, foseball table, and gun magazines from our #NRA membership subscription. This child is after my own heart. He's also the one who begs us to 'go Mennonite' so he can have a horse and buggy #tradlife . . ."

25. On interwar fascist aesthetics, see Sears 2017; Schnapp 1994, 2005.

a central role in catalyzing the Trad right's ordinary violence. Irony is its dominant political tactic, drawing on the infinite reversibility of language to generate an overidentification with its subject (see Yurchak 2005: 249–50; Yurchak and Boyer 2010; Weatherby 2019; Young 2019). Claims to post-structuralism's wearing out of identity politics motivate identitarian critiques of the performative that grasp at the imaginary of a solid and stable originary selfhood. The neotraditional thus serves both an impossible temporality, an *already-always-that-never-was-but-nevertheless-will-be*, and an impossible authenticity, an *absolutely-never-truly-true*, that exposes the precarity of the present. The trading of intention for iterability and history for prophesy offer neotraditionalism as both a solvent for and an adjoiner to a spectacular politics premised on the appeal of a contagious joke. While many may claim new media platforms make Trad right irony possible through their suturing of image to text in visceral and immediate formats, such techniques also long cemented ties to what Sianne Ngai (2020) more broadly calls the gimmickry of late capitalist modernist aesthetics. Is neotraditionalism then just the newest iteration of a faschy avant-garde?

The Trad right's reliance on prophesy lends real force to its ironic disavowal of violence, or as Hannah Arendt wrote, it functions as a "surrogate for power" in which "the form of infallible prediction . . . has become more important than their content" (1973: 345–48). Kekism, a precursor to more popular internet religions such as Q, embodies both a fictive ideology and national territory (Kekistan) that claims to have elected president Trump through "meme magick" (a numerology based on the random number assigned to 4chan posts). In this way, Kekism marks an early example of a broader trend toward occult Internet cults and their role in mobilizing the Right. Part ironic meme semiotics, part digital religion, it featured drawings of the character Pepe the Frog styled as a timeless mythological figure alongside a female anime character—"Ebola-chan"—a viral virus dressed as a nurse who called for the ritualistic summoning and transference of "thoughtforms." As one pamphlet proclaims, "He who controls the meme controls the universe" (Saint Obamas MomJeans 2016: 17). An example of neotraditionalist thought translated into 4chan idioms, it ironically claimed to recuperate "ancient eastern knowledge," drawing on the fictive mythology of Kek, the frog-headed Egyptian god of chaos, in which "the hieroglyphic spelling of KeK resembles a man sitting in front of a computer monitor and tower" (20). The term *KeK*, which is the enemy player code for LOL in the online multiplayer game World of Warcraft, literally conceals its own laughter through a self-effacing irony that extends the inside joke beyond the game platform. Kekism's brand of Internet occultism is rooted in the evolutionary biologist Richard Dawkins's (1990: 192) theory of *memetics* in which memes, or "units of cultural transmission . . . propagate themselves by leaping from brain to brain via a process that can be called imitation." "The Divine World of KeK" leads with a parodic allusion to Dawkins, "KEK, when the letters are composited together, resembles the double-helix pattern of DNA" (Saint Obamas MomJeans 2016: 4). Dawkins's theory, which retained popularity in right circles, offers a conception of memes as active, self-reproducing, and contagious systems of ideas that do not rely on any material structural foundations. As an alternative to speech acts, memetics do not affirm performative intent but nonetheless performatively spread like contagious organisms. In this case, the anime character Ebola-chan, with its "African" viral origins, travels from brain to brain, implanting the racist joke through the form of the viral transmission armed with its self-effacing irony. Through the occult ritual of meme magick, Kekism deploys ironic disavowal to spread the racist joke through its claims to a will to power in Trump's election while at the same time harnessing the force of its predictive form over its content.

The Russian New Right draws on its own ironic tradition—*stiob*—fashioned in late Soviet dissident circles, as a strategy of political resistance (Yurchak and Boyer 2010; Laruelle 2017: 5; Epstein 2000; Fenghi 2020). *Stiob* is a form of irony that requires such a degree of overidentification with its object that it is impossible to distinguish mocking from sincerity. In this way it facilitated an overidentification with formal elements in a highly ritualized official late Soviet culture, and in turn formulated a space for creative resistance and a critical relationship to the petrified language of the party (Yurchak 2005: 249–50). However, what happens to this form of ironic political disavowal when the party no longer exists? The use of *stiob* in a contemporary political context evokes nostalgia for the lost aesthetic and the Soviet system itself, while it simultaneously retains a critical distance from its object. However, what this perversion of post-Soviet *stiob* illustrates, and what I argue inhabits New Right genres of irony more broadly, is not its alleged attempts to undermine liberal electoral politics, but its insistence that white supremacist violence is the only viable form of politics available amid this extended period of crisis.

Dugin's vision of the end of times is at once indebted to Fukuyama's liberal historiography of the end of history and an abstract critique of postmodernism that draws on a violence that works through the logic of *stiob*. In the face of the triumph of unipolar liberalism, Dugin (2012: 16–17) writes that the binary between the modern and traditional must be replaced by a "battle for Postmodernity" in which the "Fourth Political Theory must draw its 'dark inspiration' from postmodernity, from the liquidation of the Enlightenment program, and the arrival of the society of the simulacra." He traces "new holes," which identify "vulnerable spots in the global system and decipher its login passwords in order to hack into that system" (16). Offering 9/11 as a vague yet concrete example, paramilitary or extra-state violence looms in the shadow of his hacking metaphor. The very ephemerality of the substantive absence of Dugin's *holes* sutures this conception of liberal postmodernity's "dictatorship of things" to the virtuality of a digital age, a problem he oddly renders analogous to a Marxist critique of capital (16). Dugin's dismissal of consumerist liberalism "mutated into a lifestyle" highlights a "biopolitical sub-individual" that traces its alternative in the very "holes" that he argues appear in the fabric of the failed political system itself (6).[26] While this obsession with a postmodern ideological wreckage is indeed easy to poke holes in, its preoccupation with liberal degeneration is an old narrative that has again imbricated the structural context of economic, political, and ecological collapse within the purview of authoritarian returns. The Trad right thus bundles these anxieties as a fear of meaning falling into the material holes of a broken infrastructure.

The irony of the meme-ified inside joke harnesses its prophetic power to reterritorialize these geopoetic fantasies of Europe, the South, and Eurasia striated by the violence that undergirds their predestined projection as organic political units. Such a predictive ironic disavowal indeed framed Russia's invasion of Ukraine. In 2009, Dugin ominously foretold its dismemberment, drawing a map marking Ukraine with the foreboding neo-imperial distinction *Novorossiya*—New Russia (see Clover 2016: 12). Putin's initial denunciation of Russian military deployment in eastern Ukraine in 2014 also conjured a fantastic conspiracy that even the militia's Russian uniforms could have been purchased at local shops (Avril 2014). This narrative, in turn, rescales state politics through its erasure or virtualizing, while in turn reifying the historical inevitability of Russian civilizational dominance as a prepolitical or, as Dugin conjures, a *metapolitical* geopolitics framed by an already, always Eurasian becoming.

26. Dugin may also be alluding to the precarity of Kremlin ideologist Vladislav Surkov's virtual illusion of democratic pluralism, which reigned roughly from 1999 to his ousting in 2011. Clover (2016: 267–306) attributes the post-Surkov illiberal turn to the increasing gravity of the violence of Kremlin-backed nationalist street gangs, from Dugin's more mild Eurasian Youth Movement to the more extreme Russian Image.

The Russian Right employs an eclectic pragmatism, drawing conservative and corporate strategies, metaphysical metapolitics, geopolitical spheres of influence, and informal militarized action into their orbit. The Kremlin's operational ecologies, as Marlène Laruelle argues, traces the interaction between branches of the presidential administration, military-industrial complex comprised of conservative red-brown private-public partnerships, and Orthodox Christian realm including the Moscow Patriarchate and Orthodox businessmen. For Laruelle, Dugin's status is less important than the "reverberance aspect of the regime," which "takes inspiration from many popular subcultures: gang and prison culture, martial arts, the tradition of *stiob* (parody) and carnivalization, neoliberal consumerist practices, and late Soviet culture" (Laruelle 2017: 5). A coherent ideology is replaced by a logic of pragmatic capture, in which a Russian national feeling is tuned to a cacophony of discursive interferences, nostalgic and imaginary, undergirded by forms of localized organization in a state of political and economic collapse. However, regardless of whether diachronic comparison reveals neo-Eurasianism as "fascist" or not (see Laruelle 2021; Snyder 2018; Clover 2016), I argue it is crucial to recognize how Dugin's (and others') manipulation of forms of postsecular Trad right politics—armed with virulent irony—obscure racial capitalism's authoritarian turns along the fault lines of crisis.

The End of History

The Right's cathexis to crisis and catastrophe, to these very forms of state failure that it blames on a "global cabal of liberals," is a frame that more accurately glosses its racism than its structural opposition to global capital. Its self-effacing globalism remains central to its mobilization of collective solidarity through powerful affective attachments—fear, hate, and disgust—the basis of what Bataille, Theodor Adorno, Max Horkheimer, and others framed as the psychological structures of fascism (Bataille 1979; Adorno 1950; Adorno and Horkheimer [1947] 2007). That this philosophy shares a romantic concern for the primacy of feeling over thought does not make it less invested in material technologies or modernist aesthetics. These visions alight along visceral catastrophic imaginaries of immigration and environmental pollution and crystallize in the crisis of the failure of the liberal international order. While, as Marx and Gramsci remind, crisis is endemic to capitalism, the topoi of the catastrophic—a term that itself invokes the denouement of Greek tragedy—formulates the basis of New

Right temporality and indexes a narrative *overturning* that at once embodies this vision of counter-modernity as it conceals its investment in the slow process of systemic collapse.

As Fukuyama (1989) famously misjudged, it was only from the singular vantage of his narrative of liberal late capitalist globalization that the end of the Cold War foretold the end of conflict, and thus the end of history. The end of multipolarity triggered by the fall of the Soviet Union and unipolar dominance of what would come to be read as a global neoliberal order with the United States at its helm intensified claims to national belonging, particularly in the case of the belated *Völkish* nationalisms of Hungary, Germany, Russia, and Turkey. As if seizing Fukuyama's end of history as its beginnings, the Right naturalizes violence by highlighting the crises of state collapse. Such deterritorialized metapolitical visions lend the Right viral, transnational appeal. However, such examples also highlight modes of reterritorialization that consolidate these geopoetic imaginaries of Europe, the US South, and Eurasia. The geopoetic imaginaries of the New Right generate not only attachments to political ideas but the reterritorialization of a supranational Trad-right political theology.

The New Right has assembled its postsecular neotraditionalist politics in the shadow of a precarious state—from post–Cold War nationalism to the COVID-19 pandemic. These right narratives project the catastrophic collapse of a secular liberal west through horrifyingly ordinary violence across an array of genres and online communities—from fascist vegan cooking vlogs to mediations on whiteness through pastoral homesteading blogs, movie review podcasts highlighting white victimization, calls for self-determination for fictional ethno-nationalist territories, Etsy fascist lifestyle branding, and folk booths at ethno-nationalist music festivals. The Right's cluster of affects and its logic of victimhood appeal to both the opportunism of a disaffected white working class that obscures their location within postindustrial suburban transport centers connected by global flows of capital alongside educated white upper-middle-class elites anxious about their "great replacement" by immigrants and people of color. Ever seeping out of its own containment, the Right's saturation by a grotesque irony stridently hacks a worldly selfhood, hails pluriversalist geopolitics and explosive ethno-nationalisms, and celebrates fantasies of multipolarity and a riotous smashing of institutional politics, law, and the welfare state straight-jacketed to deterritorialized ethno-nationalist authoritarianism. These right geopoetic imaginaries cannibalize a liberal good life, assuming its failure in a false-bottomed authenticity. Beneath the folds of its geopoetic neo-traditional imaginary, New Right literature congeals the failures of political solidarity as it assembles neofascist affects from the crises of economic, political, and ecological precarity that haunt our present.

Gayatri Chakravorty Spivak's ([1988] 1993) landmark essay "Can the Subaltern Speak?" can be instructive here. Spivak argues that the problem of representation in Marx centers on the two distinct yet intertwining meanings of representative authority in the terms *darstellen* and *vertreten*, which capture the sense of rhetoric-as-trope and rhetoric-as-persuasiveness respectively. The dangerous elision of these notions of representation can be extended to Lenin's failure to recognize the colonial foundations of the Soviet project when he envisioned the literary journal as the medium through which the proletariat could authentically represent itself for itself. This fundamental misreading has remained the central if unspoken problematic undergirding the reception of anticolonial thought in many scholarly and popular accounts of the Soviet empire, and has in turn served the Right's creation of a homogeneous vision of Eurasian whiteness. Exposing the New Right's white supremacy thus requires attending to the aesthetic and literary self-representation that its public intellectual elites have generated and the dangers they pose. While New Right politicians rotate in and out of office, the problem of right terrorism and the literature that incubates it continues to grow. As extensions of its well-oiled, crisis-prone form, the Right feeds on intertwining economic, political, and infrastructural collapse brought on by the COVID-19 pandemic, the war in Ukraine, and ecofascist nightmares on the horizon. It is only in recognizing the worldly political force of our thought and writing within and beyond the university through our attention to the nuanced politics of representation, that we can challenge the violence of New Right thought forms as they continue to mutate and spread across Russia, Europe, the United States, and beyond.

Postscript: Ukraine

Putin's invasion of Ukraine on February 24, 2022 has further consolidated this New Right worldview. Dugin's (2022) framing of the war marks the culmination of his project to create a new political semiotics for the Trad right—from his vision of Russia's attempts following the collapse in the 1990s to adopt the "broken English" of Western globalization to his rousing of support for the restoration of justice of a multipolar order long subjected to "globalist Western domination."[27] His vision of the invasion of Ukraine as a crusade for geopolitical multipolarity aims to dismantle not only the globalist forces of Euro-American hegemony but the structure of the system of signs and the set of affects (victimhood, inferiority, etc.) attached to Russia's place within that ideological worldview, making Ukraine the passe-partout, the open frame through which the New Right reimagines economic and military growth in tandem with geopolitical realignments. The New Right remains divided on the war: a faction continues to claim Russian-supremacist Eurasian sovereignty while another—the so-called anarcho-nationalist and white nationalist faction—emphasizes instead the white territorial sovereignty claims of the Ukrainian nation (decrying Putin's imperialism). Indeed, this internal fissure within the Right over the case of Russia is not a new development, but one that has begun to further blur ideological distinctions between New Right nationalists and liberal white globalists, whose support for the war stems from a combined mix of latent McCarthyism levied by liberal American nationalistic cries to defend democracy.

An increasingly shared affinity is emerging between latent liberal desires for a defense of democracy and human rights and right ethnonationalist claims to territorial sovereignty. This convergence, in part the result of a diminished critical examination of how the New Right's representational authority has emerged through its literature and media landscape, dangerously serves the Right's broader aims to align its vision of white victimhood with the violence of its white supremacist Trad right worldview. The political, historical, and epistemological recognition of Russia as an empire may finally have come to an end. However, this most recent turn to recognize Russia as an empire, and in some cases point back to the Soviets' role in empire-building, must crucially be framed alongside complex representations of race and ethnicity in (post-)Soviet Russia and the republics. The role that the increasing waves of racialized violence against ethnic and religious minorities following the collapse played in the securitization and consolidation of Putin's control in the region has perhaps been diminished by that same persistence of Leninist orthodoxy, despite the pervasive denunciation of Stalinist authoritarianism, against which Spivak's careful reading of Marx warned.

The outpouring of media and social media attention to the war is striking, not only in comparison with the scale of international awareness

27. Dugin (2022) shared his March 4 address "to Western journalists," recorded at an unnamed location, on his Telegram channel and Facebook account on March 5, 2022.

for recent crises in Syria, Palestine, or Kazakhstan but in the unflinching support for the war in the form of Euro-American armament. No doubt this attention is motivated by the proximity of the war to Europe and the economic, infrastructural, and military threats this proximity poses. However, Putin's decision to invade Ukraine also reflects the consolidation of Trad right discourses of white supremacy. Unlike Kazakhstan, Chechnya, Armenia, Azerbaijan, or Georgia, Ukraine serves as a barometer for Europe in crisis and the war has garnered a particular empathy for the figure of the white Christian refugee, in part by recalling the mass displacement and murder of Ukrainian Jews during the Holocaust. Both Zelensky's and Putin's reciprocal wielding of the term *fascist* point back to the recurring historical debate about how to read the Soviet-German pact over the partition of Poland (Ribbentrop-Molotov Pact of 1939) in relation to its defeat of Nazi Germany in 1945 (see Laruelle 2021). The doubling of fascist accusations extends a neo-Eurasianist anxiety over European threats to Russian hegemony to its historical losses in WWII.

However, the reach of Putin's control extends much more broadly than Russia's western borderlands. Civilians, students, artists, academics, journalists across the former Soviet republics have continued to be kidnapped, tortured, and murdered by political hitmen and arrested by authoritarian regimes supported by Putin since the early aughts. Russians now fleeing the draft range from those mobilizing an opposition to the war to "pacifists" evading the battlefield and seeking the comforts of a lost liberal good-life by setting up colony-like encampments in neighboring Georgia and Kazakhstan. Such mass migrations of Russians may be particularly threatening for communities in the Caucasus and Central Asia, who have, in addition to continued Russian military pressures in their own countries, such as Putin's 2008 invasion of Georgia, since the 1990s experienced increased racialized violence directed against them in Russia and abroad incubated by the Russian state since the Chechen wars and economic fallout (Sahadeo 2016, 2019). Such fears have only intensified following Putin's most recent calls in September 2022 to defend Russians abroad. Not only has the war in Ukraine and its broader effects in the region produced new narratives of white victimization in the face of the violence and horrors of war, but in so doing, they reanimate profound layers of racism that continue to render invisible the precarity of non-Christian and ethnic non-Russian people in the former Soviet empire and beyond who will also continue to feel the collateral damage of the war for years to come. If in 1997 Dugin insisted on the Hitlerian frame that "Ukraine as a state has no geopolitical meaning . . .

no particular cultural import or universal significance, no geographic uniqueness, no ethnic exclusiveness," then in 2022 Ukraine has become an opening for the Trad right's imaginary of multipolarity and its crusade to remake Eurasian whiteness.

References

Adorno, Theodor. 1950. *The Authoritarian Personality.* New York: Harper & Row.

Adorno, Theodor, and Max Horkheimer. (1947) 2007. *Dialectic of Enlightenment.* Translated by Edmund Jephcott. Redwood City, CA: Stanford University Press.

Akçali, Emel, and Mehmet Perinçek. 2009. "Kemalist Eurasianism: An Emerging Geopolitical Discourse in Turkey." *Geopolitics* 14: 550–69.

"Alexander Dugin: Either Russia Will Win or the World Will Be Destroyed by Nuclear Weapons." 2022. *Al Jazeera,* March 19. YouTube video, 0:48:44. https://www.youtube.com/watch?v=RyTbgtRNvB8.

Appel, Hilary, and Mitchell A. Orenstein. 2018. *From Triumph to Crisis: Neoliberal Economic Reform in Postcommunist Countries.* Cambridge: Cambridge University Press.

Arendt, Hannah. 1973. *The Origins of Totalitarianism.* New York: Harcourt.

Aslund, Anders. 2007. *How Capitalism Was Built: The Transformation of Central and Eastern Europe, Russia, and Central Asia.* Cambridge: Cambridge University Press.

Avril, Pierre. 2014. "Ukraine: Poutine souffle le chaud et le froid." *Le Figaro,* May 3. http://www.lefigaro.fr/international/2014/03/04/0100320140304ARTFIG00338 -poutine-sort-de-son-silence-pour-se-justifier-sans-clarifier-ses-objectifs .php.

Azal, Wahid. 2016. "Dugin's Occult Fascism and the Hijacking of Left Anti-imperialism and Muslim Anti-Salafism." *Counterpunch,* February 10. https://www.counter punch.org/2016/02/10/dugins-occult-fascism-and-the-hijacking-of-left-anti -imperialism-and-muslim-anti-salafism/.

Baranyi, Tibor Imre. n.d. "About the Term 'Nation' in Light of the Primordial Tradition." http://www.tradicio.org/baranyi/nation.html (accessed January 30, 2017).

Bassin, Mark. 2016. *The Gumilev Mystique: Biopolitics, Eurasianism, and the Construction of Community in Modern Russia.* Ithaca, NY: Cornell University Press.

Bataille, Georges. 1979. "The Psychological Structure of Fascism." *New German Critique* 16: 64–87.

Belew, Kathleen. 2018. *Bring the War Home: The White Power Movement and Paramilitary America.* Cambridge, MA: Harvard University Press.

Belew, Kathleen, and Ramón A. Gutiérrez. 2021. *A Field Guide to White Supremacy.* Oakland: University of California Press.

Berlant, Lauren. 2011. *Cruel Optimism.* Durham, NC: Duke University Press.

Berlant, Lauren. 2017a. "Big Man." *Social Text*, January 19. https://socialtextjournal
.org/big-man/.
Berlant, Lauren. 2017b. "Humorlessness (Three Monologues and a Hairpiece)."
Critical Inquiry 43, no. 2: 305–40.
Clover, Charles. 2016. *Black Wind, White Snow: The Rise of Russia's New Nation-
alism.* New Haven, CT: Yale University Press.
Dawkins, Richard. 1990. *The Selfish Gene.* 2nd ed. Oxford: Oxford University Press.
De Benoist, Alain. 2016. *The Indo-Europeans: In Search of the Homeland.* London:
Arktos.
Du Bois, W. E. B. 1915. "The African Roots of War." *Atlantic Monthly*, May. https://www
.theatlantic.com/magazine/archive/1915/05/the-african-roots-of-war/528897/.
Dugin, Aleksandr. 1989. *Puti Absoliuta.* Moscow: Arktogeia.
Dugin, Aleksandr. 2000. *Osnovy Geopolitiki.* Moscow: Arktogeia.
Dugin, Aleksandr. 2001. "Modernization without Westernization." Translated by Jafe
Arnold. Fourth Political Theory. http://www.4pt.su/en/content/modernization
-without-westernization.
Dugin, Aleksandr. 2002. "Lev Gumilev: Nauka 'zhivoi zhizni'." *Evraziia*, May 10.
http://evrazia.org/modules.php?=article&sid=634.
Dugin, Aleksandr. 2006. "Souchastie, sobornost', samobytnost'." *Argumenty i fakty*,
no. 16: 1329. http://www.evrazia.org/modules.php?name=News&file=article
&sid=3042.
Dugin, Aleksandr. 2011. *Martin Khaidegger: Vozmozhnost' russkoi filosofii.* Moscow: Gaudeamus.
Dugin, Aleksandr. 2012. *The Fourth Political Theory.* Moscow: Eurasian Movement.
Dugin, Aleksandr. 2016. "Carl Schmitt's Five Lessons for Russia." *Fourth Revolutionary War* (blog), July 26. https://4threvolutionarywar.wordpress.com/2016/07/26
/carl-schmitts-5-lessons-for-russia-alexander-dugin/.
Dugin, Aleksandr. 2020. "Let Us Create Another Culture War: Interview with Alex-
ander Dugin." In *Postsecular Conflicts: Debating Tradition in Russia and
the United States*, edited by Kristina Stoeckl and Dmitry Uzlander, 57–70.
Innsbruck: University of Innsbruck Press.
Dugin, Alexander. 2022. "Alexander Dugin Speaking on the Ukraine Conflict."
March 5. YouTube video, 0:26:09. https://www.youtube.com/watch?v=NXNIN
sOXqsM.
Dzhemal, Geydar. 2013a. "The Future Class Struggle as the Destiny of the World
Protest." Open Revolt, March 3. https://openrevolt.info/2013/03/03/geydar
-dzhemal-the-future-class-struggle-as-the-destiny-of-the-world-protest/.
Dzhemal, Geydar. 2013b. *Orientatsia: Sever.* Novosibirsk: Svarte Aske.
Elden, Stuart. 2010. "Reading Schmitt Geopolitically: Nomos, Territory, and Großraum."
Radical Philosophy 161: 18–26.
Epstein, Mikhail. 2000. "Postmodernism, Communism, and Sots-Art." In *Endquote:
Sots-Art Literature and Soviet Grand Style*, edited by Marina Balina, Nancy

Condee, and Evgeny Dobrenko, 3–29. Evanston, IL: Northwestern University Press.

Faye, Guillaume. (1999) 2010. *Archeofuturism: European Visions of the Post-catastrophic Age.* Translated by Sergio Knipe. London: Arktos.

Feldman, Leah. 2018. *On The Threshold of Eurasia: Revolutionary Poetics in the Caucasus.* Ithaca, NY: Cornell University Press.

Fenghi, Fabrizio. 2020. *It Will Be Fun and Terrifying: Nationalism and Protest in Post-Soviet Russia.* Madison: University of Wisconsin Press.

Frank, Thomas. 1997. *The Conquest of Cool: Business Culture, Counterculture, and the Rise of Hip Consumerism.* Chicago: University of Chicago Press.

Fukuyama, Francis. 1989. "The End of History?" *National Interest* 16: 3–18.

Glebov, Sergei. 2011. "The Mongol-Bolshevik Revolution: Eurasianist Ideology in Search of an Ideal Past." *Journal of Eurasian Studies*, no. 2: 103–14.

Gourgouris, Stathis. 2013. "Why I Am Not a Postsecularist." *boundary 2* 40, no. 1: 41–54.

Gourgouris, Stathis. 2019. *The Perils of the One.* New York: Columbia University Press.

Hall, Stuart. 1980. "Thatcherism: A New Stage?" *Marxism Today* 24, no. 2: 26–28.

Hall, Stuart. 2011. "The Neo-liberal Revolution." *Cultural Studies* 25, no. 6: 705–28.

İmanbeyli, Vulgar. 2015. "Failed Exodus: Dugin's Networks in Turkey." In *Eurasianism and the European Far Right: Reshaping the Europe Russia Relationship*, edited by Marlène Laruelle, 145–75. Lanham, MD: Lexington.

"Interview de Alexandre Douguine." 2013. *PAS L'info*, May 29. YouTube video, 0:23:17. https://www.youtube.com/watch?v=KLRdV9x-5qY.

Jakobson, Roman. 1962 "K kharakteristike evraziiskogo iazykovogo soiuza." In *Roman Jakobson Selected Writings 1*, 144–201. The Hague: Mouton & Co.

Johnson, Matthew Raphael. 2008. "Anarchism and Orthodox Community: The Politics of Sobornost, the Ancient Ritual, and the Destruction of Old Russia by the Petrine State." In *Sobornosti: Essays on the Old Faith.* Morrisville, NC: Lulu.

Johnson, Matthew Raphael. n.d.(a). "Globalization and the Decline of the West: Eurasianism, the State and the Rebirth of Ethnic-Socialism." RusJournal. https://www.rusjournal.org/wp-content/uploads/2016/02/Russia_Global.pdf (accessed September 11, 2022).

Johnson, Matthew Raphael. n.d.(b). "The Ukrainian Orthodox Conception of Sobornopravna: The Prophets, Nominalism, and the Ontology of Empire." RusJournal. https://www.rusjournal.org/wp-content/uploads/2016/05/Sobornapravna.pdf.

Jones, Gwen. 2009. "Daytrip to Magyar Sziget." Unpublished manuscript, August 18.

Kisilowski. Maciej. 2017. "How Eastern Europe Blew Up the West." *Project Syndicate*, January 24. https://www.project-syndicate.org/onpoint/how-eastern-europe-blew-up-the-west-by-maciej-kisilowski-2017-01?barrier=accesspaylog.

Kropotkin, Petr. 1885. "What Geography Ought to Be." *Nineteenth Century* 18: 940–56.

Laruelle, Marlène. 2008. *Russian Eurasianism: An Ideology of Empire.* Translated by Mischa Gabowitsch. Baltimore, MD: Johns Hopkins University Press.

Laruelle, Marlène. 2015. "The Iuzhinskii Circle: Far Right Metaphysics in the Soviet Underground and Its Legacy Today." *Russian Review,* no. 74: 563–80.

Laruelle, Marlène. 2016. "Digital Geopolitics Encapsulated: Geidar Dzhemal between Islamism, Occult Fascism, and Eurasianism." In *Eurasia 2.0: Russian Geopolitics in the Age of New Media,* edited by Mikhail Suslov and Mark Bassin, 81–99. Lanham, MD: Lexington.

Laruelle, Marlène. 2017. "The Kremlin's Ideological Ecosystems: Equilibrium and Competition." *PONARS Eurasian Policy Memo,* no. 493: 1–6.

Laruelle, Marlène. 2021. *Is Russia Fascist? Unraveling Propaganda East and West.* Ithaca, NY: Cornell University Press.

Miller-Idriss, Cynthia. 2018. *The Extreme Gone Mainstream: Commercialization and Far Right Youth Culture in Germany.* Princeton, NJ: Princeton University Press.

Millerman, Michael. 2015. "Alexander Dugin on Martin Heidegger: Interviewed by Michael Millerman." *Arktos,* November 3. https://www.academia.edu/17674206/Alexander_Dugin_on_Martin_Heidegger_Interview.

Mirowski, Philip. 2009. "Defining Neoliberalism." Postface to *The Road from Mont Pelerin: The Making of the Neoliberal Thought Collective,* edited by Dieter Plehwe and Philip Mirowski, 417–56. Cambridge, MA: Harvard University Press.

Mises, Ludwig von. 1941. "An Eastern Democratic Union: A Proposal for the Establishment of a Durable Peace in Eastern Europe." Mises Wire, Mises Institute. https://mises.org/library/eastern-democratic-union-proposal-establishment-durable-peace-eastern-europe.

Mitchell, W. J. T. 2000. "Geopoetics: Space, Place, and Landscape." *Critical Inquiry* 26, no. 2: 173–74.

Mitchell, W. J. T. 2002. *Landscape and Power.* 2nd ed. Chicago: University of Chicago Press.

Mufti, Aamir. 2013a. "Introduction: Antinomies of the Postsecular." *boundary 2* 40, no. 1: 1–4.

Mufti, Aamir. 2013b. "Why I Am Not a Postsecularist." *boundary 2* 40, no. 1: 7–19.

Neel, Phil. 2018. *Hinterland: America's New Landscape of Class and Conflict.* London: Reaktion.

Ngai, Sianne. 2020. *Theory of the Gimmick: Aesthetic Judgement and Capitalist Form.* Cambridge, MA: Harvard University Press.

NYU Jordan Center. n.d. "University Press Books." https://jordanrussiacenter.org/university-press-books/ (accessed September 11, 2022).

Oushakine, Serguei. 2007. "Vitality Rediscovered: Theorizing Post-Soviet Ethnicity in Russian Social Sciences." *Studies in East European Thought* 59, no. 3: 171–93.

Plehwe, Dieter. 2009. Introduction to *The Road from Mont Pelerin: The Making of the Neoliberal Thought Collective*, edited by Dieter Plehwe and Phillip Mirowski, 1–44. Cambridge, MA: Harvard University Press.

Provost, Claire. 2019. "Revealed: Trump-Linked US Christian 'Fundamentalists' Pour Millions of 'Dark Money' into Europe, Boosting the Far Right." *Open Democracy*, March 27. https://www.opendemocracy.net/en/5050/revealed -trump-linked-us-christian-fundamentalists-pour-millions-of-dark-money -into-europe-boosting-the-far-right/.

Sahadeo, Jeff. 2016. "Black Snouts Go Home! Migration and Race in Late Soviet Leningrad and Moscow." *Journal of Modern History* 88, no. 4: 797–826.

Sahadeo, Jeff. 2019. *Voices from the Soviet Edge: Southern Migrants in Leningrad and Moscow*. Ithaca, NY: Cornell University Press.

Said, Edward. 1978. *Orientalism*. New York: Vintage.

Said, Edward. 2002. "Invention, Memory, and Place." In *Landscape and Power*, 2nd ed., edited by W. J. T. Mitchell, 241–60. Chicago: University of Chicago Press.

Saint Obamas MomJeans. 2016. *The Divine Word of Kek*. Scotts Valley, CA: CreateSpace Independent Publishing Platform. https://www.amazon.com/Divine -Word-Saint-Obamas-MomJeans/dp/153364666X.

Schnapp, Jeffrey. 1994. "Propeller Talk." *Modernism/Modernity* 1, no. 3: 153–78.

Schnapp, Jeffrey. 2005. "Bad Dada (Evola)." In *The Dada Seminars*, edited by Leah Dickerman and Matthew S. Witkovsky, 30–55. CASVA Seminar Papers 1. Washington: National Gallery of Art, in association with Distributed Art Publishers.

Schrader, Stuart. 2019. *Badges without Borders: How Global Counterinsurgency Transformed American Policing*. Oakland: University of California Press.

Sears, Olivia. 2017. "A Post-Dada Superfascist Shadow." *Center for the Art of Translation Blog*, June 5. https://www.catranslation.org/blog-post/a-post-dada -superfascist-shadow/.

Sériot, Patrick. 2014. *Structure and Totality: The Intellectual Origins of Structuralism in Central and Eastern Europe*. New York: Walter De Gruyter.

Shekhovtsov, Anton. 2015. "Alexander Dugin and the West European New Right, 1989–1994." In *Eurasianism and the European Far Right: Reshaping the Europe-Russia Relationship*, edited by Marlène Laruelle, 35–54. Lanham, MD: Lexington.

Shekhovtsov, Anton. 2018. *Russia and the Western Far Right: Tango Noir*. New York: Routledge.

Slobodian, Quinn. 2018. "Perfect Capitalism, Imperfect Humans: Race, Migration, and the Limits of Ludwig von Mises's Globalism." *Contemporary European History*, no. 10: 1–13.

Snyder, Timothy. 2018. *The Road to Unfreedom: Russia, Europe, and America*. New York: Tim Duggan.

Spencer, Richard. 2017. "Richard Spencer's Interview with Europe Maxima." *Radix*,

February 15. https://radixjournal.com/2017/02/2017-2-15-richard-spencers
-interview-with-europe-maxima/.

Spivak, Gayatri Chakravorty. (1988) 1993. "Can the Subaltern Speak?" In *Colonial
Discourse and Post-colonial Theory: A Reader*, edited by Patrick Williams
and Laura Chrisman, 66–111. New York: Columbia University Press.

Stewart, Ayla. 2019a. "Introduction: Who Am I?" *Wife with a Purpose*, March 16.
https://wifewithapurpose.com/2019/03/16/re-introduction-who-am-i/.

Stewart, Ayla. 2019b. "Boy's Rooms, Milkmaid Braids, Remembering Compassion."
Wife with a Purpose, March 31. https://wifewithapurpose.com/2019/03/31
/boys-rooms-milkmaid-braids-and-remembering-compassion/.

Stewart, Ayla. 2019c. "Wife With a Purpose." Etsy shop. https://www.etsy.com/shop
/WifeWithAPurpose.

St. Julian-Varnon, Kimberly. 2020a. "The Curious Case of 'Russian Lives Matter.'"
Foreign Policy, July 11. https://foreignpolicy.com/2020/07/11/the-curious-case
-of-russian-lives-matter/.

St. Julian-Varnon, Kimberly. 2020b. "The Ties That Bind: Black Lives Matter, Ukraine's
Euromaidan, and the Realities of European Integration." *Krytyka*, May. https://
krytyka.com/en/articles/ties-bind-black-lives-matter-ukraine-euromaidan.

Teitelbaum, Benjamin. 2020. *War for Eternity: Inside Bannon's Far-Right Circle of
Global Power Brokers*. New York: Dey Street.

Trad Youth. 2015. "Forging the Traditionalist International: Uniting in St. Petersburg."
http://www.tradyouth.org/2015/04/forging-the-traditionalist-international
-uniting-in-st-petersburg/.

Trubetzkoy, Nikolai. 1925. Vol. 2 of *Nasledie Chingiskhana: Vzgliad na russkuiu
istoriiu ne s Zapada a s Vostoka*. Berlin: Evraziiskoe knigoizdatel'svto. http://
eurasian-movement.ru/archives/20246.

Trubetzkoy, Nikolai. 1991. "The Legacy of Genghis Khan: A Perspective on Rus-
sian History Not from the West but from the East." Translated by Kenneth
Brostrom. In *The Legacy of Genghis Khan and Other Essays on Russia's
Identity*, edited by Anatoly Liberman, 161–231. Ann Arbor: Michigan Slavic
Publications.

Uffelmann, Dirk. 2017. "Eurasia in the Retrofuture: Dugin's Tellurokratiia, Sorokin's
Telluriia, and the Benefits of Literary Analysis for Political Theory." *Die Welt
der Slaven* 62, no. 2: 360–84.

"We the People Will Build the Wall." 2018. GoFundMe. December 16. https://www
.gofundme.com/TheTrumpWall.

Weatherby, Leif. 2019. "Irony and Redundancy: The Alt Right, Media Manipulation,
and German Idealism." *b2o*, June 24. http://www.boundary2.org/2019/06
/leif-weatherby-irony-and-redundancy-the-alt-right-media-manipulation-and
-german-idealism/.

Wedeen, Lisa. 2019. *Authoritarian Apprehensions: Ideology, Judgement, and Mourn-
ing in Syria*. Chicago: University of Chicago Press.

Weigel, Moira. 2022. "The Authoritarian Personality 2.0." *Polity* 54, no. 1: 146–80.

Wilson, Jennifer, and Jennifer Suchland. 2017. "#BlackOctober Reading List: The Russian Revolution and the African Diaspora." *Black Perspectives*, November 4. https://www.aaihs.org/blackoctober-reading-list-the-russian-revolution-and-the-african-diaspora/.

Young, Damon R. 2019. "Ironies of the Web 2.0." *Post 45*, May 2. https://post45.org/2019/05/ironies-of-web-2-0/.

Yurchak, Alexei. 2005. *Everything Was Forever Until It Was No More: The Last Soviet Generation*. Princeton, NJ: Princeton University Press.

Yurchak, Alexei, and Dominic Boyer. 2010. "American Stiob: Or, What Late-Socialist Aesthetics of Parody Reveal about Contemporary Political Culture in the West." *Cultural Anthropology* 25, no. 2: 179–221.

Zahra, Tara. 2021. "Against the World: The Collapse of Empire and the Deglobalization of Interwar Austria." *Austrian History Yearbook* 52: 1–10.

The White Minority:
Natives and Nativism in Contemporary France

Olivia C. Harrison

Souchiens and Underdogs

In 2009, an association dubbed General Alliance against Racism and for the Respect of French and Christian Identity (AGRIF) sued Houria Bouteldja, cofounder of the French antiracist movement Indigènes de la république (Natives of the Republic), for her use of a neologism to refer to white people, *les souchiens*.[1] Founded in 1984 by Bernard Antony, a former

For their insightful comments on an early draft of this essay, I thank Arne De Boever, Lia Brozgal, Jessica Marglin, and Neetu Khanna.

1. AGRIF sued Bouteldja for "anti-white racism," using the very legal framework designed to prohibit hate speech—the 1972 loi Pleven—against an antiracist militant now accused of "racial injury" against whites. The first of its kind in France, the Pleven law sanctions "incitement to discrimination, hatred or violence against a person or group of persons in reason of their origins or their belonging or nonbelonging to a specific ethnicity, nation, race or religion" (République Française 1972). In 1991, the courts recognized AGRIF as an antiracist association, adding anti-French and anti-white racism to the repertoire of

boundary 2 50:1 (2023)   DOI 10.1215/01903659-10192131   ©2023 by Duke University Press

sympathizer of the Secret Armed Organization (OAS), a clandestine para-military group intent on blocking Algerian independence from France, in order to "struggle against all racisms and in particular anti-French and anti-Christian racisms," AGRIF has become a major player in the recuperation of antidiscriminatory legislation to nativist ends (AGRIF n.d.). The lawsuit against Bouteldja, though unsuccessful in legal terms, is in turn part of a much broader recuperation of anticolonial and antiracist discourses by the nativist Right in France, from the think tanks of the Nouvelle droite (New Right), launched in the aftermath of decolonization, to more recent associations and media outlets that might be grouped together under the label *droite identitaire* (nativist right): the recently disbanded Génération identitaire (known in English as Generation Identity), Bloc identitaire (Nativist Block), the *Journal des indigènes* (*Native Newsletter*), and, tellingly, Fdesouche, short for *Français de souche*, the expression that inspired Bouteldja's neologism.

It is worth citing Bouteldja's comments in full to capture the extent to which they were made to mean the opposite of what she was calling for: epistemic decolonization. Here is the transcript of Bouteldja's remarks on the set of Frédéric Taddeï's popular television program, *Ce soir (ou jamais!)* (*Tonight [or Never!]*), on June 21, 2007:

> So what I don't like about the way we talk about things is that we always focus on working-class neighborhoods [*les quartiers populaires*], working-class neighborhoods are lacking in knowledge, in political consciousness, we have to educate them etc., and we nev... and we completely ignore the rest of society and its privileges, the privileges of the rest of society, and what I want to say is that it's the rest of society that needs to be educated. It's to the rest of society that we have to explain, for example on the simple question of history, it's the rest of Western society, well of s... [*de souche*, of roots], those we call *les souchiens*, because we have to call them something, white people [*c'est le reste de la société occidentale, enfin de s...*, *ceux qu'on appelle, nous, les souchiens, parce qu'il faut bien leur donner un nom, les Blancs*], that need to learn the history of slavery, of colonization.[2]

---

hate speech. On the history of appeals to "anti-white racism" in France, see Charrieras 2013. All translations are my own unless otherwise indicated.

2. I base my translation of Bouteldja's remarks on an excerpt of the debate posted to the video-sharing website Vimeo (enzo bateau n.d.).

No one took issue with Bouteldja's call to historicize the stigmatization of *les quartiers populaires*, one of the metonymic expressions used to designate the ex-urban neighborhoods where migrant workers, most of them hailing from France's former colonies, were housed in the postwar era. Activists, historians, and sociologists have insisted on the need to situate racial inequality in the context of France's colonial and postcolonial history for decades, and Bouteldja's arguments were in this respect not new, although they remain controversial.[3] What lit up the blogosphere, rather, was her use of the expression *les souchiens*, synonymous in her speech to *les Blancs*. *Souchiens* was, according to her numerous critics, a racial epithet for whites.

Grammatically, the neologism *souchien* is an adjective derived from *Français de souche européenne* (French of European "roots" or extraction), an expression first used during the Algerian war of independence. An awkward biological-botanical metaphor aimed at introducing a racial distinction not present in the legal definition of nationality, the expression was meant to distinguish white French soldiers in Algeria from troops previously known as *Français musulmans d'Algérie* (French Muslims from Algeria), redubbed *Français de souche nord-africaine* (French of North African extraction) for the occasion (Shepard 2006: 51–52).[4] In truncated form, the expression

3. The call to "decolonize the Republic," in the Indigènes de la république's catchy phrase, is not new, pace current attempts to discredit postcolonial and critical race theory as US imports (PIR n.d.[a], n.d.[b]). Migrant workers from France's former colonies began to demand political recognition in France in the 1970s. In the scholarly field, historian Benjamin Stora (1992) and sociologist Abdelmalek Sayad (2004) were pioneers in situating immigration to France within colonial and postcolonial history, and helped launch the field of postcolonial studies in France. The backlash against antiracist activism and postcolonial scholarship has been fierce, particularly as these fields have grown more visible in both national and international arenas. Shortly after the Indigènes de la république was founded in 2005, the French National Assembly voted to have the "positive aspects" of French colonization, particularly in North Africa, enshrined in law. Article 4, which mandated that said positive aspects be taught in schools, was modified after mass protests by historians, teachers, and activists (République Française 2005). Best-selling books against "colonial repentance" show that the question of France's colonial past remains highly contested, sixty years after the end of French empire (Bruckner 1986, 2012; Lefeuvre 2006).
4. French colonial nationality law is a particularly convoluted matter, nowhere more so than in French Algeria. The indigenous inhabitants of Algeria were decreed "French subjects" when Algeria was annexed in 1834. The 1865 Sénatus-Consulte officially recognized indigenous Algerians as French nationals and allowed them access to citizenship under the condition that they give up their personal status or customary law—in

Français de souche was popularized in the late 1970s by Jean-Marie Le Pen, a veteran of the Algerian war and founder of the nativist Front national (FN) party, to demarcate French nationals of European, read *white*, extraction from those hailing from the former colonies, newly dubbed *immigrants*. If the mention of European roots has dropped out of the expression, its origins in colonial military jargon reveal that it has always conveyed a racial understanding of Frenchness. The neologism that Bouteldja used on television is thus both ironic and critical: a *souchien* is a French national who claims to be a *Français de souche*, with all the fantasies of racial purity that expression belies.

Most viewers, however, interpreted the term *souchien* as a racial slur, and felt authorized to return the favor. Most interesting for my purposes here are the laborious efforts users deployed to parse the meaning of Bouteldja's neologism as an example of "anti-white racism." For her critics, *souchien* was an intentional pun on a homonymous expression, *sous-chien*, literally "underdog." (Unlike *underdog*, *sous-chien* is not an idiomatic expression in French.) YouTube user Le rider fou, whose thumbnail image, a Celtic cross, is a transparent affirmation of white identity, wonders: "if we are 'less-than-dogs' [*des 'sous-chiens'*] what are they less-than-shits [*des sous-merdes*]?? No to anti-white racism!!!"[5]

On July 13, 2007, a user who goes by the handle XRolan posted an excerpt from Bouteldja's intervention on YouTube along with an ethnographic take on her "antiwhite racist puns," surreptitiously underscoring Bouteldja's Muslim and hence foreign roots: "souchiens is especially insulting because 'dog' is one of the worst insults for Muslims: example 'infidel dogs.'" Imagine the hullabaloo, XRolan continues, if a European had used such an expression to refer to Algerians or Senegalese. "This absence of reaction [in the media] is not surprising in the least, anti-white racism is the most common and only authorized form in France. Add to this the affirma-

---

this case, Koranic and rabbinic codes governing marriage, inheritance, and other civic matters. In practice, this meant that very few indigenous Algerians became fully French until the 1870 Crémieux Decree, which extended French citizenship to most Algerian Jews. Muslim Algerians had to wait until the implementation of the 1946 Lamine Gueye law extending citizenship to French colonial subjects (without the attendant universal suffrage rights, however; Muslim Algerians had their own electoral college, not proportional to their numbers). For a succinct overview of nationality law in French Algeria, see Weil 2005.

5. Le rider fou posted these comments under XRolan's (2007) video upload of Bouteldja's televised interview. As of writing, this video has been taken down.

tive action [*discrimination positive*] of Nicolas Sarkozy and others, the result is that in France Europeans are becoming second-class citizens [*sous-citoyens*] in their own land" (Xrolan 2007).[6] Note the unacknowledged inversion of roles in Xrolan's counterexample. In France, Senegalese and Algerian nationals, or more likely French citizens of Senegalese and Algerian descent, are minorities in the numerical sense. They are also, in the French euphemism, "visible minorities," racialized subjects of a postcolonial metropole that has a long history in Senegal and Algeria, two of France's most prized colonies. Xrolan's rhetorical example surreptitiously turns whites into a racialized minority in France.

The ethical problem of naming race is a longstanding issue in France. As scholars working on racism and antiracism have noted, the legal interdiction on "ethnic statistics" in France has placed hurdles before corrective policies such as affirmative action (Ndiaye 2008: 76).[7] The very translation of this term in French—*discrimination positive* or "positive discrimination"—reveals an uneasy relation to differentialist measures that risk, according to some, to imperil a republican notion of equality.[8] But the reluctance to name white privilege—*privilège* is precisely the term Bouteldja uses to speak of "the rest of society," that is, the white majority—speaks also to a self-interested race-blindness. The ideal citizen does not "see" race, and yet the identity photograph that is still compulsory on French curriculum vitae necessarily elicits reactions based on a visual identification of race. In practice, the republican moratorium on naming race serves the interests of nativist groups like AGRIF, which have paradoxically been able to use the legal interdiction against racism in defense of whiteness.[9]

6. Contra XRolan's claims that "no one reacted" to Bouteldja's "anti-white racism," mainstream media outlets relayed comparable accusations, albeit couched in secular republican terms (Péguy B 2007; Jeanpierre 2007).

7. Article 8 of the 1978 Information Technology and Freedom law bans "collecting or treating data of a personal character that directly or indirectly show the racial or ethnic origins, the political, philosophical or religious opinions, the union membership [*l'appartenance syndicale*], or any information relating to the health or sex life of persons" (République Française 1978).

8. The tension between universal values and the recognition of particularities remains a thorny issue in France, as revealed by the recent decision to remove the word *race* from the Constitution (Agence France Presse 2018). For a recent critique of French colorblindness, see Diallo 2018.

9. Although unsuccessful in court, AGRIF's lawsuit against Bouteldja for "racial injury" managed to make whiteness a protected racial category, defying decades of legislation aimed at reversing the white supremacist laws of the Vichy regime. This is notable for

The *souchien* affair is illustrative of a decades-long phenomenon that has accelerated in the age of new media: the recuperation of antiracist discourse by nativist activists who claim that white people constitute a political minority in France, one that risks becoming a statistical minority due to the "counter-colonization" of France by migrants. It also centers around a notion that is central to both sides of the debate: *indigeneity*, alternatively defined as a political identity born in the colonial contact zone or as a naturalized expression of French nativism.[10] The polemic around Bouteldja's neologism reached deep into the websites, chat rooms, YouTube channels, and blogs that together make up *la fachosphère*, the blosphère of the French alt-right.[11] It also reached into the courts, culminating in legal proceedings against Bouteldja, who was accused of "anti-white racism." Bouteldja was acquitted in 2012, and the case was closed. But the multipronged defense of whiteness mounted against Bouteldja reveals that French nativism has deep roots in French imperial history, writ large to include decolonization and colonial and postcolonial migration. This essay is an exercise in reading the colonial subtext that runs through the outraged response to Bouteldja's neologism.

In the following sections, I track the emergence of French nativist discourses from the nineteenth century to the present, with particular attention to identification with the figure of the colonized in the colonial archive—focusing on Alexis de Tocqueville's Algerian writings—and in the nativist discourses that have accompanied decolonization in France, as evidenced in the tropes of "counter-colonization," "reciprocal decolo-

---

many reasons, not least the taboo against naming race in France. Activists and scholars have recently been able to carve out a space for studies of *la blanchité* (whiteness) in France, although it remains a highly controversial field of study. See, for example, the controversy over Bouteldja's (2017) provocatively titled book *Whites, Jews, and Us*, which has virtually made her persona non grata in France. Bouteldja resigned from the Indigènes de la république in 2020, citing the "witch hunt" against her (Bouteldja and Boussoumah 2021).

10. I do not capitalize the terms *indigenous* and *indigeneity* to make clear that I am referring to the legal and discursive categories that were instituted under colonial rule, and reappropriated in nativist discourses. Against current usage, I also avoid capitalizing *indigenous* when referring to populations that were present at the time of colonial conquest. While I recognize the acute political importance of empirical claims to first of prior occupancy in ongoing settler colonial projects such as the United States or Australia, the redeployment of indigeneity as a weapon in nativist discourses demands a critical reconsideration of the term.

11. For an overview of *la fachosphère*, see Albertini and Doucet 2016.

nization," and "great replacement" deployed by Alain de Benoist, Renaud Camus, Michel Houellebecq, and others. Central to my investigation is the instrumentalization of anticolonial and antiracist discourses to nativists ends. How does one respond to accusations of racism wielded by white identity organizations such as AGRIF against racial minorities? What does one make of the use of anticolonial theorist Frantz Fanon by the likes of Benoist and Camus to advocate for remigration (the expulsion of migrants from France)? And what can a dystopian novel—Houellebecq's *Soumission* (2015)—teach us about the contest for indigeneity in France? Exposing instrumentalist misreadings of anticolonial and antiracist texts by nativist activists is one step, but it is not sufficient. What is needed now, more than ever, is an effective strategy to read, analyze, and historicize the terms that are at stake: *indigène* (native), immigrants, racism, decolonization, and minority, to name a few. In order to understand the circulation of contemporary nativist discourses in France, it is imperative that we situate these terms in the colonial context where they were forged, and study their transformations in the postcolonial present.

A note on terminology before I begin. The study of nativism in France presents an interesting and perhaps symptomatic translation problem: there is no obvious cognate for *nativism* in French, even though it is a Latinate term. The closest expression in usage is the adjective *identitaire*, based on the substantive *identité* (identity), as in *la droite identitaire*, which I translate as the "nativist right." The terms *indigène* (native) and *indigéniste* (a more literal translation of *nativist*) are also in use, as I will discuss in my reading of Michel Houellebecq's novel *Soumission* below. These derivatives of *indigène* have the advantage of exposing the colonial genealogy of nativism. But they have also been used pejoratively to refer to the colonized and, today, to their descendants, some of whom have appropriated the colonial identity *indigène* for antiracist purposes. This essay is an attempt to historicize these fluid and ever-shifting semantic fields.

Indigènes and Immigrants

Algeria looms large in the colonial genealogy of French nativism. A French colony from 1830 to 1962, Algeria was considered an integral part of France from 1848, and its indigenous inhabitants were decreed French subjects, not citizens. Algeria was also France's sole remaining settler colony in the nineteenth and twentieth centuries, with a million European settlers residing in Algeria by the time the war of independence ended in 1962.

As sociologist Abdelmalek Sayad (2004: 63) put it with respect to Algerian immigration to France, Algeria is both exceptional within and exemplary of French colonial rule.[12] The notorious Code de l'indigénat, a separate penal code governing France's colonial subjects, was first put in place in Algeria before being exported to France's other colonies in 1881.[13] Though the nomenclature *indigène* did not congeal into a legal category until the end of the nineteenth century, military, administrative, and later literary texts concerning France's empire are rife with mention of *indigènes*, the "natives" that settlers and other colonists set out to displace. A template, staging ground, and sometime foil for colonial law and governmentality in France's other colonies, the prized settler colony of Algeria offers copious evidence of the colonial roots of nativism.

It is not a coincidence that nativist discourses that emerged in postcolonial France can be tracked back to a settler colonial context. Some of the conclusions I draw from the French archive can be evidenced in other settler colonies, not least the United States, which provided inspiration for the conquest of Algeria. Surveying the vast expanse of the Algerian plains, the French conquistadores of Africa compared themselves to New World pioneers, and those they dubbed *indigènes* to American Indians. For some, "extermination" was a noble precedent in the pursuit of racial supremacy.[14] Others sought to set France's civilizing mission apart from the US race wars. "I am not one to believe," writes Ferdinand Hugonnet (1858: 119), one of the most inspired apologists for colonization-as-civilization, "that we are fatally destined to push the inhabitants of Algeria into the desert, like the Yankees chase the Indians." Whether they advocated for extermination or more benevolent forms of cohabitation, colonists in Algeria expressed a palpable anxiety about the demographic risks of colonization: how was a small minority of settlers to govern a multitude of natives?

I borrow the title of this section from colonial apologist Ismaÿl Urbain's (2002) book *L'Algérie française, indigènes et immigrants* (*French Algeria, Natives and Immigrants*), which offers an early articulation of what Ranajit Guha (1997: 487) analyzes as the "anxiety . . . of empire": the knowledge that in an imperial setting, colonial hegemony is far from assured. The immigrants in Urbain's ([1862] 2002: 59–60) title are the European set-

---

12. Mahmood Mamdani (1996: 126) makes the related point that French colonial law merely formalized the permanent state of exception that governed all African colonies.

13. For a detailed history of the Code de l'indigénat, see Le Cour Grandmaison 2010.

14. "The fate reserved for American Indians and Australian Aborigines," writes historian Olivier Le Cour Grandmaison (2005: 18), "was a precedent that was frequently invoked to advocate for [the *extermination*] of all or part of the 'Arabs'" (original italics).

tlers—French, Spanish, Italian, Maltese—just shy of two hundred thousand across the three "centers of European colonization," Algiers, Oran, and Constantine. The natives—the indigenous Jewish and Muslim populations—are, in the same cities, four hundred thousand, more than twice the number of Europeans.[15] When the anticolonial insurrection broke out in the mountainous areas of Algeria in 1954, the demographic balance had tipped to one settler for nine *indigènes*.

Writing during the heyday of anticolonial struggles in North Africa, the Tunisian writer Albert Memmi (1965: 52) captured the performative paradox inherent in the colonial venture: the settler must persuade himself that he is the legitimate occupier of the conquered land; "the usurper... knows that he is claiming a usurped place" (translation modified). "L'image d'Epinal," the "heroic portrait" of the pioneering settler tilling the land—invariably a masculine figure in colonial discourse—will serve to justify the usurpation of colonization (33, 3; translation modified). The settler takes the place of the *indigène* in order to cultivate the land, and this *mise en valeur*, in turn, will serve to naturalize the presence of France in its far-flung colonies. There is a performative dimension to this substitution: in order to consider his presence legitimate, the settler must become a native of the colony. By the time Memmi wrote *The Colonizer and the Colonized*, Algeria "was" France ("l'Algérie, c'est la France"), and French settlers had dubbed themselves *les Algériens*.[16]

Equally interesting for my purposes here is the paradoxical identification of the colonial administrator, soldier, or settler with the figure of the *indigène*, a phenomenon Achille Mbembe (2017: 57) dubs the "'indigenization' of the colonist."[17] A brief look at the colonial archive reveals that the

15. An early champion of the "civilizing mission," Urbain was not unduly concerned with the arithmetic of colonization. But the asymmetry in numbers convinced Urbain (2002: 65) of the necessity of pursuing a politics of association, rather than assimilation.

16. France annexed Algeria in 1834 and began administering the colony as a French territory in 1848. The expression "L'Algérie, c'est la France" was popularized during the war of independence, when the territorial integrity of France's empire was in question. On the adoption of the appellation *Algérien* by colonists and settlers in nineteenth-century Algeria, see Pervillé 1997. The term *pied-noir*, initially a pejorative epithet for *indigènes*, only came to designate settlers during the war of independence and was reclaimed by repatriated settlers after 1962. The origins of the term *pied-noir* remain controversial, with some claiming that the nationalist anticolonial movement Parti du Peuple Algérien coined it in 1946, while others maintain that it was first used by the OAS to rally the support of settlers (Pervillé 2007; Zerrouky 2004).

17. This is particularly true of settler colonies like South Africa, which Mbembe takes aim at here; Algeria; and of course Palestine/Israel. Indigenization is part and parcel of what Patrick Wolfe (2016: 33) calls "settler colonialism [as] a project of replacement."

appropriation of indigeneity is, from the outset, a central figure of colonial discourse. Take Alexis de Tocqueville's 1847 "Report on Algeria," commissioned by the National Assembly to support additional funding to conclude the conquest of Algeria. An erstwhile candidate for settlement, Tocqueville (2001: 89) had made several trips to Algeria and was known as a fervent proponent of all-out war and "forced expropriation." Alleging that the most fertile lands have gone to native subjects and not to European citizens, Tocqueville, previewing nativist discourse in France, insists in the report on what we might call *préférence nationale* (the privileging of French citizens over foreigners) for settlers in the colonies. His plea for settler self-governance surreptitiously turns "la population indigène" (the native population) into "sujets étrangers" (foreign subjects):

> In many places where the European civilian population is mixed with the native population, it is complained, and not without some reason, that in general it is the native [*l'indigène*] who is better protected, and the European who has more difficulty obtaining justice. . . . One will be drawn to conclude that our government in Africa pushes gentleness toward the conquered to the point of forgetting its position as conqueror, and that in the interest of its foreign subjects [*sujets étrangers*], it does more than it would do in France for the well-being of its citizens. (139–40; translation modified)

Note the terminological shift from *indigènes* to *sujets étrangers*, in opposition to European and French settlers, the legitimate beneficiaries, for Tocqueville, of the rights of citizenship. If Algerians were indeed subjects rather than citizens of France, they were, since the annexation of Algeria to France in 1834, de facto French nationals, not foreigners. Tocqueville was well aware of the legal status of *indigènes*, of course. The transformation of French colonial subjects into foreigners serves his argument that democratic representation should be reserved for Europeans. If Tocqueville (2003: 376) warned against following the American example in Algeria—what, in *Democracy in America*, he characterizes as the "destruction" of the Indians—he nevertheless advocated for extreme methods taken straight out of the US playbook, including forced displacement, burning, looting, and *enfumades*, the indiscriminate practice of "smoking out" populations sheltered in caves.[18]

18. On Tocqueville's (2003: 70) shifting and sometimes contradictory positions on what he called the "unfortunate necessities" of colonial warfare in the United States and Algeria, see Le Cour Grandmaison 2005: 91–92, 112, 193.

Notwithstanding Tocqueville's (2001: 19) fantasy of "taking...the place of the vanquished" (translation modified), Europeans never formed a statistical majority in Algeria, nor indeed in any other French colony. In Guha's (1997) felicitous phrase, the settler is "not at home in empire." Writing about the struggle for independence in Algeria more than a century after Tocqueville, Frantz Fanon (2004: 5) offers a blunt assessment of the impossible "indigenization" of the settler: "In the colonies the foreigner coming from elsewhere imposed himself using his cannons and his machines. Despite the success of his pacification, in spite of his appropriation, the settler always remains a foreigner. . . . The ruling species is first and foremost the one from elsewhere, different from the autochtonous population, 'the others'" (translation modified). The domestication of the colony, based on the desire to take the place of the colonized, is futile, for the settler will never be a native. If the *autochtone* (Greek for *indigène*) wants to take the place of the foreigner (*allochtone*), it is because it was his place to begin with. In response to the usurpation of colonization, decolonization will undertake "the replacement of one 'species' of mankind by another" (1; translation modified).

It is important to stress that Fanon is speaking of the invention of a new man here, not of racial warfare. And yet as we will see, his ironic appropriation of racial scientific discourse ("une 'espèce' d'homme") to speak of decolonization as a world-making enterprise would prove easily recuperable within nativist discourses, allowing Nouvelle droite pundit Alain de Benoist (2001: 528) to freely borrow from Fanon in his plea for "reciprocal decolonization." Fanon's poetic account of decolonization as a movement of replacement offers an unexpected preview of nativist discourses on migration in France. For the voice of the settler ventriloquized in Fanon's (2004: 5) description of the colony—"they want to take our place"—eerily resembles the voice of the *Français de souche* in postcolonial France.

I return briefly to the *souchien* affair to make visible the links between fantasies of replacement in the settler colony and postcolonial France before turning to Benoist's appropriation of Fanon in the following section. Indeed, the *souchien* affair offers ample evidence of the colonial genealogy of French nativism as a contest over indigeneity in France. Camille9340, a YouTube user who posted an excerpt of Bouteldja's televised remarks on July 5, 2007, betrays an uncanny, albeit unintentional, understanding of this genealogy when he gives the example of French expatriates in Morocco, a former protectorate of France: "Imagine that in Morocco the french call the *marocains de souche* '*des souchiens*' because we have to call them something, tanned people' [*les bronzés*] I think they'll take the first plane for France and for good reason [*sic*]." The French expatriate community in Morocco—descendants of French settlers and postcolonial *coopérants* as well as today's business and diplomatic elites—become a "visible minority" in Camille9340's telling, which manages to slip in a racial term for Moroccans. The calque expression *Marocains de souche*—why not say, simply, Moroccans?—also manages to naturalize a racialized understanding of national identity, projecting French fantasies of racial purity onto the object of France's racial paranoia, the region that is now purportedly "colonizing" France through migration. French racists are not welcome in Morocco, nor should "anti-white" racists be welcome in France. Hence, according to a YouTube commenter who goes by the transparently anagrammatic handle Faldo Itlehr, if Bouteldja doesn't like France, she can go back to her own country: "If French hospitality isn't to her liking, she's free to go back to her *bled* in Algeria" (Camille9340 2007).[19] Never mind that Bouteldja's "migrant" parents were already French nationals before Algerian independence. For Faldo Itlehr, citizenship is not commensurate with nationality.

That French imperial rule relied on a similar distinction between nationality and citizenship only underscores the colonial genealogy of these forms of nativism more clearly. Moroccans, Algerians, Senegalese, and France's colonial subject across Asia and Africa were all, legally speaking, *indigènes* (natives), French subjects bound by a separate penal code and deprived of the rights of citizenship. Camille9340's disingenuous invocation of *les Marocains de souche* reveals a displaced obsession with indigeneity: the nativeness of *Français de souche* versus the foreignness of those Bouteldja and her fellow activists have dubbed the *natives of the republic*.

What interests me here is the linguistic *détournement* that turns yesterday's natives and their descendants (*indigènes*) into immigrants (*immigrés*) and the emigrants of old (*colons*, settlers) into natives. The history of the use of these terms in the French language reveals that the story of the nativist Right in France is, in part, the story of what Todd Shepard (2006) calls "the invention of decolonization" from a metropolitan point of view. It is the story of how natives turned into immigrants, and immigrants into natives. In the words of a *pied-noir* repatriate to France: "they threw us out of the

---

19. *Bled*, from *balad*, in the sense of "town" or "village," is one of the many Arabic words that has made it into the French language via French Algeria. Although in contemporary French colloquial speech it can be used affectionately to refer to one's hometown, Faldo Itlehr's tone echoes its colonial use to speak of a purportedly backward Algerian hinterland.

country, they should stay there now" (quoted in Comtat 2018: 267). What Nouvelle droite luminary Alain de Benoist calls "reciprocal decolonization" will, in his telling, complete the process of decolonization initiated by the colonized in the middle of the twentieth century.

Reciprocal Decolonization

One of the remarkable features of the new nativist discourse that emerged in the 1970s, and has only grown stronger since, is the recuperation of *indigeneity* it relies on. If, as we have seen, the legal category of the *indigène* (native) was forged at the colonial frontier, the notion of indigeneity paradoxically returned to the metropole in the guise of *nativism*: the claim that only those with ancestral roots in France can be French. Decolonization, I argue, is the pivot that enabled this appropriation of indigeneity in the metropole. With the demise of the French empire in 1962, French settlers, many of them born in the colonies, made their definitive return to France. According to a belated nativist logic, colonial migrants—freshly minted nationals of sovereign nation-states—were no longer welcome in the metropole. Or, to paraphrase nativist discourses, from the Nouvelle droite that emerged in the late 1960s to the *identitaires* of the twenty tens: we left Algeria; now you leave France. The refusal to acknowledge the shared history of (post)colonial migrants and those newly dubbed *Français de souche* in the metropole—that is, the refusal to historicize migration—is one of the principal tactics of the nativist Right.

Like the expression *anti-white racism*, which co-opts antidiscriminatory law for the benefit of the white majority, *decolonization* has become a weapon in the arsenal of the nativist Right, redefined as the right to French self-determination. One of the principal theoreticians of the decolonization of France is Alain de Benoist, cofounder of the far-right movement Nouvelle droite.[20] Forged in the wake of decolonization, the movement Benoist helped launch is, I will argue, pivotal in the transformation of colonial nativism (settlers into natives) into postcolonial nativism (natives into immi-

---

20. For a synthetic overview of the Nouvelle droite, an appellation that encompasses various rightist movements propagating "cultural" (rather than biological) forms of racism, see Taguieff 1993. The Nouvelle droite is usually studied within a French and European tradition of xenophobic (anti-Semitic and anti-immigrant) thought, with little attention to the colonial genealogies of the movement. I focus here on Benoist's writings because they make apparent nativist identification with the colonized.

grants). As we will see, Benoist's recuperation of the terminology of anti-colonialism against immigration is particularly agile because it is couched in an apology for diversity, plurality, and self-determination. "Yesterday left-ist intellectuals turned toward the Third World to precipitate the decline of European culture," writes Benoist (1986: 222) in his essay *Europe, Tiers Monde, même combat* (*Europe, Third World, Same Struggle*). "Today we turn toward the Third World to keep all cultures alive, to try to save the diversity of the world, and to restore to the global political game its necessary plurality."[21] What Benoist proposes is the regeneration of a Europe finally disentangled from its erstwhile colonies.

Those who know Benoist's political trajectory can appreciate the irony of his self-positioning as anticolonial activist. Founder in 1968 of the unapologetically nativist Research and Study Group for European Civili-zation, the principal think tank of the Nouvelle droite, Benoist started his career as coeditor of an underground pro-OAS journal in the waning years of French empire. Still a teenager, he "saw decolonization take place" (Ben-oist 1986: 9) through the eyes of the most hardcore *algérianistes*, armed militants "ready to die for French Algeria" (Bar-On 2011: 206). His first essays, published after Algerian independence, continued to defend the actions of the OAS (Benoist 1963) and, later, apartheid and white minority rule in South Africa (Benoist and d'Orcival 1965) and Rhodesia (Benoist and Fournier 1965).

What might explain the volte-face that makes Benoist a belated apol-ogist for the right to self-determination? Against the grain of the humanitar-ian discourse that, by the 1980s, had all but replaced Third Worldism, Ben-oist (1986: 67–68) manages to resuscitate none other than Frantz Fanon in defense of an oddly French version of anticolonial nationalism:[22]

> The colonized did not affirm their right to independence as abstract individuals, but as members of a people and potential citizens of a future nation. They affirmed this right on the basis of a specific *belonging* [*appartenance*] and *heritage*, that is to say in the name of a *collective identity*, giving legitimacy to the right of a people to con-stitute itself as a nation. If they wanted to have full sovereignty of their *land* [*terre*], it's because they considered that it belonged to them,

21. Pace Benoist, the aim of French anticolonialism was not the destruction of Europe. For a thorough history of Third Worldism in France, see Liauzu 1982.
22. On the drastic shift from decolonization to human rights as "the last utopia," see Moyn 2010.

that they were there before the colonizers, in sum that they were *at home* [*chez eux*], and that this is where they could take full possession of their destiny. (original italics)

Citing Fanon, Benoist offers anticolonial nationalism as a model for French national rebirth.

Readers of anticolonial theory will recognize the selective use Benoist makes of Fanon's *Wretched of the Earth* as a template for the decolonization of France. Gone are Fanon's (2004: 160) admonitions against the reification of "custom," which he opposes to the vital force of the "culture" that emerges in the struggle against colonial rule. Gone too is Fanon's humanist understanding of decolonization as a radical upending of the colonial order, not a one-to-one operation of substitution whereby the colonized simply takes the place of the colonizer.[23] The subtle shifts between clinical, hortatory, and ironic registers in Fanon's work have made him an ideal target for appropriation by the nativist Right. Take the passage where Fanon (2004: 5) ventriloquizes the settler's fear of being replaced: "'They want to take our place.'" For Benoist, anticipating the language popularized by disciples like Renaud Camus (2018: 22), Fanon is a "replacist." No surprise, then, that Benoist's version of decolonization emphasizes terms that bear a striking resemblance to the keywords of French nativism: belonging, tradition, collective identity, *terroir*, and the self-evidence of being at home.

Benoist's instrumentalization of anticolonial theory is not merely an illustration of the maxim according to which the enemies of one's enemies are one's friends. Central to his idiosyncratic critique of imperialism is a refutation of what he identifies as the Enlightenment principles that drove France's colonial venture, initially defended, he correctly notes, by the Left (Benoist 1986: 32). Contra anticolonial theorists like Fanon, who defended the universal values of liberty, equality, and fraternity against a Europe that had betrayed its principles in the colonial venture, Benoist contends that the ideological engine of colonialism is egalitarianism.

This argument requires a remarkable rewriting of history. In order to make this claim, Benoist has to bypass the history of France's Ancien Régime empire, built on the highly lucrative slave trade and plantation economy. He also fails to mention that nineteenth-century scientific racism was largely based on phrenological "data" culled from the colonies, hardly in

---

23. I owe this point to Stathis Gourgouris, who rightfully insists that Benoist's reading of Fanon is, in fact, a misreading.

support of the argument that all men are born equal. What Benoist wants to prove is that, as a so-called egalitarian ideology, colonialism has homogenized the globe: "For the political philosophy born out of the Enlightenment, all men being equal and holders of the inalienable rights that they derive from the time that they lived in a 'state of nature,' all peoples are finally identical" (34). Against the blind universalism of the civilizing mission which extends, according to him, to the era of the free market and multiculturalism— globalization is merely an extension of European imperialism in his account— Benoist advocates for what he calls the "right to difference," redefined, as we will see, as an apology for separateness:

> The belief that the more the world is homogeneous, the more men will understand each other, is an error of judgment that has been proven wrong many times over: xenophobia, the rejection of the Other, is born less from the acknowledgment of differences [*du constat des différences*] than from the fear that they will disappear, and the excessive, pathological desire to create differences artificially where they no longer exist. The more a culture develops its difference, then, the more chances it has to reach the "universal"—a *universal* that is the exact opposite of cosmopolitanism. (93–94; original italics)

The solution to racism? The right to self-determination, in Europe as in the Third World. Or, in Benoist's (2001: 528) earlier formulation, "reciprocal decolonization" (*la décolonisation réciproque*).

Benoist's critique of multiculturalism sounds eerily like an anticolonial defense of the particular against the universal that threatens to engulf it. But his objectives in *Europe, Tiers Monde, même combat* come into much sharper focus in *Vu de droite* (*View from the Right*), an anthology of texts that elaborate what he calls a "double *critique* ... of the ideology of the left and the methodology of the right" (Benoist [1978] 2001: 26; original italics).[24] While the Left has, according to Benoist, successfully "annexed" and "inverted" the ideas of the Right, from environmentalism and regionalism to anti-universalism, the Right lazily relies on the fallacious idea of a "silent majority" that will manifest itself when the time is ripe (18, 21). The

---

24. Benoist's writings have had considerable impact outside of France, although very few of his works have been translated. Previously translated into German, Italian, and Portuguese, *View from the Right* is now available in a three-volume English translation thanks to a crowdsourced alt-right press (Benoist 2017–19). As of writing, the Kickstarter campaign that launched this translation project is still live (Arktos 2019).

intellectual movement launched by Benoist in the aftermath of decolonization aims to "frontally resist a pseudo-racism that negates differences and
a threatening racism that is also the rejection of the Other—the rejection
of diversity" (25).

Benoist is not taking aim at biological racism when he evokes a
"threatening racism." The real menace, rather, is egalitarianism. In his review
of a spate of recent publications on Arthur de Gobineau, author of *The
Inequality of Human Races* (1855), Benoist suggests that the nineteenth-
century racial scientist's magnum opus would have been more accurately
titled "Essay on the Diversity of Human Races." "Gobineau distinguishes
three great races," writes Benoist (2001: 263), "the white, the yellow, and
the black, all three with qualities and defects proper to them, none superior
in absolute terms, but which all risk to lose their personality by mixing."[25]
He concludes this patent misreading of the urtext of scientific racism by
claiming that Gobineau is for "mutual respect and *reciprocal* decolonization" (original italics).

Benoist's disingenuous reading of France's most influential white
supremacist—who was, as Tocqueville's personal secretary, also impli-
cated in the pacification of Algeria—manages to turn biological racism
into an apology for "le droit à la différence" (527). An expression coined
by antiracist activists and institutionalized by the left-wing government in
the 1980s, "the right to difference" was intended to allow for difference
within the egalitarian, universalist framework of the French Republic. In the
catchy phrase of the 1984 antiracist march Convergence, "la France c'est
comme une mobylette, pour avancer il lui faut du mélange" (France is like a
motorbike, in order to go forward it needs blend [oil]). Like his recuperation
of decolonization, diversity, and self-determination, Benoist's antiphrastic
use of "the right to difference" to mean separation (the very opposite of
mélange) is another example of what Pierre-André Taguieff (2001: 7) terms
"the strategy of 'retorsion' with respect to the words and values of antiracism" by the Nouvelle droite.[26]

25. See Gobineau (1855) 1915.
26. There is some irony in quoting Taguieff here. A leading expert on the Nouvelle droite,
Taguieff is best known today for coining the expression *islamo-gauchisme* (Islamo-
leftism) to speak of new forms of anti-Semitism that include, in his view, all brands of anti-
Zionism and pro-Palestinianism. Taguieff is also a vocal critic of postcolonial and critical
race studies. In January 2021, Taguieff launched a watchdog association on "decolonial"
studies, the Observatoire du décolonialisme et des idéologies identitaires (Observatory
of Decolonialism and Identitarian Ideologies), after publishing a book on "the decolonial
imposture" (Taguieff 2020).

There is remarkable continuity in Benoist's instrumentalization of antiracist terms, despite his recent efforts to distance himself from "ethnocentrism." Note the introduction, in the 2001 edition of *Vu de droite*, of the notion of "counter-colonization" (*contre-colonisation*; that is to say, the colonization of Europe by migrants), popularized in recent decades by the novelist Jean Raspail and the nativist thinker I turn to next, Renaud Camus:[27]

> While universalism tends to negate alterity by reducing the Other to the Same, ethnocentrism tends to reduce diversity by suppressing the Other, or by keeping the Other radically apart. In both cases, alterity is considered to be without interest, diversity without value. On the contrary, a positive conception of alterity consists in recognizing difference without using it to submit the existence of some to the desires, interests, or reason of others. Oppression not only negates the freedom of the oppressed, but also that of the oppressor. This is what Marx meant when he wrote that "a people that oppresses another cannot be free." We are familiar with the dialectic of the master and the slave: the two roles ineluctably change places. Those who have colonized ought not to be surprised when they are invaded in turn. (Benoist 2001: xxii)

In a typically selective use of the classic texts of the Left, Benoist manages to turn Hegel and Marx into the harbingers of counter-colonization. The colonial dialectic will ultimately drive the former slaves not to emancipate but to colonize their former masters. But Benoist's admonition that the master and slave will inevitably trade places also clarifies the stakes of the metaphors he uses to speak, ultimately, of segregation: diversity, difference, alterity. Reciprocal decolonization will ensure that the races do not mix, to paraphrase Benoist's reading of Gobineau. The image of role reversal is, in fact, symptomatic of Benoist's identification with the colonized. If the colo-

27. Jean Raspail offers a classic example of the trope of counter-colonization in his 1973 novel *The Camp of the Saints*. Faced with the sudden arrival of a million migrants, one of the novel's many minor characters has this to say: "Nobody has yet pointed to the essential risk, which stems from the extreme vulnerability of the white race and its tragic status as a minority. I'm white. White and Western. We are white. But what do we amount to in total? Some seven hundred million souls, most of us packed into Europe, as against the billions and billions of nonwhites, so many we can't even keep count" (Raspail 1975: 93; translation modified). Raspail's novel is required reading for the nativist Right in France, the United States, and beyond. On the recent transatlantic fortunes of *The Camp of the Saints*, see Alduy 2017.

nized could legitimately consider themselves *chez eux* in their homeland, so too can *Français de souche* in theirs. Except that France is being "invaded," and *les souchiens* are rapidly becoming a minority.

Benoist's call to decolonize France sounds relatively mild mannered compared to the more extreme uses to which his theories have been put in recent years. The most influential theorist of the invasion of France by migrants today is Renaud Camus, author of the "great replacement" theory according to which Europeans are being steadily replaced by non-Europeans. According to Camus (2015: 72, 127), "the race of ex-colonizers" is now "a people in the process of being colonized.") To his empiricist critics, who counter that Europeans are not by any stretch a numerical minority in Europe, Camus retorts that his concern is not with numbers. To the dictatorship of statistics Camus opposes the "gaze" (*regard*) of the writer capable of "apprehend[ing] the real" in the absence of "ethnic statistics." Even if the numbers proved him wrong, Camus contends, that would constitute further proof of the success of the "counter-colonization" of France. Glossing the naive sociologist who claims that "there are fewer and fewer foreigners," Camus (2017: 26–32) inserts the parenthetical remark, "of course, they were all naturalized—the Great Replacement is when there are no more foreigners (neither foreigners nor foreignness [*ni d'étrangers, ni d'étrangèreté*])." What Arjun Appadurai (2007: 52) calls "fear of small numbers"—the fear that the majority is in danger of "trading places" with the minority—cannot be supported or refuted on empirical grounds. Camus's paranoid vision offers a postcolonial spin on the anxiety of empire. If the colonizer is "not at home in empire," nor is the postcolonizer at home in the metropole (Guha 1997). Postcolonial France is *unheimlich* for the *souchien*.

President of a marginal political party named In-nocence (etymologically, the opposite of harm) and of the think tank Conseil national de la résistance européenne, and once a hopeful for the 2017 presidential elections, Camus has managed to disseminate his ideas widely, despite efforts to censor him.[28] The notion of "great replacement," popularized in English thanks to a self-translated, self-published pamphlet titled *You Will Not Replace Us!*, has become ubiquitous in no small part due to Brenton Tarrant's 2019 live-streamed mass shooting of congregants in two mosques in

---

28. In 2017 Camus tried to garner the necessary five hundred signatures to run for president but fell short. He had marginally more success with the 2017 European elections, but he backed out in 2019 because one of his colleagues, a young *gilet jaune*, was found to have "prayed" in front of a swastika ("Européennes" 2019).

Christchurch, New Zealand, allegedly in reaction to the purported replacement of Europeans by migrants.[29] Though Camus (2017: 39) was quick to distance himself from the actions of his Australian disciple, he has, at other times, explicitly evoked the threat of violence:

> One might for example accuse us of not being very in-nocent [not harmful] when we advocate for remigration, at the risk of bothering [*déranger*] quite a few people. But if, as I believe to be the case, nocence [harm, *sic*] and the upheaval [*le dérangement*] it implies . . . are the only things that can liberate us from colonization, submission, and the horrors of living together [*les horreurs du vivre-ensemble*], long live remigration! Barely independent, Algeria considered that, in 1962, it would not be truly independent if there were still among its population ten percent of people who did not pertain [*ne relevaient pas*] to its culture, its traditions, its language, its religion. The rest of the world more or less agreed at the time. Remember: "the suitcase or the coffin."

Camus's cryptic allusion to the spontaneous outbursts of violence that accompanied decolonization in Algeria is both singularly reductive and symptomatic of the process of identification with the colonized I have been tracking in this essay. "La valise ou le cercueil" was allegedly an expression used by indigenous Algerians to convince settlers to leave Algeria during the war of independence. In reality, the exodus of some eight hundred thousand settlers to France was an unexpected and unwelcome development for both parties.[30] The implicit threat of reprisals Camus makes here—Algerians ousted French settlers in 1962; now the French will return the favor by deporting its migrant population—is a familiar leitmotif in postcolonial nativist literature.[31] But what interests me here is the equivalence Camus draws

29. Tarrant's (2019) manifesto cites Marine Le Pen's defeat in the 2017 presidential elections as a catalyst in his decision to "ensure the existence of our people, and a future for white children." On Camus's influence on the alt-right, see McAuley 2019.

30. For a detailed history of the *rapatriement* (repatriation) of French settlers and Jews from Algeria to France—many of whom had never set foot in the metropole—see Shepard 2006: 207–28. According to Pierre Daum, the oft-cited number of one million *rapatriés* is inflated. By December 1962, departures totaled 802,265, while 218,735 Europeans remained in Algeria (Daum 2012: 44).

31. See for example Raspail's wistful observation that what offended no one at the moment of decolonization—the "brutal exodus" of one million *pieds-noirs*—is inconceivable today (2011: 768n4).

between French settlers in Algeria, on the one hand, and (post)colonial migrants and their French descendants, on the other. Camus's well-worn claim that the Algerians kicked out the French betrays a paradoxical understanding of the colonial genealogy of immigration.

It should not surprise us, then, that the name of Camus's (2018: 19) signature concept, "le Grand Remplacement," is modeled after an obscure episode in French colonial history: the expulsion of French Acadians by the British in the middle of the eighteenth century, an event known as "le Grand Dérangement" (the Great Upheaval). Ironically, the replacement of one settler population by another becomes a figure for the replacement of the settlers of old by the formerly colonized. Remember that "'they want to take our place'" is how Fanon (2004: 5)—whom Camus often cites—ventriloquizes the fear of the white minority in the colony. If Algerians had the right to kick out the French, those Camus calls "les archéo-Français, les indigènes" (the archeo-French, the natives) must advocate for the remigration of "les allochtones, les néo-Français" (the foreigners, the neo-French), who threaten to take power if they outnumber France's original inhabitants. A footnote clarifies what Camus (2015: 23n7) means: "On this topic, see Soumission, Michel Houellebecq's novel." The fact that Camus cites a recent dystopian novel—or is it utopian?—to buttress his claims about the Islamization of France reveals the deeply speculative nature of what I am calling the *white minority*. But it also betrays a remarkable inability to read literary texts. In fact, *Soumission* paints a rather more complex picture of the battle over indigeneity in France. I turn in conclusion to this work of fiction, which elucidates the stakes of the colonial genealogy of nativism I have begun tracing in this essay.

Civil War

Hailed as prophetic by Renaud Camus when it was published on January 7, 2015—the very day of the *Charlie Hebdo* terrorist attacks—Michel Houellebecq's *politique-fiction* about an Islamized France was immediately criticized on the left for its purported Islamophobia. Known for his glib comment, after 9/11, that "la religion la plus con, c'est quand même l'islam" (the dumbest religion, after all, is Islam), Houellebecq was no doubt prepared for a media storm around his new novel. In a long review published two days before the *Charlie Hebdo* attacks, Goncourt jury member Pierre Assouline (2015) berated Houellebecq for his political nonchalance: "What is more irresponsible than lighting a fire under the fantasy of civil war in today's France?" Hours before the *Charlie Hebdo* attacks, Radio commentator Patrick Cohen accused Houellebecq of "essentializing French Muslims by giving them a political will [*une volonté politique*; i.e., Islamism]" without leaving room in his novel for the great diversity of Muslim voices in France. More troubling still is the fact that Houellebecq presents an Islamist regime based on patriarchy, polygamy, and child marriage as the image of a "moderate Islam" (France Inter 2015). Houellebecq's chuckles do little to dispel the uncomfortable fact that such a regime is perhaps less repugnant to him than it is to his secular republican interviewers. The explosion of violence that followed the publication of the novel only fanned the flames of liberal outrage, along with sales, which surpassed the one-hundred-thousand mark within days (Bellaigue 2015).

Houellebecq's liberal critics are right, of course, that *Soumission* essentializes Muslims, presenting them as a homogenous, undifferentiated, and consensual bloc.[32] But they assume that, in the novel, the destruction of the republic is a bad thing. Against the grain of liberal critiques of *Soumission*, I propose to read the novel as a parody of nativist discourses that make Islam the unexpected savior of a decadent Europe.

It matters little if Houellebecq's parody is intentional.[33] Read through the lens of colonial and postcolonial nativist discourses, the dystopia of an Islamized France tips into the regenerative utopia of demographic explosion. Once a great empire, France is in the midst of "committing suicide," literally, by failing to reproduce (Houellebecq 2015: 214). Muslims, on the other hand, are concerned first and foremost with demographic hegemony: "What they care about is birth rate and education. . . . If you control the children, you control the future" (66). Polygamy presents the added benefit of favoring natural selection. Given that there aren't enough women for all the men, only the fittest will reproduce: "it was how the species achieved its destiny" (225). In a parodic inversion of white supremacist discourse, demographic engineering by way of immigration saves Europe from ageing out of existence. In the words of Robert Rediger, the president of the newly

---

32. Unlike the joyful cacophony of Kabyle and Arab voices, most of them fiercely secular, in Sabry Louatah's (2011–16) *Les sauvages* trilogy, which imagines an Islamist attack against the newly elected Franco-Algerian president. A much more palatable speculative thriller about Islam in France, *Les sauvages* has recently been turned into a TV series (Poussel 2019).

33. As critics have noted, the narrative ambiguity of Houellebecq's novels makes it difficult to read them as *romans à thèse*. For an astute reading of *Soumission* as an example of "degenerative realism" that defies the norms of the pamphlet genre, see Wampole 2020: 158–81.

Islamized, Saudi-funded Sorbonne where the narrator teaches, "the massive arrival of immigrant populations, with their traditional culture—of natural hierarchies, the submission of women, and respect of elders—constitutes a historic opportunity for the moral and familial rearmament of Europe. These immigrants held out the hope of a new golden age for the old continent" (231; translation modified). The electoral victory of the French Islamist Mohamed Ben Abbès, an assimilated second-generation Tunisian, against FN leader Marine Le Pen in the 2017 elections is presented as a way out of "the decadence of Europe," heralding a new era of imperialism that will see the expansion of the European Union to the southern shores of the Mediterranean, from Morocco to Turkey, and restore the French language—before English, the language of empire and global diplomacy—to its former glory (214, translation modified; 243). As Rediger notes, "the nativists [les identitaires] and the Muslims were in perfect agreement" (230).

A potpourri of allusions to the luminaries of the nativist Right, from Edouard Drumont to Renaud Camus, Houellebecq's version of Eurabia might be read as a caricatural alt-right dystopia, were it not for the fact that political Islam is what drives the regeneration of France, rather than its demise.[34] The novel is written as a mock thriller, leaving a trail of clues about the fate of the French Republic. An academic boycott against Israel and burka-clad female students, flanked by Black and Arab bodyguards, are the early warning signs of the rapid and ineluctable Islamization of France (21–24). It is only in the final line, narrated in the conditional—"je n'aurais rien à regretter" (I would have nothing to regret) (250; translation modified)—that the narrator's imminent conversion to Islam is suggested. Until the runoff between Ben Abbès and Le Pen—postponed due to a "civil war" between nativists (identitaires) and Salafists who consider both candidates too moderate—there is the added suspense of not knowing whether the nativist Right or the Islamist party will win.[35] Thanks to a new colleague

34. Other figures include J. K. Huysmans, the writer of decadence whose collected works François is tasked with editing; Léon Bloy (not an anti-Semite, according to the narrator), whose essay Le salut par les Juifs was recently republished alongside Edouard Drumont's La France juive in Alain Soral's Les InfréKentables alt-right book series; Charles Martel, the hero of the French Reconquista; and Bat Ye'or, who coined the portmanteau Eurabia to denounce the purported collusion of leftists and Islamists in Europe. Renaud Camus is rumored to be Le Pen's speech writer in the novel.

35. The novel rehearses anxieties around the 2002 elections opposing center-right candidate Jacques Chirac and FN candidate Jean-Marie Le Pen. For a dystopian graphic novel on the much more likely scenario of an FN-led France, see the trilogy La présidente (Boudjellal and Durpaire 2015–17).

who may or may not still be an *identitaire*, François learns that the random gunshots and explosions echoing throughout Paris during the electoral season, subject to a "total [media] black-out," are indeed evidence of "a civil war between Muslim immigrants and the indigenous populations of Western Europe," meant to derail the elections and precipitate France into an all-out "ethnic conflict" (48, translation modified; 43, 58). Everything changed, his informer tells him, when militants of Bloc identitaire took on a new identity: "The 'European Natives' [*les 'indigènes européens'*]. They started out as a direct response to the Indigènes de la république. They had a clear, unifying message: we are the natives of Europe [*les indigènes de l'Europe*], the first occupants of the land, and we refuse Muslim colonization. . . . They quoted Geronimo, Cochise, Sitting Bull" (55; translation modified).

That the Indigènes de la république serve as a boogeyman for Islamism in the novel is in perfect alignment with the republican outrage Bouteldja and her party have provoked since the movement was launched in 2005, ten years before *Soumission* went to press. But the matter-of-fact assessment of French nativism as an appropriation of indigeneity in the metropole—"they quoted Geronimo, Cochise, Sitting Bull"—is on the mark. To the Indigènes de la république's politico-historical understanding of indigeneity as an ascribed identity born at the colonial frontier, the *Indigènes européens* hold up the distorted mirror of an identitarian nativism, appropriating American Indian icons to claim "we were here first." Tellingly, the tract published online by *les Indigènes européens* is titled "Préparer la guerre civile" ("Get Ready for Civil War"). The war they envision opposes two groups of French citizens who both claim to be *indigènes*. It is a war over indigeneity.[36]

To be fair to Houellebecq's liberal critics, *Soumission* offers a completely dehistoricized view of the presence of Muslims in France. European civilization and Islam are presented in a great vacuum, and the only reference to the history that binds them, barring Charles Martel, the hero of the French Reconquista, is the promise of a revival of the French language through southward European expansion. The centuries-long history of French empire is evoked only through nostalgia for past greatness, and nowhere is the history of colonial and postcolonial migration from France's former colonies evoked. The Muslims that are colonizing France arrive

---

36. Although I part ways with his interpretation of the novel as an Islamophobic dystopia disguised as utopia—if anything, Islam is the foil that shores up the decadence of the French Republic—Shlomo Sand's (2018: 203–19) reading of *Soumission* offers an astute interpretation of nativism as a claim to indigeneity in France.

seemingly out of nowhere. And yet, in the novel, language functions as an implicit reminder of France's lost empire. For if Ben Abbès's Mediterranean empire can recenter the French language, it is because North Africa was once a French possession.

Whether it was Houellebecq's intention or not—there is no evidence that he would agree with my reading—*Soumission* offers a brilliant parody of what I am calling the *white minority*. Using the language dear to the nativist Right—depopulation and great replacement, colonial nostalgia and Reconquista, and above all, inequality (between men and women, inferior and superior men, the rich and the poor)—the novel offers Islam as a solution to European decadence. If the novel manages to evade the charge of Islamophobia—Islamization ends up being the narrator's saving grace—it is not by any stretch an antiracist novel. There are no anti-FN demonstrations in *Soumission*. Nor are there any non-Islamist Muslims. But there is a perhaps unintentional reminder of the antiracist movement that crystallized in opposition to the nativist Right in the 1970s, one that allows for a contrapuntal reading of Houellebecq's novel as a parody of nativism.

In a last-ditch effort to rally her base before the runoff, Marine Le Pen calls for a massive demonstration on the Champs Elysées. Watching the events on television, François observes "an immense banner stretched across the avenue, bearing the inscription 'We Are the People of France.'" Many of the demonstrators had been given small placards that read, more simply, 'We Are at Home' [*Nous sommes chez nous*]" (97; translation modified). Slogans such as these are familiar clichés within the repertoire of postcolonial nativist discourses in France. But there is nothing in their wording that betrays the ascribed or, for that matter, political identity of those wielding it. Indeed, Houellebecq's fictional FN slogans, almost naive in their self-evident tautology, could just as well be the rallying cry of antiracist activists in France. Here is how the French-Algerian protagonist of Faïza Guène's (2020: 135) novel *La Discrétion* sums up the contest for indigeneity in postcolonial France: "No, we are not in their home, mom! [*Non, on est pas chez eux maman!*] We are not "guests"! Did you get an invitation card? I didn't! Enough, I've been told the same thing for thirty-five years! We are at home [*nous, on est chez nous*]!" Or, in the phrase of antiracist activists like Bouteldja (2018), "Nous sommes ici parce que vous étiez là-bas." We are here, in France, because you were there, in the colonies.[37]

---

37. A rallying cry of the migrant rights movement in postcolonial France, the slogan "We are here because you were there" is attested in English (Mehta 2019: 3).

This is, I want to suggest, what is at stake in Bouteldja's call to "educate" *les souchiens*. By subverting the nativist expression *Français de souche*—an expression that bridges, as we have seen, the colonial and postcolonial periods—Bouteldja places whiteness within the *longue durée* history of French colonialism, and reactivates anticolonial critique in the postcolonial present. The provocative name of the movement she cofounded in 2005, les Indigènes de la république, underscores the discursive transformation of *indigènes* into immigrants. It also claims indigeneity—nativeness—in the country that precluded *indigènes* from becoming citizens of France and continues to discriminate against "populations hailing from the colonies" (PIR n.d.[a], n.d.[b]; translation modified). It is, in other words, a polemic rearticulation of indigeneity against nativism. The subversive appropriation of a semilegal colonial category—*indigène*—in the postcolonial context is emphatically not a claim to an originary identity. It is, instead, a political identity forged in the postcolonial "contact zone."[38]

As the *souchien* controversy makes clear, however, the very attempt to name *nativism* is subject to recuperation. In retrospect, Bouteldja's attempt to "out" the nativism of the expression *Français de souche* through irony and double entendre might seem like a tactical mistake. In the era of social media and user-produced content, irony is a double-edged sword. But perhaps the act of naming nativism is no longer up to the task of combating it, if it ever was. That both racist and antiracist discourses have become sites of moral posturing (who is the real racist?) shows that we are prisoners of a terminological impasse. Nor will "facts" serve us, as Camus reminds us (who cares about the numbers; everyone knows we are being replaced). In the face of an increasingly irresolvable *différend* where the terms of anticolonial and antiracist critique (colonization, decolonization, racism, minority, *indigène*) are mobilized in the interest of the white minority, it is incumbent upon us to become historians of these terms.

---

38. Mary Louise Pratt (2008: 7) dubs *contact zones* the "social spaces where disparate cultures meet, clash, and grapple with each other, often in highly asymmetrical relations of domination and subordination—such as colonialism and slavery, or their aftermaths as they are lived out across the globe today." For a recent articulation of *indigène* as a political (rather than ethnic or racial) identity, see Bouteldja 2017: 118–20.

References

Agence France Presse. 2018. "L'Assemblée supprime de la Constitution le mot 'race' et interdit 'la distinction de sexe.'" *Le Monde*, July 12. https://www.lemonde.fr/politique/article/2018/07/12/l-assemblee-supprime-dans-la-constitution-le-mot-race-et-interdit-la-distinction-de-sexe_5330615_823448.html.

AGRIF. n.d. "Qui sommes-nous?" http://www.lagrif.fr/notre-combat/qui-sommes-nous (accessed January 11, 2022).

Albertini, Dominique, and Albert Doucet. 2016. *La fachosphère: Comment l'extrême droite remporte la bataille d'Internet*. Paris: Flammarion.

Alduy, Cécile. 2017. "What a 1973 French Novel Tells Us about Marine Le Pen, Steve Bannon, and the Rise of the Populist Right." *Politico*, April 23. https://www.politico.com/magazine/story/2017/04/23/what-a-1973-french-novel-tells-us-about-marine-le-pen-steve-bannon-and-the-rise-of-the-populist-right-215064.

Appadurai, Arjun. 2007. *Fear of Small Numbers: An Essay on the Geography of Anger*. Durham, NC: Duke University Press.

Arktos. 2019. "View from the Right by Alain de Benoist." Last modified May 9. https://www.kickstarter.com/projects/grimberg/view-from-the-right-by-alain-de-benoist.

Assouline, Pierre. 2015. "Michel Houellebecq, subversif et irresponsable comme jamais." *La République des livres*, January 5. http://larepubliquedeslivres.com/michel-houellebecq-subversif-et-irresponsable-comme-jamais/.

Bar-On, Tamir. 2011. "Transnationalism and the French Nouvelle droite." *Patterns of Prejudice* 45, no. 3: 199–223.

Bellaigue, Christopher de. 2015. "*Soumission* by Michel Houellebecq, review— France in 2022." *Guardian*, February 6. https://www.theguardian.com/books/2015/feb/06/soumission-michel-houellebecq-review-france-islamic-rule-charlie-hebdo.

Benoist, Alain de. 1963. *Salan devant l'opinion*. Paris: Editions Saint-Just.

Benoist, Alain de. 1986. *Europe, Tiers Monde, même combat*. Paris: Robert Laffont.

Benoist, Alain de. 2001. *Vu de droite: Anthologie critique des idées contemporaines*. Paris: Labyrinthe.

Benoist, Alain de. 2017–19. *View from the Right: A Critical Anthology of Contemporary Ideas*. 3 vols. Translated by Robert A. Lindgren and Roger Adwan. London: Arktos.

Benoist, Alain de, and François d'Orcival. 1965. *Le courage est leur patrie*. Paris: Editions Saint-Just.

Benoist, Alain de, and Gilles Fournier. 1965. *Vérité pour l'Afrique du Sud*. Paris: Editions Saint-Just.

Boudjellal, Farid, and François Durpaire. 2015–17. *La présidente*. 3 vols. Paris: Edition des Arènes and Demopolis.

Bouteldja, Houria. 2017. *Whites, Jews, and Us: Toward a Politics of Revolutionary Love*. Translated by Rachel Valinsky. South Pasadena, CA: Sémiotext(e).

Bouteldja, Houria. 2018. "Si nous sommes ici c'est que vous étiez là-bas . . ." *Montray Kréyol*, July 16. https://www.montraykreyol.org/article/si-nous-sommes -ici-cest-que-vous-etiez-la-bas?page=1.

Bouteldja, Houria, and Youssef Boussoumah. 2021. "The Parti des indigènes de la république—A Political Success and the Conspiracy against It (2005 to 2020)." Translated by David Fernbach. *Verso Books Blog*, October 6. https:// www.versobooks.com/blogs/5167-the-parti-des-indigenes-de-la-republique -a-political-success-and-the-conspiracy-against-it-2005-to-2020.

Bruckner, Pascal. 1986. *The Tears of the White Man: Compassion as Contempt*. Translated by William R. Beer. New York: Free Press.

Bruckner, Pascal. 2012. *The Tyranny of Guilt: An Essay on Western Masochism*. Translated by Steven Randall. Princeton, NJ: Princeton University Press.

Camille9340. 2007. "Souchiens." July 5. YouTube video, 0:05:33. https://www.youtube .com/watch?v=fkXXe6_qw0s.

Camus, Renaud. 2015. *Le Grand Remplacement*. Plieux: Renaud Camus.

Camus, Renaud. 2017. *2017 dernière chance avant le Grand Remplacement. Changer de peuple ou changer de politique?* Paris: La Maison d'Edition.

Camus, Renaud. 2018. *You Will Not Replace Us!* Plieux: Renaud Camus.

Charrieras, Damien. 2013. "Racisme(s)? Retour sur la polémique du 'racisme anti-Blancs' en France." In *De quelle couleur sont les Blancs? Des 'petits Blancs' au 'racisme anti-Blancs,'* edited by Sylvie Laurent and Thierry Leclère, 244–52. Paris: La Découverte.

Comtat, Emmanuelle. 2018. "From Indigènes to Immigrant Workers: Pied-Noir Perceptions of Algerians and People of Algerian Origin in Postcolonial France." *Settler Colonial Studies* 8, no. 2: 262–82.

Daum, Pierre. 2012. *Ni valise ni cercueil: Les pieds-noirs restés en Algérie après l'indépendance*. Arles: Actes Sud.

Diallo, Rokhaya. 2018. "France's Dangerous Move to Remove 'Race' from Its Constitution." *Washington Post*, July 13. https://www.washingtonpost.com /news/global-opinions/wp/2018/07/13/frances-dangerous-move-to-remove -race-from-its-constitution/.

enzo bateau. n.d. "Souchiens." Vimeo video. Dailymotion. https://www.dailymotion.com /video/x2du97 (accessed October 17, 2019).

"Européennes / Exclusif: Une photo et une vidéo de l'ex-gilet jaune amiénoise, no. 2 de la liste 'Ligne Claire,' Fiorina Lignier, qui dessine une croix gammée dans le sable." 2019. *L'Observateur de Beauvais*, March 22. https://www .lobservateurdebeauvais.fr/2019/05/22/europeennes-exclusif-une-photo-et -une-video-de-lex-gilet-jaune-amienoise-n2-de-la-liste-ligne-claire-fiorina -lignier-qui-dessine-une-croix-gammee-dans-le-sable/.

Fanon, Frantz. 2004. *The Wretched of the Earth*. Translated by Richard Philcox. New York: Grove.

France Inter. 2015. "Michel Houellebecq: 'Mon livre est une satire.'" January 7. YouTube video, 0:16:22. https://www.youtube.com/watch?v=o5ttzXGKbSY.

Gobineau, Arthur de. (1855) 1915. *The Inequality of Human Races*. Translated by Adrian Collins. London: William Heinemann.

Guène, Faïza. 2020. *La discrétion*. Paris: Plon.

Guha, Ranajit. 1997. "Not at Home in Empire." *Critical Inquiry* 23, no. 3: 482–93.

Houellebecq, Michel. 2015. *Submission*. Translated by Lorin Stein. London: William Heinemann.

Hugonnet, Ferdinand. 1858. *Souvenirs d'un chef de bureau arabe*. Paris: Michel Lévy Frères.

Jeanpierre, Lucette. 2007. "Houria Bouteldja, un racisme de moins en moins voilé." *ReSPUBLICA*, letter no. 550, July 3. http://www.gaucherepublicaine.org/wp-content/uploads/lettres/550.htm.

Le Cour Grandmaison, Olivier. 2005. *Coloniser, exterminer: Sur la guerre et l'état colonial*. Paris: Fayard.

Le Cour Grandmaison, Olivier. 2010. *De l'indigénat: Anatomie d'un monstre juridique*. Paris: Zones.

Lefeuvre, Daniel. 2006. *Pour en finir avec la repentance coloniale*. Paris: Flammarion.

Liauzu, Claude. 1982. *Aux origines des tiers-mondismes: Colonisés et anticolonialistes en France, 1919–1939*. Paris: L'Harmattan.

Louatah, Sabri. 2011–16. *Les sauvages*. 4 vols. Paris: Flammarion.

Mamdani, Mahmood. 1996. *Citizen and Subject: Contemporary Africa and the Legacy of Late Colonialism*. Princeton, NJ: Princeton University Press.

Mbembe, Achille. 2017. *A Critique of Black Reason*. Durham, NC: Duke University Press.

McAuley, James. 2019. "How Gay Icon Renaud Camus Became the Ideologue of White Supremacy." *Nation*, June 17. https://www.thenation.com/article/archive/renaud-camus-great-replacement-brenton-tarrant/.

Mehta, Suketu. 2019. *This Land Is Our Land: An Immigrant's Manifesto*. New York: Farrar, Strauss and Giroux.

Memmi, Albert. 1965. *The Colonizer and the Colonized*. Translated by Howard Greenfeld. New York: Orion.

Moyn, Samuel. 2010. *The Last Utopia: Human Rights in History*. Cambridge, MA: Harvard University Press.

Ndiaye, Pap. 2008. *La condition noire: Essai sur une minorité française*. Paris: Calmann-Lévy.

Péguy B. 2007. "Finkielkraut vs Taddeï contre Houria Bouteldja." June 30. YouTube video. https://www.youtube.com/watch?v=uSvqYvplfvk.

Pervillé, Guy. 1997. "Comment appeler les habitants de l'Algérie avant la définition légale d'une nationalité algérienne?" *Cahiers de la Méditerrannée* 54, no. 1: 55–60.

Pervillé, Guy. 2007. "Pieds-noirs: La valise ou le cercueil." *Pour une histoire de la guerre d'Algérie*. November 23. http://guy.perville.free.fr/spip/article.php3?id _article=161.

PIR (Parti des indigènes de la république). n.d.(a). "Nous sommes les indigènes de la république!" http://indigenes-republique.fr/le-p-i-r/appel-des- indigenes-de -la-republique/ (accessed January 11, 2022).

PIR (Parti des indigènes de la république). n.d.(b). "We Are the Indigenous of the Republic." Translated by Roberto Hernández. Decolonial Translation Group. http://www.decolonialtranslation.com/english/AppelEng.php (accessed January 11, 2022).

Poussel, Marie. 2019. "'Les Sauvages' sur Canal+, le meilleur de la série française." *Parisien*, September 21. http://www.leparisien.fr/culture-loisirs/series/les-sau vages-sur-canal-le-meilleur-de-la-serie-francaise-21-09-2019-8157075.php.

Pratt, Mary Louise. 2008. *Imperial Eyes: Travel Writing and Transculturation*. New York: Routledge.

Raspail, Jean. 1975. *The Camp of the Saints*. Translated by Norman Shapiro. New York: Charles Scribner's Sons.

Raspail, Jean. 2011. "Big Other." Preface to *Le camp des saints*, 20–65. Paris: Robert Laffont.

République Française. 1972. Loi no. 72-546 du 1er juillet 1972 relative à la lutte contre le racisme. https://www.legifrance.gouv.fr/jo_pdf.do?id=JORFTEXT00000 0864827&pageCourante=06803.

République Française. 1978. Loi no. 78-17 du 6 janvier 1978 relative à l'informatique, aux fichiers et aux libertés. https://www.ilo.org/dyn/natlex/docs/ELECTRONIC /68039/77813/F938852590/FRA-68039.pdf.

République Française. 2005. Loi no. 2005-158 du 23 février 2005 portant reconnaissance de la Nation et contribution nationale en faveur des Français rapatriés. https://www.legifrance.gouv.fr/affichTexte.do?cidTexte=JORFTEXT000000 444898.

Sand, Shlomo. 2018. *The End of the French Intellectual? From Zola to Houellebecq*. New York: Verso.

Sayad, Abdelmalek. 2004. *The Suffering of the Immigrant*. Translated by David Macey. Cambridge, UK: Polity.

Shepard, Todd. 2006. *The Invention of Decolonization: The Algerian War and the Remaking of France*. Ithaca, NY: Cornell University Press.

Stora, Benjamin. 1992. *Ils venaient d'Algérie: L'immigration algérienne en France, 1912–1992*. Paris: Fayard.

Taguieff, Pierre-André. 1993. "From Race to Culture: The New Right's View of European Identity." Translated by Deborah Cook. *Telos* 98–99: 99–125.

Taguieff, Pierre-André. 2001. *The Force of Prejudice: On Racism and Its Doubles*. Translated and edited by Hassan Melehy. Minneapolis: University of Minnesota Press.

Taguieff, Pierre-André. 2020. *L'imposture décoloniale: Science imaginaire et pseudo-antiracisme*. Paris: Editions de l'Observatoire.

Tarrant, Brenton. 2019. "The Great Replacement: Towards a New Society." Uploaded April 13. https://archive.org/details/TheGreatReplacementManifesto.

Tocqueville, Alexis de. 2001. *Writings on Empire and Slavery*. Edited and translated by Jennifer Pitts. Baltimore: John Hopkins University Press.

Tocqueville, Alexis de. 2003. *Democracy in America and Two Essays on America*. Translated by Gerald E. Bevan. London: Penguin.

Urbain, Ismaÿl. (1862) 2002. *L'Algérie française, indigènes et immigrants*. Paris: Séguier.

Wampole, Christy. 2020. *Degenerative Realism: Novel and Nation in Twenty-First-Century France*. New York: Columbia University Press.

Weil, Patrick. 2005. "Le statut des musulmans en Algérie coloniale: Une nationalité française dénaturée." *Histoire de la Justice* 16: 93–109.

Wolfe, Patrick. 2016. *Traces of History: Elementary Structures of Race*. London: Verso.

XRolan. 2007. "Bouteldja: 'Il faut éduquer les souchiens: les blancs.'" July 13. YouTube video, 00:00:36. https://www.youtube.com/watch?v=t6-FQuzhrwM.

Zerrouky, Hassane. 2004. "OAS 'la valise ou le cercueil.'" *L'Humanité*, October 28. https://www.humanite.fr/node/314732.

Green Walls:
Everyday Ecofascism and the Politics of Proximity

April Anson and Anindita Banerjee

Whiteness is the ownership of the earth forever and ever, Amen.
— W. E. B. Du Bois, "The Souls of White Folk"

Ecologies of Fascism

On August 3, 2019, a twenty-one-year-old man drove more than two hundred miles across the breadth of Texas to a Walmart in El Paso that stands just across the bridge straddling the US-Mexico border. In the parking lot, he opened fire with an automatic weapon, leaving twenty-three dead and an equal number grievously injured in fewer than five minutes. According to a lengthy screed posted on the Internet minutes before the massacre, the author had been planning this mission to "kill some Mexicans" for a considerable time (Attanasio 2019). But while the document offered a proximate rationale of "stop[ping] the Hispanic invasion of Texas" (Confessore and Yourish 2022), it also embedded the individual act of extreme violence in a

boundary 2 50:1 (2023) DOI 10.1215/01903659-10192145 ©2023 by Duke University Press

set of overlapping, contiguous narratives whose scale and scope extended far beyond the geopolitical borders and demographic particularities of any single city, state, nation, or region.

"The Inconvenient Truth," as the El Paso murderer's text was titled, transparently invoked the iconic 2006 documentary film in which former vice president Al Gore issued dire warnings about the combined effects of global warming and toxic pollution on the geo-bio-physical systems of the entire planet (Crusius 2019). But it was not just the imminent threat of "a worsening environment" on all forms of life that drove the self-defined "ecofascist" to promote genocidal violence as a pathway toward "a more sustainable way of living" (Joyce 2022). What provided focus and purpose to his actions was an altogether different specter of extinction that concerned the diversity of human life itself, one captured by the equally pithy catchphrase "the great replacement." Unlike the multifaceted, immensely complex, and largely imperceptible reality of what has come to be shorthanded as climate change—a web of wicked problems that is not just unthinkable but also intractable from the perspective of any single individual or community— the great replacement put a name to a visible threat that was possible to address in the here and now, and in fact had already proven actionable by a recent predecessor who had also taken on the mantle of an "ecofascist." "The Inconvenient Truth" paid elaborate and effusive tribute to another text, titled "The Great Replacement" and posted online only a few months earlier in March 2019, which announced the live-streamed massacre of fifty-three worshippers in two mosques all the way across the world in Christchurch, New Zealand (Tarrant 2019).

By the same logic, it now seems entirely predictable that over the ensuing years, punctuated by an ongoing pandemic and accompanied by unrelenting demonization of immigrants and minorities around the world, the ecological prefix of contemporary fascism has remained largely unexamined even as the great replacement has evolved into its most legible through line. Although it remains unclear whether either the Christchurch killer or his acolyte in Texas knew the source of the phrase (Charlton 2019), it was immediately traced to the title of a 2010 treatise of the same name by the French author Renaud Camus. By the time the great replacement showed up in the ecofascist screeds of 2019, Camus's coinage had become a viral meme in extremist networks around the globe. As far back as 2017, it rang through the streets of Charlottesville, Virginia, when tiki-torch-bearing Unite the Right marchers chanted "You will not replace us!" and "Jews will not replace us!" In October 2018, it provided a gunman at the Pittsburgh

Tree of Life synagogue with the justification for eliminating putative supporters of HIAS—the Hebrew International Aid Society, dedicated to assisting
the stateless since the interwar years of the early twentieth century—for the
alleged crime of seeking to replace the American electorate with darker-
skinned Muslim refugees. On May 13, 2022, the great replacement burst
into public view again following the live-streamed massacre of thirteen people at a supermarket in a predominantly Black neighborhood of Buffalo,
New York. The perpetrator was an eighteen-year-old white man armed with
an assault weapon whose barrel was prominently emblazoned with a racist
slur. The proximity of this last event to the time of this writing makes it difficult to hypothesize whether the extensive media attention paid to the connections between the Buffalo shooting and the continuum of violence outlined above was triggered by an unprecedented mainstreaming of Camus's
once-obscure formulation—just a few weeks earlier, the *New York Times*
had documented at least four hundred instances in which the television
anchor Tucker Carlson had invoked replacement in prolific tandem with
other Fox News hosts and an array of current and former Republican lawmakers over the course of the last two years (Farhi 2022)—or the transmu-
tation of targets from enemies abroad to enemies at home in the wake of
the Black Lives Matter protests of summer 2020.

What is clear, however, is that the Buffalo shooting was directly
inspired by Christchurch and El Paso. According to an analysis conducted
by the Anti-Defamation League, some two-thirds of the one-hundred-eighty-
page screed consisted of verbatim citations from the 2019 document titled
The Great Replacement (Stanley-Becker and Harwell 2022). Yet in conspicuous contrast with all the close readings of replacement theory, the
fact that the Buffalo perpetrator also identified himself as an "ecofascist"
received scarcely any attention. While a few news reports noted that the
phrase "our White lands" provided something of a refrain in both the text
and the live-streamed video (Confessore and Yourish 2022; Stanley-Becker
and Harwell 2022), the eco-logic that rendered those who have long lived in
shared proximity indistinguishable from the demonized figures of new immigrants—"those who invade our lands, live on our soil, live on government
support, and attack and replace our people" (Confessore and Yourish; Farhi
2022)—has not been subjected to any substantive analysis. If mentioned at
all, the desire for a green future that preoccupied the killers in Christchurch,
El Paso, and Buffalo alike at least as much as their shared dreams of a
white-supremacist retro-utopia continues to be treated as a supplemental
metaphor at best to the overwhelming histrionics of demographic panic.

Worth noting, then, is the fact that equally extensive portions of the Buffalo shooter's document—also mirroring the precise language of Christchurch—are devoted to a deep concern for the "industrialized, pulverized, and commoditized" "natural environment" (Tarrant 2019). And just like its predecessors in 2019, the genocidal solution for countering this degradation seems logically aligned with the scientific consensus that the climate crisis is anthropogenic and therefore attributable to and actionable by human agency. Emulating the Christchurch killer's assertion that immigration, demographics, and environmental action constitute multiple facets of the same problem, the Buffalo killer declared, "There is no conservationism without nature, there is no nationalism without environmentalism. . . . The protection and preservation of these lands is of the same importance as the protection and preservation of our own ideals and beliefs" (Joyce 2022). If El Paso was a response to the Christchurch call to "kill the invaders, kill the overpopulation and by doing so save the environment" (Tarrant 2019), the Buffalo shooter's text both expanded the range and scaled down the definition of surplus, and therefore disposable, human lives that need to be exterminated for securing a sustainable future. From "invaders" crossing distant borderlands to refugees separated by international waters, it zoomed in on those whose continued trauma is historically inextricable and inescapably visible within the nation's own body politic.

This confluence of extremism and environmentalism, in which the latter is generally perceived to be an enduring legacy and current preoccupation of the progressive Left rather than the reactionary Right, perhaps explains the media's reluctance to delve into what Alex Amend (2020), in the wake of Christchurch and El Paso, called "a daisy chain of replacement theory and ecofascism." Yet it is precisely at the limits where the two seemingly oppositional concepts collide, converge, and shape each other that we must begin to look for environmentalist topologies and tropologies of embodied, racialized violence. This is the zone of discomfort that provides a potent point of departure for our exploration of ecofascism here—not in terms of isolated hyperperformative acts, but as an ongoing, metamorphosing politics of proximity in the places and practices of everyday life.

Camus's phraseology, far from being marginal to our purview, is integral not just to understanding the aforementioned "daisy chain" but also for untangling its constituent elements of natural and human ecology in the *longue durée* and transnational flow of environmentalism itself as a doctrine. The most obvious and well-documented strain of their co-constitutive relationship, identified by Amend as well as many others before him, traces contemporary ecofascism back to the "soil and folk" imaginary of nineteenth-century German romantic nationalists—a green xenophobia infamously taken up by early twentieth-century eugenicists in the United States and subsequently reexported and repurposed in Europe under Nazi occupation. In this transatlantic triangulation, Madison Grant's *The Passing of the Great Race* (1916) and Lothrop Stoddard's *The Rising Tide of Color against White World Supremacy* (1920) would later merit citations in Adolf Hitler's *Mein Kampf* (Churchwell 2019).

But less obvious examples of the same aesthetic, spanning the ideological spectrum from the plutocratic Right to the anti-capitalist Left, can be found not in overt ideological documents but rather amid enduring classics of the American canon. As if referring to contemporary fears of rising temperatures and waters, Tom Buchanan in the very first chapter of *The Great Gatsby* warns over a sumptuous dinner, "If we don't look out the white race will be—will be utterly submerged" (Fitzgerald 1925). Jack London's science fiction story "The Unparalleled Invasion" (1910) strikes a very similar chord in the current pandemic. The invasion in question is bidirectional: concerned about overpopulation in China and the resultant outflow of labor migrants to the shores of Europe and the New World, Western powers unleash a bioweapon that instantly solves both crises. Like the recent ecofascist screeds, moreover, the particularity of Sinophobia in the story is at best incidental to London's biographical context of Oakland, California, and the demographics of immigration in the proverbial Golden State. The plague is but a metonym of a broader, universal telos that was first articulated by the author in the 1902 essay "Salt of the Earth": the triumph of "a race of mastery and achievement," consisting of "English-speaking Anglo-Saxons," over "lesser breeds" by means of "natural selection" (London 1902). The imaginary virus in the far future of 1976 merely accelerates in historical time what was scientifically, and therefore incontrovertibly, preordained in evolutionary terms.

These latter instances of benignly naturalized Malthusianism and Darwinism—whose traces linger to this day in the commonplaces of "human flows" and "rising tides" with regard to migration and the atmospheric nebulousness of "climate" as an index of both race relations and ethno-religious tolerance—are as crucial for understanding the attractions of replacement at the current moment as the eugenicist environmentalism of a century ago. In our second gilded age, a materially manifest reality in which an astoundingly small class of the global ultrarich has not just left practically everyone else behind but seems destined to claim what remains

of the planet's rapidly dwindling resources, it is no wonder that the generation most burdened by the prospects of dire inequality on an uninhabitable
planet is hyperaware of the ways in which environmental depletion and
political conflict increasingly fuel each other while terms such as "resource
wars" and "climate refugees" visibly evolve from dystopian neologisms to
factual signifiers of displacement and dispossession across the world (Garcia 2017; Lustgarten 2020).

Climates of Contagion

That the zoonotically transmitted novel coronavirus is both a terrifying symptom and anticipated outcome of what the novelist Margaret
Atwood (2015) eloquently called "not just climate change but everything
change" has lent a distinct ecotone to xenophobic biopolitics in recent
years. Large-scale outbreaks of transmissible diseases, as Susan Sontag
(1988), Roberto Esposito (2002), and Priscilla Wald (2007) have famously
theorized, illuminate how easily the diseased body becomes conflated with
demographic threats to the body politic during times of emergency and
states of exception. During the current pandemic, likewise, hashtags such
as #ChinaVirus and #KungFlu in the United States and #Biojihad in India
emerged overnight to shorthand what social scientists call "the parasite
stress theory": immunological fears, expressed in simultaneously economic
and ecological terms, of not just visibly marked immigrants and minorities
but also those who may be phenotypically familiar but estranged in their
values and ways of life (Thornhill and Fincher 2014). The bioweapons conspiracy that emerged on the eve of Russia's invasion of Ukraine and was
widely promoted by right-wing media outlets in the United States is an illu-
minating case in point. Its claim, that Western intelligence agencies were
developing new respiratory viruses in the Chernobyl Exclusion Zone to be
sent into Russia on the bodies of migratory birds (Frenkel and Thompson
2022), demonstrates the extent to which scientific evidence of interspe-
cies disease vectors, triggered by climate change and habitat loss, can
be seamlessly appropriated into rationales for retaliatory violence against
human communities.

At a time of contiguous, compound, and chronic catastrophe, such
conflations of inconvenient facts and malignant fabulations proliferate across
what the sociologist Cynthia Miller-Idriss (2021) calls the "post-organizational"
networks of the Far Right, sustained not by unified ideologies and centralized leadership but by vastly dispersed assemblages of on- and offline com-

munities. But the interface between environmental activism and xenophobic violence can no longer be analyzed in metaphorical terms of media ecosystems alone. The January 6 storming of the US Capitol—a hitherto commonplace political metaphor now symbolically freighted with the QAnon anticipation of an apocalyptic "storm"—vividly demonstrated the dizzying speed at which catastrophist tropes once confined to the fascist fringes had come to capture the imagination of wide swathes of the populace. But the very anticipation of an environmental disaster that suffused the term with such urgency also spoke to the ways in which Sontag's "illness as metaphor" has now coalesced with the poetics and politics of what we term "climate as metaphor" in the growing vocabulary of informal violence. In France, Eric Zémmour inaugurated his presidential bid in December 2021 with a slickly curated video on the dangers posed not by a "rising tide" of unwashed, contagious masses in the far future as Jean Raspail imagined in his 1973 dystopia *Camp of the Saints* but by insidious others, pictured in images interspersed with numerous scenes of fires and floods, who have already spread across the homeland and transformed it in their own image (Gopnik 2021).

These distinctly unromantic visions of unwanted excess that tie the sheer magnitude of natural disasters to the number of human bodies that can inhabit a given area on the surface of the planet represent a perversion of William Wordsworth's "the world is too much with us," a fragment of poetry equally beloved by literary ecocritics (Ghosh 2016: 69) and geological theorists (Yusoff 2013). But they do provide a startlingly clear view of the paradoxical parallels between left-leaning environmentalism and the recurring ecofascist logic of saving "nature" by combating "overpopulation." Raspail's Nouvelle droite fantasy, published three years after the first Earth Day protests at the height of the Cold War, indexes the crucial turn at which the disavowal of eugenicist Darwinism, starkly visible in Fitzgerald's and London's writings discussed earlier, metamorphosed in the shadow of Hiroshima and the Holocaust into a different set of scientific and social ecologics. Mae Ngai (2004) and John Hultgren (2015) have extensively documented this postwar "second wave of environmentalism," which eschewed ethno-supremacist and nativist arguments in favor of advocating for the limited "carrying capacity" of nonhuman planetary systems (Hultgren 2015: 41–43). Against the cross currents of third-world developmentalism on the one hand and civil and immigrant rights on the other, concern for the "natural environment"—a recurring motif in the recent ecofascist documents as well—was externalized onto an anticipated "population explosion," analogous to a nuclear apocalypse, that would originate from the recently decolonized Third World (Ngai 2004: 257). Among the many figureheads of this late twentieth-century movement, only one, John Tanton, was invoked in the context of El Paso (Cagle 2019). Contemporary ecofascists' obsession with "overpopulation," far from being anachronistic or anomalous, thus draws directly from well-respected antecedents. Like the great replacement, the trope has only gained momentum over the course of the pandemic. While submergence by "Third World" people and their attendant inferior value(s) remains a refrain for the American Right long after the January 6 "storm," a recent UMass poll finds a sizable majority of Republican voters convinced that the pandemic has given Democrats a devious excuse for replacing the populace with "third world" substitutes (UMass/YouGov 2021).

It is this creeping continuum between aberration and habit in which we theorize everyday ecofascism. We do not approach the term as an unprecedented peculiarity of the Anthropocene, a kind of human counterpart to the monstrous, ontologically confounding "hyperobjects" that Timothy Morton (2013) identified as unique (by)products of the current peak of the environmental crisis. Instead, the objective here is to rescale ecofascism from a hypervisible series of unthinkable acts into a *method* and *practice* for negotiating a planetary eschaton of degradation and extinction. Although we focus on its proximate and recognizable forms in a vein very similar to the ways in which analysts of the great replacement look simultaneously backward and forward, the aim of this study is neither to arrive at a unified theory of contemporary ecofascism nor to elucidate its particulars within singular geographical or historical contexts. The canvas on which we trace everyday ecofascism instead consists of aesthetic forms and performative practices, fertile breeding grounds for cultural imaginations and political imaginaries that can provide both insights and interruptions to its alarming naturalization across the globe.

Everyday Ecofascism

Racism in America is like dust in the air. It seems invisible—even if you're choking on it—until you let the sun in. Then you see it is everywhere. As long as we keep shining that light, we have a chance of cleaning it wherever it lands. But we have to stay vigilant, because it's always still in the air. . . . So what you see when you see black protesters depends on whether you're living in that building or watching it on TV with a bowl of corn chips on your lap, waiting for "NCIS" to start.
—Kareem Abdul-Jabbar

These words by Kareem Abdul-Jabbar (2020), the basketball legend and recipient of the Presidential Medal of Freedom, appeared in the *Los Angeles Times* at an inflection point in the summer of 2020. They were published a week after George Floyd's plea, "I can't breathe," became the clarion call for forsaking pandemic protocols and taking to the streets, and a day before federal forces violently dispersed Black Lives Matter protesters to clear the way for the president's photo-op in front of a historical Black church across from the White House. The column perfectly captured the climate of the moment in the intimate urgency of its tone, yet the "double pandemic" to which it urges the audience to bear witness has little to do with the unthinkable magnitude and scale of the toll that the novel coronavirus was exacting across the nation and the world. Instead, it asks readers to "see" the visceral fear of two familiar vectors of death: long-term exposure to pollution in inferior and unsafe housing, and the equally endemic possibility of being snuffed out in a few minutes by the hand of the law. Far from representing isolated and mutually exclusive causes of death, they are but constituent elements of the same ambient necro-ecology for those long condemned to disposability. It is only the proximity of the virus with the viral video of Floyd's last moments that make their interface of flesh and place momentarily flare into view.

As if underlining the contrast between hypervisible discourses and performances of extreme violence and the invisible eliminationism of everyday life, the dispersal of protestors the next day in Lafayette Square finally broke the media taboo on what Robert Reich (2020) pointedly called "the f-word" on Twitter. "This is Fascism," declared Adam Weinstein (2020) in the *New Republic* on a similar note. Soon thereafter, the floodgates broke on linking systemic violence wreaked upon minority bodies by agents of the state and the informal vigilantism visited upon those, like Ahmaud Arbery, who merely stumble into what Abdul-Jabbar (2020) called the "open season on Black bodies" that arrives as regularly as springtime. Over the following weeks as protests continued to gain momentum, provoking yet more retaliation from police who were frequently backed by federal forces, the image of multiple and nested contagions became ubiquitous in the US media. The model of a "triple pandemic" generated by researchers at Harvard University's Joint Center for Housing Studies added a crucial economic dimension to the reckoning with systemic violence and structural racism (JCHS 2020). The survey attributed the disproportionately high rates of morbidity and mortality in communities of color not just to the concentration of high-risk, low-income occupations and concomitant job losses, but also the endemic lack of access to nutrition, healthcare, and educational resources (Corne-lissen 2020).

The novel coronavirus indeed opened a "window," to invoke Abdul-Jabbar's metaphor of claustrophobic, inescapable violence punctured by a thin beam of dust-suffused light, to a particular intersection of inequal-ity whose discussion was previously limited to an interdisciplinary field of knowledge and action known as environmental justice. It focused on the long-entrenched nexus of warehousing the bodies of the poor, dispropor-tionately of color, in particularly polluted places, and the routine and tar-geted concentration of state violence in those same enclaves of racial and economic segregation. The term environmental justice itself became a prominent platform in the presidential elections at the end of the year. But worth noting alongside the macrostructural analyses by social scientists and legal scholars cited by the media is the equally powerful body of stud-ies that literary scholars of environmental justice have been conducting for some time on the semiotic and affective roles of language, both as an agent of acclimatizing us to environmental inequities and for exposing, naming, and mobilizing against its constituent and entangled elements. Lindsay Dil-lon and Julie Sze, to cite only one prominent example, conducted precisely such a pioneering study in 2016, when the initial Black Lives Matter move-ment took up Eric Garner's last words, "I can't breathe," as its animating slogan. Under the resonant title "Police Power and Particulate Matters," the authors issued a call for engaging not just metaphors but also materialities that transform homes and neighborhoods into zones of simultaneously slow violence and swift death (Dillon and Sze 2016).

It is this mandate that also inspires our own attempts to move eco-fascism from a constellation of viral metaphors in which fears of climate catastrophe and paranoias of demographic extinction lead to the inexorable logistics of determining life or death according to varying degrees of vulner-ability. Our analysis, consequently, emerges from the interpenetration of bodies, natural elements, and built environments that materially shape the conditions of being at home and being in the world. And it is Abdul-Jabbar's evocative deployment of stay-at-home orders that returns us to confined places of the *oikos*, the Greek signifier of hearth and home that provides the shared root for the abstract concepts of both economy and ecology. This is the microcosm of materiality through which the following sections examine everyday ecofascism in a virally interconnected world.

The Home and the World

"The air quality is excellent today—the storm last night cleared all the germs" (Bong 2019). These words could be uttered by anyone in any of the springs that have marked successive waves of the pandemic. But it is the opening line of the climactic scene in a film called *Parasite*, directed by Bong Joon-ho, that became a global icon in the short time between the eco-fascist massacres of 2019 and the lockdowns of 2020. Winner of the Palme d'Or in Cannes, *Parasite* won Best Picture at the Academy Awards ceremony that took place two weeks after South Korea and the United States had announced their first confirmed cases of COVID-19.

The violent denouement of the film is staged at a child's birthday party on an expanse of impeccable lawn visible from the plate-glass living-room window; a green wall of hedgerows that protect the property from public view serves as the backdrop. The scene could be drawn from any of the world's dramatic traditions: ancient Greek drama; Shakespeare's tragedies; operas, Italian and Chinese; or indeed the cinematic epics of Akira Kurosawa. Gathering all the characters in one enclosed space as these traditions demand, *Parasite* nevertheless depends on two crucial elements that are just as easy to overlook as the evidence of people who literally live and die underfoot. The first is the party theme, a kitschy reenactment of the American Indian Wars salvaged from a consumerist fantasy of American cultural capital that the rich family strives to accumulate at every opportunity; the second is the timing of the performance in elemental rather than human terms. A dramatic rainstorm, witnessed through the same living-room window the night before, has rendered half the actors into refugees the morning after. Forced out of their home by another routine flooding of the city's sewer system, yet with no options of retreating from domestic service, the costumed selves of the domestic workers boil over in a murderous cascade.

Both the setting and the storyline of Bong's most recent film look startlingly realistic compared with his previous works. *The Host* (2006), *Snowpiercer* (2013), and *Okja* (2017), though explicitly devoted to environmental concerns in seemingly conspicuous contrast with *Parasite*, were all speculative fictions, replete with the ultimate anxieties of a profoundly unequal world haunted by imperial capitalism and hurtling toward destruction. Not just the title but also the timing of *Parasite*, however, resonated eerily with the ways in which the coming pandemic would expose both bodies and body politics as fragile ecosystems. Predating the pandemic, *Parasite*'s parasites are represented by the working poor, a family called the

Kims who impersonate long-time staff members in order to infiltrate the domestic realm of the ultrawealthy Parks. Critics were quick to place *Parasite*'s economic critique within the context of settler colonialism, a "hegemony, ideology, epistemology, and ontology [that] requires the possession of indigenous lands as its proprietary anchor within capitalist economies" (Dunbar-Ortiz 2015: xix) and is, according to Kyle Whyte (2018) and many others, a form of ecological violence (see also Park 2020; Vassar 2020). Still, the same critics bypassed the environmental concerns embedded in *Parasite*'s relentless examination of economic inequality—and in fact are intimately related to the film's titular metaphor, an anti-Semitic and xenophobic biological trope for "not even a visible organism" (Steuter and Wills 2009: 82). The Parks' house sits high on a hill while the Kims' semi-basement apartment is halfway underground; Park-like privilege is lit in full sun, while those struggling to survive are weighted with low light; the Parks' pristine property is cloaked in the aesthetics of the "natural"—wood, metal, and "wilderness" artwork—while the Kims' space is littered with disposable pizza boxes, beer cans, urine, and brown toilet water. The fumigation scene toward the beginning, a "free extermination" for the Kims courtesy of the city government, is an early reminder that this is a natural order in which waste—as both noun and verb, trash and elimination of life—freely extends from vermin and microbes to include people who dwell in close proximity to both. Even when inside the Park property, the Kims are expected to "disappear" out of sight.

The single object that transgresses these distinctions is the "scholar's rock" treasured by the family, which first appears as a predictor of wealth but becomes a climactic instrument of violence. Cementing the danger of crossing the line in the film's geographies of waste, the rock reinforces the "natural" inequality densely plotted onto the Parks' property. As the Parks' large front windows lord over a wide, lush lawn punctuated by a lone teepee, they are barricaded by high, verdant hedges. This walled Eden backdrops the wannabe Western of the film's bloody climax, where the Parks' pastoral garden party, going-Native games, and revulsion at the visible proximity of the poor converge to trigger the vengeance of the "parasites." From inside the Park property, anxieties of replacement, extinction, and contagion plague *Parasite*'s plot in both a material and a metaphorical sense.

The Parks' illusions of immunity from the contagion of particular populations exemplify the everyday politics of proximity that this essay seeks to clarify. Just like the overwrought cosplays of frontier fantasies, both the family's verdant property and their notions of "proper" demeanor telegraph an oiko-logic and oiko-nomics of the "natural order" of colonial capitalism. As characters relinquish parts of their identities to inhabit positions of relative power—mastering English, using English names, and, most importantly, assimilating anxiety about their own immunity through the transnationality of a multicultural whiteness—they embody "a racialized line separating the deserving from the undeserving," as Joe Lowndes and Dan HoSang (2019: 28) describe in *Producers, Parasites, Patriots*. This racialized line is defended by Mr. Park throughout most of the film, exemplifying Lowndes and HoSang's (2019: 10) reminder that the geographies of white supremacy no longer need white people (see also Baldwin 2012: 171). Just as what Toni Morrison (1992: 60) calls "the parasitic nature of white freedom" morphs into a racially ambiguous category in the real world, so, too, do the Parks stand in for a natural order built on geographies of waste, their property aestheticizing this same order that dooms the Kims and protects the Parks. The green walls of the opulent estate green screen the sociobiological terror that shields the Parks from the inequality their wealth is built on—until, as Mr. Park puts it as he lies dying at the film's bloody climax, the parasites "cross the final line," take over the green-walled paradise, and expose the playactors' frontier as a killing field. *Parasite*'s environmental tropes simultaneously telegraph and deconstruct a vision of nature that naturalizes violence as acceptable, even necessary: an ecofascist logic that transgresses racial categories, national borders, and our most intimate alliances, revealing just how quotidian this logic can become.

The Park property plots the topography of this familiar ecofascism through the nature tropes of American settler colonialism: tamed wilderness, unoccupied frontiers, and the pastoral tranquility of taking "empty" space. The maximum-security gates of the Park estate protect their property through the prism of a prison, emphasizing a type of fortress conservation that quickly converts into an arcadian aesthetic once the action of the film moves inside, mirroring the logic of "conservation protection . . . bordered and guarded to keep wildlife in and unwanted humans out" (Dowie 2009: xvi). Living walls frame the interior of the Parks' idyllic paradise, and in the middle of the expanse sits the Parks' son Da-song, lone occupant of an "authentic" American teepee and a character defined solely through his obsession with playing Indian and the Cub Scouts, ideals of American innocence beloved by American eugenic conservationists (Vassar

2020).[1] Even indoors, Da-song is "surrounded by dreamcatchers and rep-licas of actual Native regalia," a repetition of Native stereotypes frequently attending the American environmental imaginary (Krech 1999). Inside the Parks' domestic space, a conquered wilderness—an "image of a forest made of stainless steel wire mesh"—hangs on their modern walls, a piece that production designer Lee ha Jun said evokes the feeling of "falling into a silent, solitary space in the forest" in a tribute to the self-reliance of American environmental thinking secured by barbed wire (Wallace 2019). In short, the Parks' greenspace is a miniature, highly claustrophobic terra nullius—or empty space—that is at once nostalgic, utopian, aspirational, cloistered, and, above all, coded white.[2]

At the top of this natural order stands Mr. Park, the latest patriarch in a white-masculinist tradition that ties environmental conservation to the safeguarding of the white race. Introduced in a promotional poster declaring "Mr. Park Hits Central Park," the film weds Park's power to one of the most recognizable projects in American environmental history, a place that "embodies the physical and spatial manifestations of white supremacy" and was planned by Frederick Olmstead, a major figure in US conservation whose later design of the Midway Plaisance of the 1893 Chicago World's Fair featured "trophies of colonialism" and "trophies of scientific racism" jux-

---

1. In *Minor Feelings: An Asian-American Reckoning*, Korean American writer Cathy Park Hong (2020: 69, 71) notes that "the alignment of childhood with innocence is an Anglo-American invention" originating in nineteenth-century nature poets but on full display in the "scrubbed white" nostalgia of *Moonrise Kingdom*, a film largely set in a scouting camp. Huhndorf's (2001: 71) *Going Native* documents the Scouts' "effort to reinscribe white racial dominance" through their choices of "pioneers and Indians as role models," and deems it exemplary of what Renato Rosaldo calls imperialist nostalgia. Phil Deloria's (1998: 134) *Playing Indian* ties the Scouts' nostalgic playing-Indian performances to a newly subsurface code of biological determinism. These displays promised protection from "the urban environment's filth" through the "doctrine of a strenuous life," subduing nature, and the scientific management of natural resources, ideas in debt to the colonial war-making, in the Americas and abroad, that gave rise to the Scouts (Mayer 2005: 64–65). As exemplary of the connection between scouting, white supremacist mass murder, and colonial capitalism, Frederick Russel Burnham took his scouting experience from Indian raids and his military service to colonial Africa, particularly Rhodesia's "own equivalent of the bloody Alamo massacres and Custer's Last Stand in the American West," which he fought on behalf of the British South Africa Company (Gann 1965: 118).
2. The affiliations between American nature tropes and white supremacy are too well documented to cite. The links are found in a transcendent Edenic nature, the wild wilderness, the lawless frontier, pastoral tranquility, and sublime rapture.

taposed against the White City (Rinehart 2012: 409, 405). Central Park was not just built on occupied Lenape lands and "seized by eminent domain in 1857, which displaced over 250 . . . Black middle- and working-class property owners" (Low 2019: 129). It was envisioned as a new Eden according to the Sturm und Drang principles shared by German Romanticism, the Hudson River School, and the Green Nazis of the Third Reich: an urban pastoral planned to preserve the threatened raw masculinity that drove the conservationist concerns of the time (Sachs 2013: 118–21; Ray 2013: 13–22; Spence 2000; and D. Taylor 2016). In *Parasite*, Olmstead's whitewashed park becomes Mr. Park's playground, both patriarchs in a masculinist nature tradition that uses the logics of white supremacy to smooth the travel of colonial capitalism into transnational frontiers.

The film's terror turns on the tranquility of the Park home—the serenity hides the threats of environmental or economic disaster internal to its order. Below the Parks' aristocratic porcelain and behind walls of food preserves, concealed by the ruse of both nobility and self-sufficiency, a bunker promises protection from a nuclear attack from North Korea or for someone escaping creditors. The Parks' bunker is an architectural allegory for settler modernity, as described by Jodi Kim (2018: 53): survival depends upon the military empire of perpetual debt. As a paradigmatic figure of this living debt, the housekeeper Moon-gwang's husband, Geun-sae, lives in the bunker literally underfoot. His "Respect!" for Mr. Park signals his subservience. In a hierarchy of value, his absorption, or "disappearance," is both architectural and biopolitical (C. Hong 2020: 35). Geun-sae performs a defining feature of settler colonial capitalism as described by Iyko Day (2016: 62), where the historical alignment of Asian bodies with capitalism's negative dimensions has "parasitic effects" on "concrete white labor." Hiding in the concrete foundation of the Parks' property, Geun-sae pleads to Mr. Kim to let him continue to live in the shelter, crying, "It feels like I was born here" (Bong 2019). Geun-sae's pleas fortify the bunker as a shelter for the disaster-prepping politics of twenty-first-century energy markets, settler modernity's military logics, and the eugenicist fictions of biological determinism.

These fictions are built into the bunker, an architectural allegory for the "natural order" that franchises colonialism by fissuring class solidarity, just as it leads to the film's climax. Building up to the climactic scene, Mr. Kim deceitfully describes Moon-gwang as a contagious tuberculosis patient, using the eugenicist rhetoric of public health and hygiene in his attempt to replace the original housekeeper with his wife, an exemplary ventriloquism of the language of imperial settler colonialism. As an agent of the "franchise colonialism" that Grace Hong (2015: 7) details, Mr. Kim dutifully performs his allegiance to the natural order of colonial white-male supremacy where the exploitation of nonwhite bodies becomes a pathway to success and property (see also Bhandar 2018). Mr. Kim then rejects Moon-gwang's pleas for solidarity among the working poor while the Parks are away performing a favorite colonial pastime: camping (Wenham 2015; Young 2017). In this way, Mr. Kim sustains his place in the dispossessive order of capitalist things until the slaughter in the film's narrative apogee, when the revenge of the "parasites" clarifies the true *terrere* of colonial capitalism's terra nullius (Simmons 2019: 103; Murdock 2021).

The cartography of the Parks' party metaphorizes a historical, ideological, and ongoing connection between the "safety" of colonial capitalism and the horror of fascism. In preparation, Mrs. Park directs Mr. Kim to arrange the tables in a crane's wing formation "like Admiral Yi" of the 1592 Battle of Hansen Island around the empty teepee. Here, a sixteenth century military battle with Japan becomes the nostalgic context surrounding the party's frontier fantasy. Da-Song plays a "good Indian" who saves a woman from the threat of the "bad Indians." Rather than playing cowboys and Indians, the Park family perform the standard settler trope of going Native, all the while preserving the threat of savagery crucial to settler modernity. This play, framed in the context of Japanese conflict, invokes the history of Japan as colonial occupiers of Korea from 1910 to 1945 as well as North Korea's invasion of South Korea in 1950 under the transposed Nazi ideology of *Herrenvolk*. Walled within this genocidal military formation, the blooming florals of the Parks' party aesthetically mirror the rebirth rituals of settler capitalism, the regeneration through violence that defines what Roxanne Dunbar-Ortiz (2015) calls "settler parasite" by the logics of extermination. The geography and aesthetics of *Parasite*'s climax confirm the transnational influence of this genocidal nature tradition. Indeed, Korea's *ilmin*, or "one people" principle, was the "equivalent of the *herrenvolk* principle that promoted organic nationalism based on ethnic homogeneity. Widely regarded as fascist by later scholars, the *ilmin* principle germinated from the works of German-educated philosopher and minister of education An Ho-Sang" (Hwang 2016: 93).

This mashup of colonial fascism is aestheticized by the "nature" environing the aristocratic order. The gathering's first moments feature a guest's performance of Handel's "Mio caro bene," a song Mrs. Park requested in the cryptic "So you know the one" language of a "natural" in-group, signaling an artist whose compositions have accompanied every British coronation since George II (Salazar 2019). Looking out over the patrician party, Ki-woo's pronouncement that "everyone looks so natural" parrots the environmental logics of colonial invasion, where appeals to "nature" define who and what belongs. Ki-woo turns to the Parks' daughter Da-hye and asks, "Do I fit in here? In this setting, do I fit in?" (Bong 2019), his anxiety about his "fitness" in this aristocratic spring scene ventriloquizing the language of celebrated American conservationist and eugenicist Madison Grant (1918: 45) who declared, "The laws of nature require the obliteration of the unfit." From the semi-basement and bunker to the Parks' green-walled celebration, the environmental topologies of waste and walls mimic the "deeply spatialized stories" of white settler society (Razack 2002: 3). Here, the film clarifies the oligarchy of white entitlement abstracted from an American nature tradition, the ways whiteness transcends national borders but still transits through the dispossession originary to settler colonialism's bloody terrain (Byrd et al. 2018: 3).[3]

The bloody climax of the film condenses the sadism of this white terrain into an absurdity splashed across the Parks' sun-lit stage. Geun-sae uses the symbol of capitalist promise, the scholar's rock, to smash Ki-woo's head in before proceeding to attack the garden party. Splattering the fresh French baguette with blood, Geun-sae is the paradigmatic threat to the "natural law," the threat that the parasite will kill the host. Moon-gwang wounds Geun-sae with a barbeque skewer, a tool of the "first food" of American empire used to confirm both "ideas of savagery and innocence" (Warnes 2008: 3). At the height of the climax, Mr. Park plugs his nose at the bloodied Geun-sae, showing the disgust that comes from describing people through vermin and parasite metaphors (Marshal and Shapiro 2018). Mr. Park's desire to block the senses in his walled-off Eden is the paradigmatic fantasy of deciding who and what should live, the fantasy of immunity fueling Frantz Fanon's (2007: 48) question, "What is fascism but colonialism?" that persists into our surreal present and anticipated future.

Mr. Park holding his nose crosses a different line for Mr. Kim, who tears the headdresses off his and Mr. Park's head, removing the icon of "American Indian" stereotypes so popular in the Western genre before

3. Linda Martín Alcoff's (2015: 95) *The Future of Whiteness* defines the "racial project of whiteness" as "in effect, an oligarchy," and Gary Brechin (1996: 236) makes clear this white oligarchy depended on, "more than anything else, the 'laws of nature' as defined by the oligarchs on both sides of the Atlantic [that] served to link the early eugenics and conservation movements." In *Transit of Empire,* Jody Byrd (2011: xx) shows how this "imperialist planetarity" depends upon, and transits through, Indigeneity.

he stabs at the heart of the Park patriarch. In this short sequence, both Kim parents show the brutality of crossing the lines of colonial capitalism, rejecting the structure of "dispossession as a present mode of imperialism" (Barker 2018: 31) and refusing the transnational transit of extermination and replacement plotted through, and green screened by, tropes associated with settler capitalist empire. The scene links the original and ongoing structure of Indigenous dispossession to a nature tradition that continues to naturalize who and what should live, who and what fits the fantasy of innocence made through murder. Green walls protect this terra nullius, but they cannot hide the threat of *terrere* (terror) underwriting colonial capitalism's terra (land) (Simmons 2019: 104). Indeed, when a German couple replaces the Parks at the film's close, *Parasite* suggests that Germans merely moved into a place preoccupied with settler colonialism's transnational ecofascism.

Ecofascism and Colonialism

While scholarship consistently locates the origins of ecofascism in Nazi Germany, the succession suggested in *Parasite* illuminates an integral but oft-invisibilized genealogy of ecofascism embedded in the history of settler colonial capitalism. As ecofascism uses claims of nature to justify racist violence and totalitarian national renewal, it is most often associated with the eugenicist belief in the "natural" supremacy of (certain) white people. *Ecofascism Revisited* originates ecofascism in Nazi Germany, where closeness to nature secures the life of the German people and identifies the influence of figures like Madison Grant (due to Hitler's oft-cited reference to Grant's *Passing of the Great Race* as his "bible") alongside the Jeffersonian agrarianism underlying *volkisch* thought (Biehl and Staudenmaier 2011: 17). Charles Darwin's theories of racial science and American expansionism similarly served as models for Nazi Germany's *lebensraum* policies (Biehl and Staudenmaier 2011: 18, 27, 29, 123). Kyle Boggs (2019: 301) theorizes the blood and soil environmentalism of *lebensraum* as exemplary of "practices of settler colonialism not radically different from the guiding principles and polices of 'Manifest Destiny' that continue to drive settler entitlement to stolen Native land in the United States today" (Boggs 2019: 235). Scholars like Nancy Ordover, Frank Uekoetter, and Gary Brechin all connect Nazi Germany to American territorial conquest, slavery, and Manifest Destiny. Indeed, America provided the "natural geopolitical model for Nazi Germany," where the racial codes of US citizenship, blood quantum and sterilization laws, immigration policy, and the reservation system were all held up as aspirational targets for the Third Reich (Whitman 2017: 181). A main architect of the Holocaust, Heinrich Himmler, articulated the Third Reich's settler order: "the new *lebensräume* (living spaces) are to become a homeland for our settlers, the planned arrangement of the landscape to keep it close to nature is a decisive prerequisite. It is one of the bases for fortifying the German *Volk*" (quoted in Staudenmaier 2021: 29). The transnational exchange of a white nature tradition suggests ecofascism is tied less to swiftly shifting national boundaries or fickle political affiliations than to the circulation of a narrative tradition where violence is a part of the "natural" order, of people and planet. The ordinariness of this ecofascist environmentalism elides its circuit, mimicking the operations of settler colonialism itself as a system that has, as its end goal, a complete erasure of its own structure.

Parasite's "natural order" extends this enduring structure into a contemporary global phenomenon in which ecofascist thought transits through settler colonial tropes of elimination, invasion, and genocide: the blood sacrifice internal to settler colonial capitalism. The El Paso murderer's invective offers a compendium of ecofascist fictions straight from the same American nature tradition (Kaufmann 1998). Replacing Al Gore's "A" with a totalitarian "The," its first lines detail the motive to defend the "country from cultural and ethnic replacement" by "Hispanic invasion" (quoted in Ehsan and Stott 2020: 12). It also updates Wilmot Robertson's 1992 *The Ethnostate*, which spins white genocide conspiracy theories from the actual endangerment of the American redwoods in a rhetorical move popularized by Madison Grant (Stern 2019: 60), exemplifying the self-referential intellectualism that defines contemporary "far-right manifestos" (Ehsan and Stott 2020).

Indeed, the El Paso shooter's screed follows this self-referential tradition from the fear of white race suicide explicit in Grant and others. Its environmental logic is internal to settler colonial capitalism, a vision that regenerates through the violent trope of "frontier settlers replacing Native peoples as historical destiny"—the template for social Darwinism, according to Roxanne Dunbar-Ortiz (2019: 118), and persisting in the globalized white possessive imagination (see also Moreton-Robinson 2015; Staudenmaier 2021). The El Paso murderer's screed claims, "the nearly complete ethnic and cultural destruction brought to the Native Americans by our European ancestors just reinforces my point. The natives didn't take the invasion of Europeans seriously" (Crusius 2019).

Here, the murderer enacts a version of the "settler absorption" that Audra Simpson (2018: 167) describes, where lived experience of Indigenous peoples is absorbed into a settler ontology. Through these absorptive assertions, the mass murderer updates the old colonial story of natural law with the new context of climate chaos, claiming violence is the only way to protect from "invaders" who inevitably become parasites in the United States. His opening paragraph alerts us to an omission in contemporary understandings of both fascism and ecofascism as singularly state-sponsored violence. Instead, like the Parks' property, the El Paso murderer's ecofascism participates in what Jodi Byrd (2011: 76, xiii) calls a "transferrable" Indianness, where ideas of the "Indian" are the "contagion" through which US empire orders the people in its purview. As just such a foot soldier, rather than targeting the systems of colonial capitalism, the author of the El Paso murderer invokes the genocide of Native peoples to project threat onto an "imagined community summoned from the frontier" (Grandin 2019: 464). His document is a metonym for settler colonial ecofascism—the ways settler capitalist logic is "framed as natural" but obtains "through blood sacrifice" (Dunbar-Ortiz 2019: 40, 54). The rise of ecofascist sentiment today across the global Right continues this trend, transiting through transnational colonial fictions that exploit the ambiguity between state and citizen (Staudenmaier 2021: 162).

Even as the walls around who counts as white morph in the context of climate chaos, ecofascism's durability lies in its persistent speculative imagination. When the first lines of the El Paso murderer's text uses the historical realities of invasion and genocide as illogical evidence for obsessions about white genocide, it confirms Joanne Barker's (2018: 31) reminder that "dispossession is not normal, nor is it a thing of the past. It is not done—it is a doing."

That "doing" happens through the virality of settler colonial ecofascism, speculative fantasies of invasion and extinction that stand in obstinate contrast to historical fact as well as the breakneck speed of the sixth extinction among nonhuman species. The now-transnational idea of "natural law" extends the security of immunity across borders, oceans, identities. It speculates upon an ever-looming threat of contamination, contagion, conquest, and, ultimately, elimination, plagiarizing promises of protection straight from the settler fictions of blood and soil, stories naturalizing both German and American genocide. However, just as the targets of those genocides remain to testify to them, acknowledging the depth of the ecofascist intellectual tradition, too, is absolutely critical to outliving its transnational creep today.

Ecofascist Speculations and Planetary Responses

Pairing *Parasite* with the El Paso murderer's so-called manifesto points to the defining features of an ecofascist literary tradition that is at once global and virally settler colonial (Guidi 2022). Just as Mark Rifkin (2019: 64) warns, "the attempt to secure the future of white supremacy, settlement, and capital involves a range of speculative technologies that project forward current conditions of subjugation as the basis for what's to come," ecofascism remains a speculative literary project. It is best understood through the lens of the literary because of its claims to narrate the near future, but also because, as Richard Dyer (1997: 12) declared so long ago, "whiteness does not name a set of stereotypes so much as a set of narrative structural positions, rhetorical tropes, and habits of perception." Indeed, ecofascism is a *literary* project. It willfully ignores the historical and ongoing realities of genocide and species extinction in favor of a dystopia where "'whites are an endangered race' whose extinction is being expedited by the bulldozing combination of 'habitat loss, invasive species, hybridization, and predation,'" to follow Alexandra Stern's (2019: 132) quotations from Greg Johnson's *The White Nationalist Manifesto* (see also B. Taylor 2019).

The El Paso murderer's text pairs with *Parasite* to suggest that speculative fiction plays "an outsized role" because it offers "a space of plausible deniability in which to discuss activities that might otherwise provide grounds for prosecution" (Trimble Young 2020). This kind of in-group signaling is paradigmatically performed in *Parasite*'s party scene, but also in the self-referential "manifestos" of real-life ecofascist mass murderers (Guidi 2022). From the Al Gore allusion in "The Inconvenient Truth," to the citations of the Christchurch murderer introduced through a Dylan Thomas poem, to the concluding colonial-apologist exemplar Rudyard Kipling, this suffocating, self-referential, and speculative literary tradition projects a disastrous end of a white world in the near future, supposedly secure in the safety and immunity of settler colonial capitalism.

The tropes that open the El Paso murderer's tirade transgress national boundaries, as *Parasite* suggests. They are just the latest green screen behind the same ecofascist imagination, the contours of which include a once empty, now besieged wasteland; the thirst for a new frontier; fantasies of going Native, taming the land via sexual violence or replacement; and the "too late"-ness of injustice that makes history irrelevant but bolsters the moral superiority of taking violent action in the present. Recent ecofascist speculative fictions have appropriated even more environmental science, claiming that "whites needed to be protected with their own border, like an endangered species": rhetoric that transcends the distinction between the open frontier and the border wall to collapse any threats to settler colonial capitalism as a speculative threat to the white body (Stern 2019: 9). This tradition transits through tropes of the promised land, from American Eden to the high green walls protecting imagined immunities across the globe. It turns the settler capitalist into the *sacer*, the sacred patriarchal sovereign lording over the *terrere* of terra nullius.

Climate chaos, and more recently COVID-19, increase opportunities to circulate ecofascist dog whistles like "humans are a cancer" or "we are the virus" (Anson 2020). *Parasite* warns of the danger of these speculative fictions. Just as Mary Heglar (2022) astutely reminds us that "ecofascism is climate action," we must acknowledge the rhetorical green walls that perpetually protect the plots of settler colonial capitalism and its neoliberal eco-logics that continue to define our existence, or extinction, at home and in the world. We must speculate with something other than the roots and branches of a transnational, genocidal tradition of envisioning the present continuous and future imperfect.

References

Abdul-Jabbar, Kareem. 2020. "Don't Understand the Protests?" *Los Angeles Times*, May 30. https://www.latimes.com/opinion/story/2020-05-30/don't-understand -the-protests-what-youre-seeing-is-people-pushed-to-the-edge.

Alcoff, Linda Martín. 2015. *The Future of Whiteness*. New York: Polity.

Amend, Alex. 2020. "Blood and Vanishing Topsoil: American Ecofascism Past, Present, and in the Coming Climate Crisis." *Public Eye*, July 9. https://politicalresearch .org/2020/07/09/blood-and-vanishing-topsoil.

Anson, April. 2020. "No One Is a Virus: On American Ecofascism." *Environmental History Now*, October 21. https://envhistnow.com/2020/10/21/no-one-is-the -virus-on-american-ecofascism/.

Attanasio, Cedar. 2019. "El Paso Shooting Suspect Said He Targeted Mexicans." *El Paso Times*, August 9. https://apnews.com/article/shootings-e-paso-texas -mass-shooting-us-news-ap-top-news-immigration-456c0154218a4d378e 2fb36cd40b709d.

Atwood, Margaret. 2015. "It's Not Climate Change—It's Everything Change." *Medium*, July 27. https://medium.com/matter/it-s-not-climate-change-it-s-everything -change-8fd9aa671804.

Baldwin, Andrew. 2012. "Whiteness and Futurity: Toward a Research Agenda." *Progress in Human Geography* 36, no. 2: 172–87.

Barker, Joanne. 2018. "Territory as Analytic: The Dispossession of Lenapehoking and the Subprime Crisis." *Social Text* 135, no. 2: 19–39.

Bhandar, Brenda. 2018. *The Colonial Lives of Property: Law, Land, and Racial Regimes of Ownership.* Durham, NC: Duke University Press.

Biehl, Janet, and Peter Staudenmaier. 2011. *Ecofascism Revisited: Lessons from the German Experience.* Oakland, CA: AK Press.

Boggs, Kyle. 2019. "The Rhetorical Landscapes of the 'Alt-Right' and the Patriot Movements: Settler Entitlement to Native Land." In *The Far Right and the Environment: Politics, Discourse, and Communication*, edited by Bernhard Forchtner, 293–309. Abingdon, UK: Routledge.

Bong, Joon-ho, dir. 2019. *Parasite.* Seoul: Barunson E&A. 132 min. https://www.hulu.com/movie/parasite.

Brechin, Gary. 1996. "Conserving Race: Natural Aristocracies, Eugenics, and the American Conservation Movement." *Antipode* 28, no. 3: 229–45.

Byrd, Jodi. 2011. *The Transit of Empire: Indigenous Critiques of Colonialism.* Minneapolis: University of Minnesota Press.

Byrd, Jodi, Alyosha Goldstein, Jodi Melamed, and Chandran Reddy. 2018. "Predatory Value: Economies of Dispossession and Disturbed Realities." *Social Text* 36, no. 2: 1–18.

Cagle, Susie. 2019. "Bees, not Refugees: The Environmentalist Roots of Anti-immigrant Bigotry." *Guardian*, August 16. https://www.theguardian.com/environment/2019/aug/15/anti.

Charlton, Loretta. 2019. "What Is the Great Replacement?" *New York Times*, August 6. https://www.nytimes.com/2019/08/06/us/politics/grand-replacement-explainer.html.

Churchwell, Sarah. 2019. "American Immigration: A Century of Racism." *New York Review of Books*, September 26. https://www.nybooks.com/articles/2019/09/26/american-immigration-century-racism/.

Confessore, Nicholas, and Karen Yourish. 2022. "A Fringe Conspiracy Theory, Fostered Online, Is Refashioned by the GOP." *New York Times*, May 15. https://www.nytimes.com/2022/05/15/us/replacement-theory-shooting-tucker-carlson.html.

Cornelissen, Sharon. 2020. "A Triple Pandemic? The Economic Impacts of COVID-19 Disproportionately Impact Black and Hispanic Households." *Housing Perspectives: Research, Trends, and Perspectives from the Harvard Joint Center for Housing Studies* (blog), July 7. https://www.jchs.harvard.edu/blog/a-triple-pandemic-the-economic-impacts-of-covid-19-disproportionately-affect-black-and-hispanic-households.

Crusius, Patrick. 2019. "The Inconvenient Truth." *Randall Packer: Reportage from the Aesthetic Edge* (blog), August. https://randallpacker.com/wp-content/uploads/2019/08/The-Inconvenient-Truth.pdf.

Day, Iyko. 2016. *Alien Capital: Asian Racialization and the Logic of Settler Colonial Capitalism.* Durham, NC: Duke University Press.

Deloria, Philip J. 1998. *Playing Indian*. New Haven, CT: Yale University Press.

Dillon, Lindsey, and Julie Sze. 2016. "Police Power and Particulate Matters: Environmental Justice and the Spatialities of In/Securities in U.S. Cities." *English Language Notes* 54, no. 2: 13–23.

Dowie, Mark. 2009. *Conservation Refugees: The Hundred-Year Conflict between Global Conservation and Native Peoples*. Boston: MIT Press.

Dunbar-Ortiz, Roxanne. 2015. *An Indigenous People's History of the United States*. Boston: Beacon.

Dyer, Richard. 1997. *White: Essays on Race and Culture*. Abingdon: Routledge.

Ehsan, Rakib, and Paul Stott. 2020. "Far-Right Terrorist Manifestos: A Critical Analysis." Henry Jackson Society, February 28. https://henryjacksonsociety.org/publications/far-right-manifestos/.

Esposito, Roberto. 2002. *Immunitas: The Protection and Negation of Life*. New York: Wiley.

Fanon, Franz. 2007. *The Wretched of the Earth*. Translated by Richard Philcox. New York: Grove Atlantic.

Farhi, Paul. 2022. "Conservative Media Is Familiar with Buffalo Suspect's Alleged 'Theory.'" *Washington Post*, May 15. https://www.washingtonpost.com/media/2022/05/15/buffalo-suspect-great-replacement-theory-conservative-media/.

Fitzgerald, F. Scott. 1925. *The Great Gatsby*. https://www.gutenberg.org/files/64317/64317-h/64317-h.htm.

Frenkel, Sheera, and Stuart A. Thompson. 2022. "How Russia and Right-Wing Americans Converged on War in Ukraine." *New York Times*, March 23. https://www.nytimes.com/2022/03/23/technology/russia-american-far-right-ukraine.html.

Gann, Lewis H. 1965. *A History of Southern Rhodesia: Early Days to 1934*. London: Chatto & Windus.

Garcia, Maria Cristina. 2017. "Migration Forced by Climate Change." Interview with Jackie Swift. News & Features, Cornell Research, May 15. https://research.cornell.edu/news-features/migration-forced-climate-change#highlight-1491414467292.

Ghosh, Amitav. 2016. *The Great Derangement: Climate Change and the Unthinkable*. Chicago: Chicago University Press.

Gopnik, Adam. 2021. "The Ultra-Nationalist Eric Zémmour Makes a Bizarre Bid for the French Presidency." *New Yorker*, December 3. https://www.newyorker.com/news/daily-comment/the-ultra-nationalist-eric-zemmour-makes-a-bizarre-bid-for-the-french-presidency.

Grandin, Greg. 2019. *The End of the Myth: From the Frontier to the Border Wall in the Mind of America*. New York: Macmillan.

Grant, Madison. 1918. *The Passing of the Great Race*. New York: Charles Scribner's Sons.

Guidi, Ruxandra. 2022. "Don't Call it 'Ecofascism.' It's Just Plain Hate." *Sierra*

Club, May 21. https://www.sierraclub.org/sierra/don-t-call-it-eco-fascism-it-s-just
-plain-hate.

Heglar, Mary Annaïse. 2022. "Climate Denial's Racist Roots." *Atmos*, June 15. https://
atmos.earth/climate-denial-mass-shootings-white-supremacy/.

Hong, Cathy Park. 2020. *Minor Feelings: An Asian American Reckoning*. London:
One World.

Hong, Grace. 2015. *Death Beyond Disavowal: The Impossible Politics of Difference*. Minneapolis: University of Minnesota Press.

Huhndorf, Shari. 2001. *Going Native: Indians in the American Cultural Imagination*.
Ithaca, NY: Cornell University Press.

Hultgren, John. 2015. *Border Walls Gone Green: Nature and Anti-immigrant Politics
in America*. Minneapolis: University of Minnesota Press.

Hwang, Su-kyoung. 2016. *Korea's Grievous War*. Philadelphia: University of Pennsylvania Press.

JCHS (Joint Center for Housing Studies). 2020. "A Triple Pandemic?" Harvard
University, July 7. https://www.jchs.harvard.edu/blog/a-triple-pandemic-the
-economic-impacts-of-covid-19-disproportionately-affect-black-and-hispanic
-households.

Joyce, Kathryn. 2022. "What Is Ecofascism? And What Does It Have to Do with the
Buffalo Shooting?" *Salon*, May 18. https://www.salon.com/2022/05/18/what
-is-ecofascism-and-what-does-it-have-to-do-with-the-buffalo-shooting/.

Kaufmann, E. 1998. "Naturalizing the Nation: The Rise of Naturalistic Nationalism
in the United States and Canada." *Comparative Studies in Society and History* 40, no. 4: 666–95.

Kim, Jodi. 2018. "Settler Modernity, Debt Imperialism, and the Necropolitics of the
Promise." *Social Text* 2: 41–62.

Krech, Shepard. 1999. *The Ecological Indian: Myth and History*. New York: Norton.

London, Jack. 1902. "The Salt of the Earth." *Anglo-American Magazine*, August.
https://thegrandarchive.wordpress.com/salt-of-the-earth/.

London, Jack. 1910. "The Unparalleled Invasion." https://americanliterature.com
/author/jack-london/short-story/the-unparalleled-invasion.

Low, Jennifer. 2019. "Design Is Political: White Supremacy and Landscape Urban-
ism." *Agora Journal of Urban Planning and Design* 13: 126–36.

Lowndes, Joseph E., and Daniel Martinez HoSang. 2019. *Producers, Parasites,
Patriots: Race and the New Right-Wing Politics of Precarity*. Minneapolis:
University of Minnesota Press.

Lustgarten, Abrahm. 2020. "How Climate Migration Will Reshape America." *New
York Times Magazine*, September 15. https://www.nytimes.com/interactive
/2020/09/15/magazine/climate-crisis-migration-america.html.

Marshal, Shantal R., and Jenessa R. Shapiro. 2018. "When 'Scurry' vs. 'Hurry'
Makes the Difference: Vermin Metaphors, Disgust, and Anti-immigrant Attitudes." *Journal of Social Issues* 74, no. 4: 774–89.

Mayer, Neil M. 2005. "A Conflux of Desire and Need: Trees, Boy Scouts, and the Roots of Franklin Roosevelt's Civilian Conservation Corps." In *FDR and the Environment*, edited by Henry L. Henderson and David B. Willner, 49–83. London: Palgrave Macmillan.

Miller-Idriss, Cynthia. 2021. "Extremism Has Spread Into the Mainstream." *Atlantic*, June 15. https://www.theatlantic.com/ideas/archive/2021/06/us-fighting-ex tremism-all-wrong/619203/.

Moreton-Robinson, Aileen. 2015. *The White Possessive: Property, Power, and Indigenous Sovereignty*. Minneapolis: University of Minnesota Press.

Morrison, Toni. 1992. *Playing in the Dark: Whiteness and the Literary Imagination*. Cambridge, MA: Harvard University Press.

Morton, Timothy. 2013. *Hyperobjects: Philosophy and Ecology after the End of the World*. Minneapolis: University of Minnesota Press.

Murdock, Esme. 2021. "Conserving Dispossession? A Genealogical Account of the Colonial Roots of Western Conservation." *Ethics, Policy, and Environment* 24, no 3: 235–49.

Ngai, Mae. 2004. *Impossible Subjects: Illegal Aliens and the Making of Modern America*. Princeton, NJ: Princeton University Press.

Park, Ju-Hyun (Jyuhundred). 2020. "Reading Colonialism in 'Parasite.'" *Tropics of Meta*, February 17. https://tropicsofmeta.com/2020/02/17/reading-colonialism -in-parasite/.

Razack, Sherene H. 2002. *Race, Space, and the Law: Unmapping a White Settler Society*. Toronto: Between the Lines.

Ray, Sarah Jacquette. 2013. *The Ecological Other: Environmental Exclusion in American Culture*. Tucson: University of Arizona Press.

Reich, Robert (@RBReich). 2020. "I have held off on using the f-word for three and a half years." Twitter, June 1, 9:10 p.m. https://twitter.com/RBReich/status /1267986930139951104?s=20.

Rifkin, Mark. 2019. *Fictions of Land and Flesh: Blackness, Indigeneity, Speculation*. Durham, NC: Duke University Press.

Rinehart, Melissa. 2012. "To Hell with the Wigs! Native American Representation and Resistance at the Columbian Exposition." *American Indian Quarterly* 36, no. 4: 403–42.

Sachs, Aaron. 2013. *Arcadian America: The Death and Life of an Environmental Tradition*. New Haven, CT: Yale University Press.

Salazar, David. 2019. "Opera Meets Film: How Joon-Ho Bong's [*sic*] 'Parasite' Develops Ironic Narrative through Handel's 'Rodelina.'" *OperaWire*, October 31. https://operawire.com/opera-meets-film-how-joon-ho-bongs-parasite -develops-ironic-narrative-through-handels-rodelinda/.

Simmons, Kristen. 2019. "Expanse." *Journal for the Anthropology of North America* 22, no. 2: 103–6.

Simpson, Audra. 2018. "Why White People Love Franz Boas; or, The Grammar of

Indigenous Dispossession." In *Indigenous Visions: Rediscovering the Work of Franz Boas*, edited by Ned Blackhawk and Isaiah Lorado Wilner, 166–81. New Haven, CT: Yale University Press.

Sontag, Susan. 1988. "AIDS and Its Metaphors." *New York Review of Books*, October 27. https://www.nybooks.com/articles/1988/10/27/aids-and-its-metaphors/.

Spence, Mark. 2000. *Dispossessing the Environment: Indian Removal and the Making of the National Parks*. Oxford: Oxford University Press.

Stanley-Becker, Isaac, and Drew Harwell. 2022. "Buffalo Suspect Allegedly Inspired by Racist Theory Fueling Global Carnage." *Washington Post*, May 15. https://www.washingtonpost.com/nation/2022/05/15/buffalo-shooter-great -replacement-extremism/.

Staudenmaier, Peter. 2021. *Ecology Revisited: Environmental Politics between Left and Right*. Porsgrunn, Norway: New Compass.

Stern, Alexandra Minna. 2019. *Proud Boys and the White Ethnostate: How the Alt-Right Is Warping the American Imagination*. Boston: Beacon.

Steuter, Erin, and Deborah Wills. 2009. *At War with Metaphor: Media, Propaganda, and Racism in the War on Terror*. Lanham, MD: Lexington.

Tarrant, Brendan. 2019. "The Great Replacement." *Ilfoglio*. https://img-prod.ilfoglio. it/userUpload/The_Great_Replacementconvertito.pdf.

Taylor, Blair. 2019. "Alt-Right Ecology: Ecofascism and Far-Right Environmentalism in the United States." In *The Far Right and the Environment: Politics, Discourse, and Communication*, edited by Bernhard Forchtner, 276–93. New York: Routledge.

Taylor, Dorceta E. 2016. *The Rise of the American Conservation Movement: Power, Privilege, and Environmental Protection*. Durham, NC: Duke University Press.

Thornhill, Randy, and Corey L. Fincher, eds. 2014. *The Parasite Stress Theory of Values and Sociality*. New York: Springer.

Trimble Young, Alex. 2020. "The Necropolitics of Liberty: Sovereignty, Fantasy, and United States Gun Culture." *Lateral* 9, no. 1. https://csalateral.org/forum /gun-culture/necropolitics-of-liberty-sovereignty-fantasy-us-gun-culture -young/.

UMass/YouGov. 2021. "Democratic Party Is Trying to Replace the Current Electorate with Voters of Poorer Countries around the World." December 19–21. https://polsci.umass.edu/research/umass-poll/recent-polls.

Vassar, Shea. 2020. "How the Movie *Parasite* Confronts Native Stereotypes." *Zora*, January 13. https://zora.medium.com/how-the-movie-parasite-confronts -native-stereotypes-f89ec8399b8c.

Wald, Priscilla. 2007. *Contagious: Cultures, Carriers, and the Outbreak Narrative*. Durham, NC: Duke University Press.

Wallace, Rachel. 2019. "Inside the Houses from Bong Joon Ho's *Parasite*." *Architectural Digest*, October 31. https://www.architecturaldigest.com/story/bong -joon-ho-parasite-movie-set-design-interview.

Warnes, Andrew. 2008. *Savage Barbeque: Race, Culture, and the Invention of America's First Food.* Athens: University of Georgia Press.

Weinstein, Adam. 2020. "This Is Fascism." *New Republic*, June 2. https://newrepublic .com/article/157949/fascism-america-trump-anti-police-george-floyd-protests.

Wenham, Simon M. 2015. "The River Thames and the Popularization of Camping, 1860–1980." *Oxoniensia* 80: 57–74.

Whitman, James. 2017. *Hitler's American Model: The United States and the Making of Nazi Race Law.* Princeton, NJ: Princeton University Press.

Whyte, Kyle. 2018. "Settler Colonialism, Ecology, and Environmental Injustice." *Environment and Society: Advances in Research* 9: 125–44.

Young, Terrence. 2017. *Heading Out: A History of American Camping.* Ithaca, NY: Cornell University Press.

Yusoff, Kathryn. 2013. "Geologic Life: Prehistory, Climate, Futures in the Anthropocene." *Environment and Planning D: Society and Space* 31, no. 5: 779–95.

The Grannies of Shaheen Bagh: Hindutva Power and the Poetics of Dissent in Contemporary India

Aamir R. Mufti

The last three to four decades have seen a marked increase in a whole host of social, political, and cultural tendencies in India that are collectively referred to in the political argot of the country as "communalism": the "Hinduization" of regional and national politics; the socially and culturally separatist tendencies among religious minorities, especially Muslims and even Sikhs; the social and political marginalization of minorities; repeated outbreaks of interreligious conflict; organized acts of mass pogrom-like violence. The most visible sign of these transformations is the rise to prominence and power of the Bharatiya Janata Party (Indian People's Party; BJP), whose current stint of national power started in 2014, but they have a much wider social, political, and cultural scope. At the core of the far-right-

I wish to thank a number of individuals for sharing with me their personal impressions of the Shaheen Bagh protest: Pankaj Butalia, Ruchira Gupta, Farida Khan, Mohammad Yousuf Nomani, and Kavita Singh. I am also grateful to Nasser Mufti for his comments on a draft of this essay.

boundary 2 50:1 (2023)   DOI 10.1215/01903659-10192159   ©2023 by Duke University Press

wing Hindu-nationalist social and political ecology throughout the history of postcolonial India has been the neofascist Rashtriya Swayamsevak Sangh (National Volunteer Organization; RSS), founded in open imitation of the Italian fascists in the 1920s and inspired a decade later by Hitler's systematic expulsion of Jews from German society (Basu et al. 1993: 25–27). The RSS exercises more or less direct control over a now vast group of large and small organizations informally referred to as the *sañgh parīvār*, or "family" of the Sangh. It is now openly acknowledged that since its founding in 1980, the BJP has simply been the political-electoral wing of the RSS, as, for instance, the Vishwa Hindu Parishad (World Hindu Council; VHP) is its religio-cultural subsidiary and the Bajrang Dal (Hanuman Brigade) consists of its street-level enforcers. Since the 1980s, scholars in several disciplines have been tracking this rise of the politics of Hindutva—literally, "Hinduness," but signifying majoritarian and supremacist Hindu nationalism (see Gopal 1991; Ludden 2005; Hansen 1999; Jaffrelot 1996; Van Der Veer 1994; Basu 2020). Even when the Congress Party has been in power in these decades, it has not been able to dent significantly this rise of Hindutva as a whole, and it has itself engaged in communalist politics repeatedly over the decades—most notoriously in perpetrating the anti-Sikh pogroms of 1984—despite having been officially committed for well over a century to the secular nature of Indian politics and state. This essay is an attempt to explore some of the preoccupations and modalities of what we might call *Hindutva power*, both in some of its social-capillary (that is, ground-level) and state-sovereign forms. Wherever and whenever in contemporary India we observe the political and social consolidation of Hinduness across a range of social fissures and hierarchies through the crafting of distinctions from "other" modes of being, we are likely witnessing the exercise of Hindutva power. In addition, this essay also seeks to explore some of the modes of dissent, challenge, and resistance to Hindutva power that have emerged in recent years.

Contemporary Hindutva politics are anchored in a concept of *the indigenous*—which makes possible a powerful cultural machinery for distinguishing the native from the alien in a whole host of social and cultural fields, including linguistic usage, religious beliefs and practices, cultural and historical imaginaries, social and cultural institutions, and demographics itself. In the all-consuming power of this concept, which appears to be able to divide in this manner any field it encounters, the ideological complex of Hindutva departs even from some of its acknowledged (and much revered) antecedents, such as Vinayak Damodar Savarkar (1883–1966), who put the idea itself into wide circulation for the first time. To take one example, in his pamphlet *Hindutva* (first published in 1923), which is the classic program-

matic text of the whole movement, Savarkar ([1923] 2003) has no problem in conceiving of the Vedic peoples, to whom he refers, with the Vedic
term Aryans, as outsiders who entered India from the West and eventually blended with the indigenous population to create a single, though hierarchical, society—something that is largely anathema in the contemporary
discourse with its obsession with indigeneity, and a huge ideological effort
has been undertaken in recent years to refute the so-called Aryan Invasion
(or Migration) Theory (see Doniger 2009; Swadeshi Indology 2019). In the
latest phase, this has even led to the use of advanced paleo-genetics to
establish the genetic (that is, racial) purity and continuity of the population
of the subcontinent (see Shinde et al. 2019). In this project of indigenization,
not surprisingly, the most energy has been expended on rendering anything
marked "Muslim" as alien to India and destructive of its national coherence
and continuity, a gargantuan and inherently contradictory task, directed as
it is at a population mostly of descendants of converts from the lower rungs
of Indian caste society. Both "Hindu" (marked as indigenous) and "Muslim"
(marked as alien) in contemporary discourse are enormous fabrications
that either conceal or try to entirely eradicate highly differentiated fields of
social and cultural experience. Above all, what these religious designations
seek to conceal is the politics of caste, arguably the most violent dimension
of social relations across the societies of the subcontinent (see Lee 2021).

Possibly the most spectacular event in this wider historical process, including in the theatrical sense of the word, was the destruction
on December 6, 1992, of the Babri Masjid, a sixteenth-century mosque in
the town of Ayodhya in north India, as the culmination of a yearslong systematic mobilization headed by BJP and RSS leadership to demolish the
mosque and replace it with a Hindu temple dedicated to the god Rama
(see Gopal 1991). In the vast, heterogeneous, and ancient epic tradition
associated with Rama, he is the prince of Ayodhya, and the movement
rests on the claim that the mosque was built during the reign of the first
Mughal Emperor, Babur (1483–1530), on the exact place of Rama's birth
(*Rāmjanmabhūmī*) after the temple that had marked the spot was demolished (see Thapar 1991; Doniger 2009). News footage showed that the final
attack was planned well in advance and executed with discipline, by militants including RSS cadres in uniform, with state and federal security forces
involved in the coordination (see Business Standard 2017).

After decades of legal wrangling, the temple is now being built with
the imprimatur of a Supreme Court decision, after the performance of
bhūmīpūjan, or ritual sacralization of the ground and the construction, by
a sitting prime minister himself in the company of priests and the leading

and most notorious figures of his party and movement, including the head of the RSS. Finally successful in Ayodhya, the temple movement has moved on to other mosques, including one in Varanasi (Benares) and another in Mathura, both of which now seem headed inexorably toward the same fate as the one in Ayodhya. In the former case, the campaign has resulted in the supposed discovery of a *shivliñg* (Shiva lingam) in the basement, leading to a somewhat bizarre polemic in the public sphere about whether it is a phallic fertility symbol or a fountain. And even the iconic Taj Mahal has now appeared on the demolitionist wish list. The demolition of the Babri Masjid and the outbreak of widespread violence in its wake in 1992–93 represented a significant event in the history of the subcontinent as a whole, seeming to have momentarily erased the boundaries instituted at the Partition of India in 1947, producing, forty-five years after the partition, a subcontinent-wide map of communal violence, with tit-for-tat riots and acts of violence on both sides of the border. In Bombay, anti-Muslim pogroms led to counterviolence in the form of bombings across the city apparently carried out by a Muslim organized-crime syndicate. The full significance of the Babri Masjid event is not as the destruction of a place of worship of one religious community by members of another, a specific case of violation of the rights of a minority. The destruction of this somewhat undistinguished late medieval structure carried meaning far beyond itself. As I have argued elsewhere, what appeared to have come crashing down that day, without the change of a single word in the Constitution of India, was "the structure of secular citizenship itself" (Mufti 2007: 2). The monumental nature of this event has lent a certain sense of historical inevitability to a decisive shift in the place of Muslims and other minorities in the space of Indian citizenship and nationhood.

Ayodhya was thus a turning point in the history of majoritarianism and struggles for minority rights in India and in the history of the Indian state as such. Beyond the comings and goings of political parties and coalitions at both the state and federal levels, the road from Ayodhya has been marked by the steady intensification of the symptoms of majoritarianism and the fraying of the very fabric of society. After 9/11, the distinctly Indian variety of anti-Muslim ideology coalesced with the global trends that are now referred to as Islamophobia. This new international imprimatur for a set of tawdry local prejudices sometimes creates hilarious misunderstandings and acts of overreach. In 2020, some Indians residing in the United Arab Emirates were called to account by an Emirati princess for openly participating in violently Islamophobic banter on social media platforms and reminded that they lived and worked in an officially Muslim country and under sufferance of its government, reducing them to awkward silence (see "UAE" 2020). And domestic and foreign policy crashed into each other in the summer of 2022 when a senior BJP spokesperson's derogatory remarks on TV about the Prophet of Islam's sexual morality—replicating motifs from the notorious "Rangeela Rasool" ("The Colorful Prophet") controversy nearly a hundred years ago—caused diplomatic uproar in India's relations with countries of the Islamic Middle East, leading to an embarrassing retreat and the firing of the individual, with a strong statement of the party's commitment to respect-ing Islam and all religions that produced paroxysms of despair among many of its constitutionally anti-Muslim followers. Since the BJP's return to power in 2014 under the leadership of Narendra Modi, some invisible Rubicon has been crossed seemingly forever. Open calls for genocide of Muslims and Christians can be voiced in front of cameras at public forums by supposed religious leaders known to be close to the party leadership and are routinely met with the latter's studied silence. Until his ascent to his present office, Modi had been a regional politician, chief minister of the state of Gujarat since 2001, where he began the following year to burnish his credentials for national BJP leadership by presiding over anti-Muslim pogroms that lasted over a year and led to deaths in the thousands (see Ayyub 2016; ANHAD 2022). It was in Gujarat that Modi honed the politics of studied silence in the face of brutal violence as an active posture of political affiliation rather than simply as a lack of concern or indifference. So well established is his role and that of those around him in the 2002 violence that he was banned from traveling to the United States for several years.[1] But in a judgment issued in the summer of 2022, the Supreme Court in essence absolved Modi and his henchman, home minister Amit Shah, also opening the way for the arrest and prosecution of journalists and activists and even a former police offi-cial who had spent two decades helping to document the violence and the complicity of the state government.

Since the party has returned to power in New Delhi, every few months the country is faced with new outrages and further degradation of the norms of public life and of everyday sociality. It is worth recalling some of the more visible tendencies. "Cow lynching," meaning the beating or

---

1. It is not often remarked that it was Barack Obama who rehabilitated Modi internation-ally, for instance nominating him for the "Time 100" list of global leaders with an enco-mium to his great status as a "reformer" (Obama 2015). But then many of Obama's foreign policy positions seemed designed to prove that he was a realist in foreign policy, not the wild-eyed radical and anti-imperialist that he had been made out to be by the Republican machinery during the election.

murder of individuals by mobs accusing them of the consumption or possession of beef, is now a commonly used term in Indian English and the vernaculars. These mobs have typically targeted Muslims and Dalits and, of course, Dalit (*pasmāñdā*) Muslims. Early in the COVID crisis, Muslims were widely blamed for the pandemic. There are ongoing efforts nationally to expunge Muslim-sounding place names from streets, neighborhoods, and entire cities. There are repeated campaigns in different parts of the country to boycott Muslim-owned businesses, and petty vendors eking out a basic living serving visitors to Hindu temples are to be removed from the holy spaces. The realm of private life has not been left unscathed either: militants of the Bajrang Dal routinely harass young lovers in public, especially on Valentine's Day, and a hysterical campaign has been launched in recent years against interreligious romance and marriage, recoded as "love jihad," a now common expression in all Indian languages, referencing a supposedly programmatic sexual predation of Hindu women undertaken by Muslim men. An app was recently launched that purported to auction off a number of prominent Muslim women, especially journalists and activists, to the highest bidder, presumably to be used as sex slaves. A veritable army of online trolls, including the organized IT cell of the BJP, work nonstop to police online speech and punish dissenters.

In just the first few months of 2022 there were several separate anti-Muslim campaigns in various parts of the country. The first of these occurred in January in Karnataka, starting with a local ban on the wearing of the hijab in schools that spread quickly throughout the state and beyond—a laughable assertion of French-like *laïcisme* in a region like the subcontinent, drowning in an excess of publicly expressed religiosity. Another took place in April, when the relatively minor Hindu festival of Rama Navami drew nationwide attention as organized mobs of young men and women invaded Muslim neighborhoods across the country, blasting loud music in front of mosques and raising the saffron Hindutva flag over some of them. The young people in these mobs revealed in their frenzied dancing to the music the proximity of mob violence and sexual excitement. Such confrontations had not been unknown during this festival period in the past but, unlike this time, had been more or less local affairs. This organized nationwide campaign reinforced another BJP-inspired neologism—"bulldozer politics" (*buldōzar rājnītī*)—as local governments razed the homes of Muslims accused of physically confronting the mobs, or of being ringleaders of the riots that have erupted in protest against the Prophet controversy, summarily and without legal proceedings (see Chakraborty and Ranjan

2022). The bulldozer has acquired a complex semiotic charge in the process, emerging, as one commentator has noted, as a symbol for Hindutva itself, a "flat, brute, massive, spectacular machine" whose only goal is to flatten everything in its path (Prakash 2022). In a recent interview with Al Jazeera (2022), the novelist, essayist, and activist Arundhati Roy placed the bulldozer in the larger context of the rise of Hindutva:

> We're being ruled by gangsters outfitted as Hindu Godmen. And when you look at how this phenomenon of bulldozing Muslim homes is being represented or written about, it's pretty chilling because you see the bulldozer being invested with a kind of divine avenging power. And to watch the spectacle of this violent sort of crushing of the enemy, it's like a kind of comic book version of an avenging God slaying demons. And this spectacle is now beamed into every Indian home. What we're seeing now in India, it's the political equivalent of scorched earth policy where everything is being destroyed, every institution is being depopulated and sort of repopulated and redirected into the service of fascism. (Al Jazeera English 2022).

This "bulldozer politics" very quickly spread beyond the Rama Navami incidents to other Muslim neighborhoods—including Shaheen Bagh in New Delhi, a now legendary neighborhood to which I return in some detail below—under the guise of "anti-encroachment" drives, as if only Muslim property owners engage in illegal construction in India. And after the home demolitions in the Prophet controversy in June 2022, United Nations rapporteurs apparently accused the Indian government of the collective punishment of Muslims (Wire 2022).

At the intellectual level, these everyday activities of Hindutva are undergirded with a widespread effort—unfolding in numerous institutions and organizations, public as well as private—to rewrite the history of the subcontinent across millennia, especially in school curricula. In popular culture, the last thousand years have come to be rewritten as an eternal battle between Indian polytheism and Abrahamic monotheism in the form of Islam, and later, Christianity, including Christianity secularized into liberal modernity. On one side in this agon is an endless stream of selfless and courageous patriots; on the other, rapacious outsiders seeking to subjugate and exploit India. Any historical detail that does not conform to this black-and-white narrative is to be ignored or actively erased from view (Basu et al. 1993: 2–3). Such senior and respected historians as Irfan Habib and Romila Thapar, with more than half a century of landmark scholarship behind them, have come to be treated as Public Enemy #1, forced, in their sunset years, to defend their craft and discipline (see Bhattacharya 2021). And US-based scholars of the Sanskrit world have not been spared either. Wendy Doniger, Sheldon Pollock, and Audrey Truschke, for instance, have been subjected online to mass vilification and threats of violence for refusing to follow the Hindutva line on ancient India. The maximalist desire expressed in this effort—the erasure of the history of the last millennium and the recoding of ancient mythology as history—is of course an impossible one, whose impossibility of attainment can only lead to more and more desperate escalations.

The police in states controlled by BJP governments (and in the national capital) often seem to have become so close to the party and the *sangh parīvār* as to be indistinguishable from them. The bulk of the mainstream media often operate like the publicity wing of the party, and independent and critical journalists and student activists are frequently harassed and hauled to jail. And even storied institutions of Indian democracy like the judiciary and the Election Commission repeatedly appear to be compromised. For religious minorities and the socially marginalized—Muslims, Christians, Dalits, among others—and all political dissidents, a sense of foreboding and fear has been palpable in recent years and gets steadily worse with time. The production of such fear appears now to be an aim and a modality of Hindutva power, at whichever level of the social structure it happens to be exercised. All these developments have produced a visible weakening of democratic norms, a steep rise in the use of force and violence in public life, and the sense of an inexorable slide toward an authoritarian Hindutva acquiring hegemonic status in society—leading to a now widespread discussion, public as well as scholarly, regarding whether Indian state and society, long proudly touted as the largest democracy in the world, are moving toward a partial, incipient, or even outright fascist dispensation (see Banaji 2016a; Sarkar 2016; Simeon 2016; Patnaik 2021; Nigam 2020; N. Menon 2020). At the very least, we can say that this recent stint of the BJP in power has resulted in dramatic changes in the structure of the exercise of sovereign power in India, a topic to which I shall return. Outside the country, much of this has gone largely unnoticed or is actively ignored, and Western leaders—including Barack Obama, Joe Biden, Justin Trudeau, Boris Johnson—have streamed in regularly or invited Modi and his mouthpieces to their capitals and provided the BJP's authoritarian politics with international respectability. Modi's India is too important to the global neoliberal economic order, with the added advantage of demonstrating how to harness frustrated popular aspirations to an increasingly authoritarian exercise of power. And in their turn Modi and his foreign minister constantly tout India's democracy when abroad, even as democratic culture is more and more hollowed out within the country. The vote bank of the BJP may be an expanding swathe of the population, but its patrons are elements of the industrial capitalist class, whose support is rewarded generously by the government in the form of "lavish grants of land and unhindered access to the leader himself" (Banaji 2016a: x; see N. Menon 2020; Patnaik 2021).

However, so far as the figurations of "the Muslim" that are put in circulation by Hindutva power are concerned, it would be wrong to see them as emerging ex nihilo. The history of minoritization of the figure of the Muslim in the subcontinent is coextensive with bourgeois modernity itself. The very emergence of the national idea in the early nineteenth century under colonial rule entailed the question of the problematic nature, origin, and social place of the Muslim population of the subcontinent. Even the secular nationalism associated at least since the 1930s with the figure of Jawaharlal Nehru inherited this problem, namely, how to conceive of India's civilizational "continuity" given the long period of Muslim rule and the mass presence of a population of one form or another of Islamic affiliation. Nehru ([1946] 1985: 62, 72–74) dealt with it, most notably in his *Discovery of India* (written in prison during the war and published on the threshold of independence in 1946), by speaking of the great *assimilative* power of the civilization, capable of turning successive waves of outsiders into Indians. This was above all the case, Nehru argued, with the Muslim rulers, who went on to create a distinctly Indian culture that Nehru considered his own. Remarkably for a radical nationalism, Hindutva thought does not share this view of the strength and continuity of Indian civilization. It typically views the period of Muslim rule—a colonial historiographic category—and its long aftermath as a major disruption and near destruction of Indian (that is, Hindu) civilization whose repair and healing has only just begun. The figure of the Muslim was thus already an *ambiguous* presence in the discourses and practices of secular nationalism in late colonial times. But this concept of Muslim-as-minority remained inadequate to the real structure of social relations in colonial society, failing to account, for instance, for the political power and cultural influence of the Muslim *ashrāf* caste elites. It required for its actualization in society the Partition of India—that is, the turning of two-thirds of the Muslims of India into non-Indians (Mufti 2007; Mohapatra 2014; Kidwai 2020). The partitioned (secular) Indian postcolonial state thus rested on this minoritization and ambiguity of the figure of the Muslim. This figure is now undergoing a violent recoding, each escalation of rhetoric and each perpetration of atrocities seeking to resolve the ambiguity by pushing the Muslim to the very margins of the space of citizenship and beyond, and contributing to the consolidation of Hindutva as a political and social habitus.

How are we to understand these remarkable developments centered around the idea of Hindutva within a broader conception of modernity in this colonial and postcolonial society? As recently as the late 1990s, one of the leading international scholars of Hindutva could write that

> Hindu nationalism could not consolidate any major constituency among the millions of marginalized poor and illiterate Indians, the xenophobic discourses of Hindu nationalism developed in the heart of the large and expanding middle class, which political common sense today holds to be the very prerequisite for creation of stable democracies in the postcolonial world. It was in these mainly urban environments, rich in education, associational life, and . . . "civic engagement" and "social capital," that the Hindu nationalist movement has found its most receptive audiences. (Hansen 1999: 7)

The present conjuncture presents a dramatically different vista in at least two ways. On the one hand, the middle class has dramatically expanded in the midst of the massive neoliberal transformation and globalization of the economy over the last three decades (see Brosius 2010; Varma 2014; Kaur 2020). On the other hand, it appears to be the case that what I am calling the Hindutva habitus—a whole set of orientations and dispositions concerning religious identity, the everyday experience of encounters with religious difference, notions of ritual purity that extend from the personal realm to the national, a contradictory approach to the hierarchies of caste as both essential to the Hindu social order and something to be overcome in order to achieve a standardized and universalized Hinduism, and a complex emotional mix of shame, pride, resentment, and rage toward the history of India over the last millennium, all held together by the sentiment expressed in the slogan *"Hindu khatrē mēñ hai"* ("The Hindu is in danger")—has now broken free of the constraints of urban lower middle-class spaces and spread to both vast swathes of the rural as well as urban subaltern social formation and the urban Anglophone professional and managerial bourgeoisie (see Menon and Nigam 2007). The *sañgh parīvār* movement now finds it possible, at least in some places in the country, to mobilize Dalits in campaigns of violence against Muslims (D. Menon 2006: 1–31). One of the overarching contradictions of politics in India today is that the same political forces that more than any other have pushed the globalization of the economy, and therefore massive disruption and transformation of culture and society, are in fact also the ones that embody the desire (and periodically genocidal drive) for continuity and authenticity (Patnaik 2021).

Ranajit Guha (1997: 1–99) argued some decades ago that the historical situation of the bourgeoisie in colonial and postcolonial India could be characterized as a case of "dominance without hegemony," of coercion over consent, rather unlike the situation of the bourgeoisie in the metropolis itself, whose universalist project sought to recreate all of society, to quote Marx and Engels ([1848] 1978: 477), "after its own image," converting society at large to the universalism of its values. The nationalist bourgeoisie sought to create a historical bloc in order to mobilize the peasant masses in the interest of its project to seize the state from the colonial rulers, and Gandhi was the instrument of this "moment of maneuver" (Chatterjee 1993). Its characteristic attitude toward them was therefore an "instrumental" and pedagogic one, seeking to induct them into the Indian national movement through such mythological forms of identification as Mother India (Bharat Mata), which Jawaharlal Nehru considered appropriate to the backward realm of rural life, as against the cities, which called for "stronger fare" (Mufti 2007: 27; Nehru [1946] 1985: 59). As Hansen (1999: 10) notes, the postcolonial Nehruvian elite maintained "a paternalist sense of being part of a 'civilizational mission' of modernity vis-à-vis the masses." The manner and extent of the systematic spread of the Hindutva habitus in recent years raises the question whether the *sañgh parīvār* is in the process of attempting to achieve a *hegemonic* domination through a standardized and universalized Hinduism, a dramatic transformation in the exercise of sovereign power in this postcolonial society and in the nature of religion as belief, practice, and basis of social and political identity. An orthodox-Brahminical, patriarchal, and middle-class religious complex is thus being recoded as "the eternal tradition" (*sanātana dharma*) of "the Hindus" as such, seeking to eradicate the vast diversity of religious belief and practice across class, caste, gender, sexuality, language, region, sect, and locality (see Basu 2020; Shepherd [1996] 2019). But it is crucial to understand and to emphasize that this social and political field remains open to challenge in a range of domains and through a range of modalities and languages of dissent. In parallel to the growth and transformations in Hindutva power is the emergence of a whole series of modes of *contestation* concretized in political acts big and small that seek to question and interrupt the exercise of power, up to and including the sovereign power exercised by the higher agents and institutions of the state (see Menon and Nigam 2007).

The overarching sense of inevitability attached to Hindutva on the rise has in fact been significantly interrupted nationally since 2014 on two major occasions of the staging of dissent, both centered on (but by no means limited to) the nation's capital, in each of which religious minorities, in particular Muslims and Sikhs, respectively, have played a prominent role. The more successful of these was in fact the more recent of the two, the so-called farmers' movement against proposed neoliberalization of the agricultural sector, which in all likelihood would have decimated small producers in favor of massive agricultural conglomerates. Farmers have already been under immense pressure from market forces and government-sanctioned theft of their land and have been suffering almost a pandemic of suicides. The vast sit-in by farmers, often on their tractors, at the northern reaches of the Delhi region lasted sixteen months and eventually forced a retreat by the government on the neoliberal legislation that was in dispute. A fascinating movement in its own right, it is nevertheless beyond the scope of this study. The first disruption, which I focus on here, occurred during the winter of 2019–20.

On December 11, 2019, with its new overwhelming majority in the lower house of the Indian Parliament, the BJP government passed into law the Citizenship (Amendment) Act, or CAA, which stipulates the conditions under which refugees from neighboring countries may be granted Indian citizenship, singling out non-Muslim refugees from three neighboring Muslim-majority countries for swift naturalization. The legislation immediately became highly controversial, for reasons I shall discuss shortly in some detail. We need merely recall here that it codified religion into the definition of citizenship for the first time and singled out Muslims and Islam as markers of state and individual identity. Protests against the act had started even before its passage. But after the bill was passed by both houses of Parliament and received the assent of the president, making it law of the land, protests spread into the main metropolitan centers, including, above all, the capital itself. These protests were focused first in universities, including all the main public universities in Delhi, and after brutal police suppression of the student demonstrations—especially at Jamia Millia in Delhi, widely shared live on social media—spilled out into the streets in numerous cities throughout the country. At some institutions, like Jawaharlal Nehru University (JNU), these new protests simply fed into the protest movement that had been launched against the BJP's multipronged attack on progressive public educational institutions at least since 2016, with, among other things, student leaders arrested under spurious charges of "antinational" behavior and outright sedition (see Nair 2016). It seemed pretty evident that young women played a leading role in the protest movement in the universities (see Sengupta 2020). In a number of well documented incidents, they stood up repeatedly to the violent tactics of the Delhi police and to at least one concerted attack (on JNU) by members of the student wing of the RSS-BJP, the largest party-affiliated student organization in the country.

What is now considered an iconic event of resistance to the new citizenship legislation took place on December 15, 2019, in southeastern New Delhi, when a large number of women of all generations, including now-famous matriarchs in their seventies and eighties, emerged from their homes in a working- and lower-middle-class neighborhood called Shaheen Bagh (or Falcon Park), children and grandchildren (including toddlers and infants) in tow in the midst of a Delhi winter, and took over a busy thoroughfare in a seemingly spontaneous rearticulation of the politics of assembly and occupation that has become familiar globally in recent years from such cities as New York, Athens, Madrid, and Istanbul, but drawing, closer to home, on the long-established protest form of the *dharnā* or sit-in. Among the surprising things about this development was the fact that these were primarily Muslim women of decidedly nonelite background in class and caste terms, speaking recognizably nonstandard and "rustic" forms of Hindi-Urdu, most practicing one or another form of the so-called Islamic veil, ranging from the traditional cross-communal *chādar* (shawl) to the full-body black burka and the modern international head-and-shoulders hijab. They clearly had little or no experience not only of political activism but of simply emerging visibly in public as such, let alone holding press conferences and appearing in television interviews. This sit-in lasted more than three months despite official and nonofficial pressure and succumbed finally to the imperatives of the COVID-19 pandemic. While it lasted, it generated an entire social ecology around itself and inspired dozens of similar protests in many other cities and regions, each coming to be referred to as the Shaheen Bagh of that particular city (Mustapha 2020). The "grannies of Shaheen Bagh"—the vernacular term for *grannies* is *dādīs*, or paternal grandmothers—has now entered the vernacular as the name of a new and (for many) baffling political actor at the center of the mass protests. The wider protest movement led in January 2020 to a nationwide general strike that has been billed as the largest in world history, involving a quarter of a billion people. One of the remarkable things about this movement is the way in which the women of Shaheen Bagh, despite their relatively marginal social backgrounds, seemed to have understood that the proposed citizenship policy marked a dramatic shift in the exercise of sovereign power in this constitutional republic that represented a serious danger not only to themselves but in fact to the country as a whole. Their own remarkable framing of their protest as a defense of the Constitution must be understood in this context.

The Shaheen Bagh protest itself, and others like it in Delhi and numerous other cities, spontaneously drew masses of supporters of a range of religious, caste, class, age, and ethnic backgrounds. A sort of spontaneous organization quickly emerged. One group of young people created a protective cordon around the protest site, especially at peak hours; another handled the media rush, and so on. The daily roster of events included political speeches, poetry recitals, music and dance performances, lectures on history and politics by scholars and academics, scripture readings and prayer sessions of the different faiths side by side, and communal meals prepared in a makeshift kitchen established spontaneously in the sacred Sikh tradition of providing *lañgar* or free communal meals to strangers. On certain days, like New Year's Eve and India's Republic Day, the crowds at Shaheen Bagh reportedly approached a hundred thousand (Chauhan 2020).

The makeshift stage, festooned with hand-painted posters, the national flag, and portraits of such icons of the anticolonial freedom movement as Mahatma Gandhi, Bhagat Singh, and B. R. Ambedkar, the lead author of India's Constitution and leader of the Dalit rights movement, became, in the words of the artist and critic Shuddhabrata Sengupta, "a stage for an autonomous, spontaneous, totally self-organized, leaderless rehearsal of a new vision for citizenship" (Sengupta 2020). The foregrounding of Ambedkar in particular is not without significance. There is, of course, Ambedkar's leading authorial connection to the Constitution of India. But Ambedkar-Dalit-Constitution is a dense text rich with meaning when it is invoked in the midst of *this* protest movement, led by *this* group of women— no other name of that period continues to be so actively linked in the present moment to a political project of mass emancipation. The density of this "text" appears to have been immediately recognized by Chandrashekhar Azad Ravan, the young Dalit leader, a lawyer and head of the activist group Bhim Army, whose personal style—including his clothes, the grooming of his facial hair, the aviator sunglasses he sports, and even the motorcycle he typically rides—is seen as provocative behavior for a supposed untouchable within the codes of the violent caste hierarchy of the semirural area of western Uttar Pradesh where he was born and raised and continues to be based. Using a common Hindi-Urdu word meaning "freedom" or "liberation" that is charged and controversial in contemporary politics due to its connection to the Kashmiri struggle against the repression of the Indian army, one observer has memorably referred to the politics of his style as "azadi with swag" (Kabir 2019). He was drawn irresistibly to Shaheen Bagh and the wider anti-CAA movement, and his remarkable emergence, despite a police injunction, on the steps of Delhi's historic Jama Masjid, holding aloft a copy of Ambedkar's Constitution, in the midst of a huge throng (presumably of Muslim worshipers) protecting him from police arrest, is one of the iconic images of the movement. What this explicit encounter with this particular strand in the politics of Dalit rights makes clear is that Shaheen Bagh broke free from the pregiven script of "Muslim protest"—a script that seems to have been partially restored in the more recent Rama Navami and anti-Prophet controversies. The maintenance of this script, with its inherent codes of legibility of the protestors as lawbreakers, as alien threat to the social order, and as "antinational elements" in general, is of course a significant interest of the *sangh parīvār*, at the core of its ability to expand and mobilize its base. Instead of reaffirming the predetermined and already-given margins of the nation-space—the identity politics defined by these supposedly distinct zones marked as "Muslim" or "Dalit," for instance—Shaheen Bagh represents a revisioning of citizenship and nation from the perspective of an actively imagined and reconstructed "undercommons" of national life, to borrow an evocative formulation from a geopolitically different context—acts of social and political imagination made possible, paradoxically (but, of course, not surprisingly), by the more and more egregious exercise of Hindutva power itself (see Harney and Moton 2013).

The broader anti-CAA movement was thus sparked by a collective political action undertaken by a group of urban "subaltern" women who seemed, on the one hand, unapologetic and unselfconscious about their social and religious background and, on the other, actively alert to *the commonality of different forms of marginality* under the ruling dispensation. It is thus another index of Shaheen Bagh's departure from the "Muslim protest" script, to which Hindutva power would like to reduce it, that it bypassed entirely the traditional so-called leadership of the Muslim community as a whole—conservative and patriarchal clerics and social and political elites who are almost all men and belong to the *ashrāf* caste elites of the Muslim population. In the script, the collective marked as "Muslim women" is typically figured as the passive object in a tussle between this upper-caste religious patriarchy and the supposedly secular state. Much like the BJP government and its henchmen, this supposed religious leadership was left in the discomfiting position of passive observers as the *dādīs* of Shaheen Bagh took center stage.

Two key earlier moments in which this script has been played out on the national stage deserve to be recalled here. The first is the so-called Shah Bano controversy in the 1980s in which the Congress-led national government succumbed to the demand of the conservative Muslim leadership that it find a legislative workaround against a Supreme Court ruling in favor of a Muslim divorcée who had filed a suit demanding "maintenance" from her former husband beyond the provisions of the so-called Muslim Personal Law, a body of patriarchal family law inherited from colonial jurisprudence. This notorious controversy is considered a key moment in the history of majority-minority relations in India, in the history of the Hindu nationalist movement, and in the history of feminism and its relationship to the Congress and the state (see Pathak and Rajan 1989). The second instance is a more recent but related one, the so-called Triple Talaq ("triple divorce") controversy, in which the Modi government passed a law banning a Muslim mode of divorce that privileges the prerogatives of the husband to the detriment of the wife. Most feminists and various sectors of the Left more broadly support the creation of a Uniform Civil Code, as it is called, to replace the religion-specific codes of family law that are presently the norm. What I am drawing attention to here, however, is the terms in which the controversy played out: the "secular" state, at the behest of a Hindu nationalist party in power, plays the protector of Muslim women from the depredations of Muslim patriarchy. In one sense, Shaheen Bagh, which began a few months after the BJP's Triple Talaq gambit, represents the rebuke, by one group of Muslim women, of the essentialized identity and fake protection offered to them by Hindutva power.

Aside from the *social ecology* consisting of forms of interaction across class, caste, and religion, social and political commentary and discussion, and experimentation with the forms of leadership and community, the protests at Shaheen Bagh and elsewhere also generated what we might call an *arts ecology*, the insertion of the various arts into this social and political event. Poetry, music, performance, theater, and visual arts all had a prominent presence in them. I wish to draw attention in particular to the prominent role of poetry in the demonstrations nationwide, which is hardly unique to this particular moment in the history of protest movements in the subcontinent and continues a long tradition of poetry's involvement in political protest. From anonymously and collectively authored slogans that take poemic form—like the famous refrain "Jāmiā kī larkīyōñ nē rāstā dikhāyā hai" ("The girls of Jamia have shown the way")—to the recitation or singing of well-known political poems, about which more below, and the sensational emergence of new and young poets, like Varun Grover and Aamir Aziz, these cadences and rhythms have provided the "prosody of the revolt," to borrow Elliot Cola's (2011) felicitous phrase, coined with respect to the practices of Tahrir Square and the Arab Spring uprisings. But a curious thing about these demonstrations in India, almost every single one of them at least in the northern and central "Hindi belt," is that the three poems most often sung or recited are in Urdu, a language often considered to be endangered in India due to its association with the Muslim minority, accused by right-wing nationalists of being antinational by nature. Adding a further complexity, two of these three poems are written by Pakistani poets, namely, Faiz Ahmed Faiz (1911–84) and Habib Jalib (1928–93). The third is by Ram Prasad Bismil (1897–1927), who was tried and executed by the colonial state on charges of sedition twenty years before India's independence from colonial rule and the creation of Pakistan. One poem by Faiz in particular, which uses a high Islamic and Quranic vocabulary and images, has become indelibly associated with the broader prodemocracy movement in India and its large and small mobilizations against the authoritarian politics and behavior of the government and the broader right-wing nationalist sphere. In the midst of the Shaheen Bagh protests, its spread and spontaneous popularity became subject to sustained attacks from the *sañgh parīvār* and the broader Hindutva world. Faiz, well known for his persistent critique of religious orthodoxy and of the Partition of the subcontinent on religious lines, was accused bizarrely of being anti-Hindu. So unconvincing and farcical is this claim that it was apparent that even many of those mouthing it were themselves unconvinced and merely going through the motions. I shall presently turn to Faiz and his role in the poetics of protest in contemporary India in some detail.

How are we to understand the new citizenship politics of the Modi government, embodied in and symbolized by the CAA? What is its place and role in the physiology of Hindutva power? What is the exact significance of the protests nationwide against the CAA? And, finally, why this connection to Muslims and Muslim women, in particular? On the surface, the purpose of the act appears to be a humanitarian one, as it formalizes in law the granting of Indian citizenship to refugees having fled religious persecution from three neighboring countries before a certain cutoff point in time, and the BJP and its allies instrumentalize this surface humanitarian tone in their responses to critics of the law. However, as already noted, the countries in question all happen to be Muslim-majority ones—Pakistan, Bangladesh, and Afghanistan—and the minorities to be protected are specified by their religion as Hindus, Sikhs, Buddhists, Parsis, Christians, and Jains, in other words, followers of all the major religions of the region with the exception of Islam. Aside from the patent absurdity of the claim made repeatedly by officials from home minister Shah down that no self-professed group of Muslims in a Muslim-majority country could be considered an oppressed minority—we need only think of Ahmedis, Shia Hazaras, and Shias in general in Pakistan—the law also leaves out some of the largest producers of refugees in the region, which happen not to be Muslim-majority countries, such as Myanmar, Sri Lanka, and the People's Republic of China. Both these suggestions, either implicit in the law or explicitly mobilized by its defenders, like the home minister, are evidently counterfactual, but the thing to note here is that the wording of the act singles out Muslims in a number of ways, both symbolic and material and concrete. In other words, the CAA introduces a religious element into the definition of citizenship itself, in the admittedly limited domain of the naturalization of refugee populations, and thus is at least problematic from the perspective of the vaunted secularism of the Indian Constitution, its "equality" clauses (numbers 14 and 15, for example) in particular (see Wire 2020).

But the full significance of the provisions of this new law begin to come into view in conjunction with another policy measure, the National Register of Citizens (NRC), distinct from the census and required by a law passed by a previous BJP-led government almost two decades earlier, whose implementation was finally announced by the BJP government in the midst of the national debate about the submission of the CAA draft bill to Parliament. Simplifying the actual situation a little bit for the sake of our collective sanity—because the legal and bureaucratic reality is so grotesquely complicated, as is possible only in a former British colony—the NRC would require all self-described citizens to prove their citizenship by producing specific types of documents, but not including the voter ID card, the biometric national ID card, nor even the passport, and including in many instances documents concerning parents and even grandparents. Given the realities of Indian bureaucracy, and given the reality of at best spotty documentation of births, deaths, and other major and minor life events in between those two extremes in any of the countries of the subcontinent, this is an unprecedented scenario that will impact every single one of India's nearly 1.4 billion citizens, in effect suspending their citizenship and placing the burden of proof for regaining it entirely on individuals and families.

The final twist, however, is provided by the language of the CAA: among all those rendered aliens in India by the NRC, those who are determined by the state to conform to the approved religious categories of the CAA—Bangladeshi Hindus or Pakistani Christians, for instance—could be brought back into the citizenship fold through naturalization as stateless aliens, but Muslims who failed the NRC test of Indianness could be rendered not only noncitizens but *nonnaturalizable* according to the categories established by the new law. Internment camps for "illegal immigrants" are already in operation in the state of Assam, the only state where the NRC has been implemented, and more are reportedly under construction in other states in anticipation of its nationwide implementation. It's been argued that millions, possibly tens of millions, of Muslims could thus be removed from the citizens' registry and therefore from the voter rolls. In Assam, it is reported, close to two million individuals have been declared to not be Indian citizens (Kidwai 2020).[2] As of mid-2022, given the strength of the nationwide dissent—the movement triggered as well as symbolized by the *dādīs* of Shaheen Bagh—the CAA-NRC combination has not yet been implemented nationally.

This entire scenario calls immediately to mind the conceptual framework that Hannah Arendt began to develop during the World War II years for understanding the upheavals in European politics in the aftermath of the previous war: the dramatic transformation of political practices, institutions, ideas, concepts, and categories in the disappearance of a number of multinational empires in Eastern and Central Europe and the establishment in their stead of a system of nation-states. Arendt speaks of the stateless (as opposed to the national citizen) as "the most symptomatic group in contemporary politics," embodying in their very political, legal, and social condition the larger crisis of the modern system of states, the inherently split and unstable nature of the nation-state as a form, a hyphenated articulation of two vastly different political logics—that of nation, people, ethnos, language, culture, and the mythos of common origins, on the one hand, and that of state, citizenship, and equality before the law, on the other. In the rise of Nazism to power, Arendt ([1951] 1979: 277, 275) argued, nation had over-

2. In another twist, in that state the opposition to the CAA is driven by motives more or less opposite to those that have animated Shaheen Bagh and other protests inspired by it: Assamese nationalists have long been opposed to the presence among them of ethnic Bengalis, whether Hindu or Muslim, whom they would like to see deported to Bangladesh, something that couldn't be done unless they were declared to be non-Indian aliens.

powered and conquered state. Whether the ongoing degradation of democracy in India represents a similar historical transition is one of the most challenging questions of our times, and I shall turn shortly to this debate. At the very least, however, we might say that under the guise of a humanitarian law offering ease of acquiring citizenship to (some) asylum seekers from (some) neighboring countries, India is poised, given the demographic scale, to become potentially one of the larger producers of stateless refugees in the region and possibly the world.

Degradation of the rights of the citizen has been formally encoded in the CAA-NRC combine, but this devaluation has been at work repeatedly in a series of national policies that have had devastating consequences for the citizenry. We may think here of such political acts as the so-called demonetization in 2016 that forced tens of millions of Indians to line up for hours and days at banks to exchange the old currency for the new one; or the brutal COVID lockdown declared with four hours' notice after the emergence of the Delta variant, which threw millions of newly unemployed and homeless migrant workers out on the streets and highways, forced to make their way back to their home villages and towns, often hundreds of miles away, on foot, receiving beatings from the police along the way. In the media, the use of the word *migrant* facilitated their refashioning as a threatening outsider presence for the middle-class residents of the cities and towns in which they suddenly found themselves to be aliens. The scale of the catastrophe in this instance may be judged by the fact that it is widely thought to be the largest mass movement of people in the subcontinent since the Partition and transfer of populations in 1947. As a range of commentators, such as Pratap Bhanu Mehta, Siddharth Varadarajan, and Apoorvanand, have recently noted, while no emergency has been formally declared, the government routinely uses emergency-like powers to intimidate its critics and stifle dissent. Apoorvanand echoed a widespread sentiment when he observed that the BJP's overall approach to governance appears to be to create a constant state of "anarchy" (*arājiktā*) in the country (Wire 2022).

How are we to understand this aspect of the life of Hindutva power in contemporary India? The apparent intention to unleash chaos on the citizenry from time to time is itself an authoritarian one. To be a bit more precise, we can perhaps say that some of the BJP's most consequential policies in recent years embody an *authoritarian definition of the sovereign*, capable of bypassing key norms and institutions of liberal democracy without abrogating (for now) the constitution as such. It is this recurring bypassing of the normative that produces the perception of anarchy. In the case of CAA-NRC, this authoritarianism reaches an apogee of sorts. A government elected by its citizens—or, to be more precise, by about 37 percent of those who cast their votes and a mere quarter of all registered voters—once elected, suspends their citizenship, putting the entire citizenry in abeyance, as a step toward its selective remaking and reestablishment. This appears to be the remarkable intention inherent to this multifaceted policy. It reimagines the citizen as a pliant subject of sovereign power that owes its very membership in the political community to the sovereign.

The most well-known authoritarian definition of the sovereign is of course the one offered in the 1920s by Carl Schmitt ([1922] 2005: 5) in his book *Political Theology*, eleven years before Schmitt emerged as the leading jurist and political theorist affiliated with the National Socialist German Workers' Party after its rise to power: "Sovereign is he who decides on the exception [*Ausnahmezustand*]." A brief analysis of Schmitt's framework is not out of place here for our goal of throwing light on the modalities of Hindutva power. As a decisionist in political and legal theory, Schmitt views the sovereign decision as one unhampered by "the checks and balances" of "a liberal constitution" (7). For Schmitt, therefore, "all tendencies of modern constitutional development point toward eliminating the sovereign in this sense" (7). Against these tendencies in political theory and practice, he argues for the priority of the sovereign with respect to the law. But the constitutional procedures and prescriptions for the application of abstract rules to concrete situations require, Schmitt argues, a "homogeneous" social medium for their operation and fail in moments of chaos or true emergency—"a case of extreme peril, a danger to the existence of the state, and the like" (13, 6). A state of emergency is thus viewed as a condition of social *heterogeneity*, making necessary the linkage between the sovereign decision and the state of exception. For Schmitt the sovereign is thus the individual, collective, or institution (though always preferably the first) that decides both when such a state of emergency exists and what to do about it, that is, how to re-create a legal order when the existing one is threatened with chaos and destruction. But it becomes clear from the very beginning that for Schmitt, "sovereign" is also a limit or "borderline" concept (*Grenzbegriff*) of the prior decision that undergirds *any* juridical or constitutional order, however normative or rule-bound it might claim to be (5). In other words, sovereign power is in its essence *constituent* power, and the (Schmittian) study of sovereignty is thus the study of "the locus and nature of the agency that constitutes a political system" (Strong 1985: xi).

Political Theology contains a theory of sovereignty as such, not of dictatorship, let alone of the distinctly fascist form of authority. Schmitt's ([1921] 2014) interest in dictatorship itself is a fairly narrow one having to do with constitutional provisions for the granting of (temporary) dictatorial authority, more specifically in the Weimar constitution. Nevertheless, the authoritarian nature of his conception of the sovereign obliges us to ask what relation sovereignty in this sense has to dictatorship and, ultimately, to fascism itself. We may begin to formulate an answer to these questions by noting that for Schmitt, the sovereign and dictator were typically distinct in history, in both Rome and early modern absolutism, for instance. In fact, the dictator exercises his extra-legal power, or rather, is constituted as ("commissarial") dictator, under the authority of the sovereign. It is the mass event of revolutionary politics in the late eighteenth and early nineteenth centuries—once the sovereign is redefined and reorganized as the body of the citizenry, that is, once it is reconstituted as the popular sovereign as the characteristic form of legitimate authority in modernity—that leads to the historical fusion of sovereign and dictator. In critiquing the nineteenth-century Catholic reactionaries who rejected outright a whole range of consequences that followed from Enlightenment philosophy and revolutionary politics in the eighteenth century, Schmitt concedes that monarchy can no longer be the basis of legitimation of a political order. But his definition of the sovereign is in part an attempt to vitiate, to hollow out from the inside, the very notion of popular sovereignty by making the sovereign decision on the exception prior to the democratic constitutional order. According to Schmitt, liberal constitutional democracies try to disperse and erase the overt signs of sovereign power, making the sovereign and the sovereign decision illegible to the citizenry. But since for Schmitt the constituent power of "the people" under conditions of popular sovereignty is in reality prior to any legal or constitutional order, this raises at once the question of the constitution of the people as such. This is what makes necessary Schmitt's ([1927] 1996: 26) famous "criterion" for a definition of "the political": "The specific political distinction to which political actions and motives can be reduced is that between friend and enemy." The making of this distinction is *constitutive* of the community and way of life that is to be protected from the "enemy"—"friend" and "enemy" are mutually constituted in the very process of being distinguished from each other. The "popular" sovereign dictator, far from simply expressing or restating the "will of the people," *creates* the "homogeneous" social and cultural space that makes the populace, and therefore the popular will, possible. Taken together, these writings of Schmitt's from his pre-Nazi era already indicate the way in which social engineering, the fabrication of the populace, is imbricated with the exercise of sovereign power as he conceives of it, and the latter depends upon it for its very functioning.

Whatever reservations Schmitt may have had about the Nazis and their brand of politics as they gradually increased their political power in the late Weimar Republic, as one of the parties that were hostile to the republic but given, he feared, free rein by its constitution to operate and engage in political competition, once they came to power, his views shifted dramatically. In the immediate aftermath of the Reichstag fire four weeks after his becoming chancellor, Hitler (and Hermann Goering, then president of the Reichstag), blaming the Communists and the Comintern for the arson, convinced von Hindenburg to issue a decree—under the same Article 48, section 2 of the Weimar constitution that had been Schmitt's main object of analysis in the book on dictatorship a decade earlier—suspending most civil rights. The decree explicitly mentioned the supposed imminent threat of Communist subversion. Then, nearly four weeks later, in a truncated Parliament devoid of Communist and even some Social Democrat deputies, all of whom had been arrested, the Nazis and their parliamentary allies passed the so-called Enabling Act, giving the chancellor and his cabinet the right to rule by decree. Throughout its existence, the Third Reich was based on this act, which had to be renewed on two subsequent occasions (see Rabinbach and Gilman 2013: 47–48, 52–53). In the midst of these developments in 1933, Schmitt came to see in Hitler what he thought Germany desperately needed: a politician who could without ambiguity "decide on the exception." He had spent the years of the Weimar Republic arguing for a strengthened authoritarian presidency that could introduce the friend-enemy distinction into politics and prohibit the participation of anti-republican parties. In the events of early 1933, he now saw the Nazis outstripping all he had dared to hope for within the constraints of the Weimar constitution. Almost immediately he threw in his lot with them, and quickly emerged as the leading jurist associated with the party (Mehring 2014).

A certain type of Schmitt apologia has it that his personal political opinions and actions have nothing to do with, and can tell us nothing about, his work as political and legal thinker. This is the position associated, for instance, with the editors of the journal *Telos*, which did more than possibly any other group or institution to introduce Schmitt for the first time to the Anglophone world. This is a spurious and ultimately nonsensical claim, because, of course, his theoretical work concerns precisely the kinds of processes at stake in the political and constitutional developments he lived through and took positions on, developments to the understanding of which he mobilized his theoretical vocabulary. The two are inseparable from each other. Translating these political positions of Schmitt's into the terms of his conceptual system, we might say that Schmitt's theorized and imagined sovereign is already involved in the exercise of what we would normally take to be dictatorial power, and the latter contains within itself the scaffolding for the fully fascist form of authority. His entire conceptual framework accommodates the possibility that the sovereign may *create* the concrete emergency (*Notfall*) that appears to bring about (more abstractly speaking) a state of exception (*Ausnahmezustand*) that is then "recognized" and "decided on" by the sovereign. Schmitt's political actions from 1933 on make clear that the ultimate motivation of the theoretical apparatus built in the 1920s was to explain what it would take to, first, eliminate the Left from politics entirely and, more broadly, refashion society as a whole as a "homogeneous medium."

In one of the very earliest writings of his Nazi period, Schmitt claimed that the Nazi conception of the "tripartite organization" of the social and political "totality" (*Einheit*) into state, movement, and *Volk* was restoring to the German nation "the great traditions of German thinking about the state as founded by Hegel," which "had been displaced from the consciousness of the German *Volk* in the second half of the nineteenth century under the influence of liberal and alien thinkers and writers" (Rabinbach and Gilman 2013: 59; for the original German, see Schmitt 1933: 13). In another, he commended the Führer for clearly understanding the "false neutrality" and "inner contradictions of the Weimar system, which destroyed itself with this legal neutrality and turned itself over to its enemies" (Rabinbach and Gilman 2013: 63). The significance of Schmitt for a project like the present one, concerned with a contemporary case of the slide from a distinct type of liberal democracy to right-wing authoritarianism, is that his work lays out a frank and unapologetic case for what it sees as the need for such a transition from a liberal-constitutional dispensation to an authoritarian one as well as a demonstration of how the incompleteness and remaining hesitations of the latter can be overcome in a fully fascistic order.[3] In other words, Schmitt is useful and important for us *because*, not despite the fact that, he was, for a certain period in his life, from 1933 to the destruction of the Third Reich in 1945, formally speaking a Nazi. On the other hand, the use I have made of Schmitt here represents a *worldly* reading of his work against the ways

3. I am grateful to Paul Bové for a conversation in which we discussed this question.

in which concepts like state of exception have been treated as free-floating theoretical concepts that do not require an excavation of the historical density of their elaboration and dissemination.

There is no doubt that after eight years of Modi's tenure as prime minister, the political culture of India has undergone significant transformations toward authoritarian and violent forms of political relations and interactions. The historian Jairus Banaji (2016a: x) has gone so far as to argue that "the public culture of democracy is so radically hollowed out and degraded that in the end it yields a mere mask, a form of legitimation, for a regime immersed in criminality." But in what way precisely does the concept of *fascism*, which comes to us from the 1920s and 1930s in Europe, come into play in our assessment of the Indian present? It is now a routinely used description of Hindutva politics in public debates in India—*fāsīvād* is the word in at least the north Indian languages. And for a whole range of deeply learned and perceptive commentators, including Nivedita Menon, Prabhat Patnaik, Dilip Simeon, Aditya Nigam, Aijaz Ahmad, Sumit Sarkar, and Banaji, the fascism of the *sangh parīvār* is not (or not anymore) a debatable question.

Let us consider this question in some detail. First of all, to begin as it were at the top, there is clearly a cult of personality surrounding the prime minister, tinged with a definite sense of menace toward nonbelievers and dissenters, that is immediately familiar to students of fascism from such cases as Mussolini as Duce or Hitler as Führer. Like his European forebears, the Narendra Modi of this cult of personality is made up of sometimes contradictory elements. It emphasizes his political as well as personal prowess, an asceticism as well as a warrior ethos: he is a self-described fakir and yogi, on the one hand, and in possession of a *chhattīs inch kī chhātī* (a fifty-six-inch chest), on the other. The list of those who have, with varying degrees of seriousness, accused Modi of being a Führer extends from opposition leader and Nehru family scion Rahul Gandhi and former prime minister of Pakistan and one-time cricket star Imran Khan to Pink Floyd cofounder Roger Waters and actor John Cusack! However, the widely expressed fear that the BJP's endgame is to amend the Constitution to both declare a Hindu Rashtra and install Modi in an authoritarian presidency is real and palpable, and its realization would be in line with the line of development of Hindutva in power since 2014.

Second, Hindutva ideology has circulated a radical right-wing nationalism—a sine qua non of fascist movements—for which the nation is a disfigured and mutilated entity whose restoration to its ancient glory has only just begun and is resisted at every step by its internal and external enemies. In this regard, the German nationalism of grievance that morphed into Nazism is far outshone by Hindutva: the former displayed a narcissism of recent injury—the crushing terms of the post–Great War Versailles settlement—while the latter extends it over a millennium. The spread and inculcation of the Hindutva habitus has made this culture of grievance part of the political instincts of vast swathes of the social spectrum. Third, the vast and organized cadres of the *sañgh parīvār* engage in what Arthur Rosenberg, in his early analysis of Nazism as a mass movement, referred to as the "stormtrooper tactic": taking extra-legal action against perceived enemies that is either ignored entirely by the legal system or results in perfunctory and pro forma punishment (Banaji 2016b: 262). These cadres can be mobilized seemingly at moment's notice, in small or large numbers, to threaten or actively punish those deemed to be recalcitrant elements in open defiance of this or that prescription of Hindutva power. Finally, the historical transformation of the figure of the Muslim from secular nationalism to Hindutva parallels in some ways fairly closely the reinscription of the Jew from the ambiguous insider-outsider figure in post-Enlightenment liberal culture to the implacable enemy and threat in fascism. In light of all these developments over the last several decades, it is a measured judgment to say that in all these ways, India appears to be approaching the edge of a chasm, and a leap or tumble into this abyss will likely change things irrevocably and forever.

Georgio Agamben (2005: 84–85) has argued that the *Führerprinzip* of the original and personal power of a unique leader that emerged in Europe in the early twentieth century combined *charismatic* authority (in Max Weber's sense) with *auctoritas*, as conceived in and derived from the Roman tradition. But Agamben does not note that for Weber ([1922] 1978: 246–50), "charisma" is a sort of liminal condition, recurringly subject to "routinization," a return to the ordinary and unexceptional, whereas fascism in power seems to attempt to permanently defer this routinization of the leader's authority and to revive and repeat its originary moment of the foundation of an original (that is, radically personalized) form of authority. Consequently, much of fascist politics may be comprehensible as an open-ended series of attempts at the deferral of the routinization of the charismatic authority of the leader—hence the permanent sense of crisis that typically surrounds fascism in power, and hence the endless series of escalations that seem only to lead to catastrophe. The recurring anarchy (*arājiktā*) characteristic of Modi's rule is of this order, each episode arising out of what can only be called the *infliction* of major policy instruments on the citizenry, which leave the latter scrambling to survive in social (and even simply physical) terms. The policies—demonetization, the CAA, the farm laws, and the recent military recruitment "reforms"—are formulated typically without much (or no) debate in Parliament, and entirely without extended public discussion. While each purports to be merely *responding* to one emergency or another, in reality it *brings about* conditions of crisis and emergency. It is almost as if democratic good governance would be destructive of Modi's charismatic authority, the instrument of its routinization.

The development of fascist movements in and out of power has taken different forms in each society and polity where it has occurred. In the content and the genealogy of its ideas, in its nature as an organized movement, in its ability to inculcate more and more sectors of society into its sense of an elect Hindu nation, and in its creeping subversion of different aspects of the democratic state, Hindutva presents a distinct case and variation in the global history of fascist movements in power. But it also appears to be the case that authoritarian Hindutva power may be objectively constrained, at least for the moment, from evolving into a recognizably and classically fascist state and societal dispensation by the unmistakable (if considerably reduced) strength of democratic political culture in the country and its tradition of organized dissent. Even the country's participation in the neoliberal economic world order and its geopolitical system of alliances might act as an objective constraint to some extent. While the world powers with which it is partnered, especially the United States and the European Union, may be indifferent to, or even tacitly support, authoritarian management of restless populations by their allies, they might have more difficulty ignoring, for instance, acts of mass genocide. The BJP leadership in power and even the leaders of the RSS have so far not heeded the call of many of their followers for an outright dictatorial dispensation, especially with respect to Muslims, other minorities, and what they deride as *adharmī* (that is, "unrighteous" or "heretical") Hindus. Society itself still does not conform entirely to the Hindu nationalist idea of India. For legions of the foot soldiers of the *sañgh parīvār*, this situation of unprecedented (but necessarily not total) power is experienced as a form of "suffocation" (*ghutan*), as one BJP leader recently put it (DO Politics 2022). Hindutva in power displays many of these features of what is sometimes spoken of as the "fascist minimum," but it has still not quite reached the level of the "fascist maximum," a movement radicalized in this manner that is in totalitarian possession of society and state (Paxton 2005: 206). However, the popular pressures produced by the failure of the state to create an economy that responds adequately to the needs of India's huge population, and especially the youth facing rising underemployment and unemployment—in other words, the very pressures produced by the imbalances of participation in the neoliberal global economy—lead in the direction of the "maximization" of authoritarianism in a fascist direction, the mobilization of the youth for actions against perceived enemies rather than economic redistribution and social justice.

This possible passage to the maximum is in many ways what the protest movement and the scene of contestation of the CAA-NRC combination are about. Coming back to the politics of citizenship embodied in the latter in light of the foregoing discussion of sovereign power and sovereign decision, authoritarianism, and the nature and structure of fascist authority, we might now say that *this* political gambit is meant to restructure the exercise of sovereign power by first gathering sovereignty at the very top of the power structure of the ruling party and its parent organization, the RSS. Discrete functions of this centralized sovereign power are then redistributed to critical sites within state and society, such as local "law and order" institutions—police, magistrates, judges—and the party's and its affiliates' various street-level cadres, in order to create an extra-constitutional network for the exercise of sovereign power in which state and nonstate institutions and personnel begin to lose their distinctness. This transformation has already been underway at rapid pace since the BJP's return to power in 2014. Here too there is a convergence with the authoritarian concept of politics that comes to us via Schmitt: the aim of the CAA-NRC policy appears to be to establish the social contours of "enmity" and "friendship" in the very institution of citizenship and, we might say, to bring into being a *wholesale state of exception*, redefining the structure of the sovereign exercise of power in order *to found a new polity*—referred to in the political vernacular of Hindutva as Hindu Rashtra. Paraphrasing Brecht ([1953] 2003) from another context a long time ago and a long distance away, the BJP's manifest intention appears to be "to dissolve the people / and electing another."

This fantasy of totalized constitutive power was unexpectedly interrupted by the actions of a new and most unlikely actor in the mobilizations of late 2019 and early 2020. In fact, this event marked the emergence of *a new political subject*, "the *dādīs* of Shaheen Bagh," producing a politics of citizenship and constitutionality from the imperiled margins of the nation-space—a quintessentially democratic event, in Jacques Rancière's ([2000] 2013) sense of that phrase, in which those who are "uncounted," who cannot be heard or seen, penetrate the order of power in the very process of being constituted as subject, transforming the "aesthetic" coordinates of the community, the communal "distribution of the *sensible*." Modi's knowing remark to a rally of his followers during the Shaheen Bagh protests that the identity of the malcontents could be determined by their clothing is not simply a dog whistle to his base. It also reveals a deep anxiety about a new mode of subjectivization of the demos. Modi and his henchmen, clearly spooked by these developments, sought to recode this subjectivized form of the demos as in reality its primordial enemy—the Muslim, the Pakistani state, Islam itself. But this attempt to neutralize this subject qua subject via long established codes of visibility and legibility of the Muslim missed its mark and failed to eliminate the possibility of the claim to political subjectivity and citizenship on the part of the protestors.

The Shaheen Bagh protests were a unique event, despite their final outcome, for they momentarily shattered the fear of breaching the semiotic or aesthetic order of power in BJP-ruled India—the fear that had been, in the then five years of its rule, a modality of the functioning of the order itself. New types of speech act became possible immediately in the aftermath of the protests, drawing on longstanding speech practices and speech genres that, for instance, involve ridicule, satire, and shaming, which had been suspended and suppressed in the order of power inaugurated with the national rise of Modi and his enforcer, Amit Shah. To use just one small anecdotal example, whereas just a few months earlier, stand-up comics would routinely confess on stage to being afraid of making even mild jokes about the duo, in the midst of the protests the two came to be openly mocked in public as Ranga and Billa, the nicknames of two notorious gangsters convicted and executed for the kidnapping, (possible) rape, and murder of two teenaged siblings in Delhi in the 1980s. Laughter diminishes the authority of the one being laughed at, as Dimitris Vardoulakis (2020) has reminded us recently. And it is also a strategy of controlling one's own fear instead of letting one's actions be controlled by it. As Hindutva in power extends and expands its repressive apparatus, this managing of fear presents itself as an endless and recurring task.

By way of a final elaboration, however, I turn to a very different aesthetics and poetics of dissent in the face of sovereign power than that of mockery and laughter, considering instead a poem in Urdu to whose appearance in the protests, and the firestorm of dissensus in which it is now enmeshed in India, I have already drawn attention. The poet in question is

Faiz Ahmed Faiz, and the poem is known popularly as "Ham dēkhēñgē" ("We Shall See"). It is not an exaggeration to say that it has become more or less synonymous with prodemocracy and anti-fascist protests in India, drawing often deranged responses from Hindutva forces. In order to understand this complex literary, political, and social phenomenon, we need to consider certain aspects of the history of Urdu literature and its entanglement in the history of the Muslim question in colonial and postcolonial India. Faiz is the towering presence in Urdu poetry in the second half of the twentieth century. Over a few decades starting in the late 1930s, Faiz and his generation of poets largely refashioned the place and role of poetry in society, liberating it from the mannered and socially isolated existence of the elite (and "feudal") *ashrāf* social castes of north India, a language and a poetic tradition that had formerly been associated with a declining Mughal Empire and the rise of British rule in India (Lelyveld 1978). These remarkable individuals were mostly associated with the All-India (and later, Pakistan) Progressive Writers Association, which was founded in the mid-1930s in London by young Indian writers and conceived from the start as an umbrella organization of writers associated with the anticolonial cause, but retained at its core a group of revolutionary writers linked to the Communist Party of India (see Coppola 2017). Faiz has long been considered its most significant poet, although he was never formally associated with the party. Perhaps the greatest aesthetic accomplishment of Faiz and his contemporaries was opening up poetic expression to the social field and its questions while also remaining strictly attached to the subjective demands of the Urdu poetic tradition and its characteristic lyric forms, above all the ghazal.

A fuller analysis of the historical nature of Urdu as an Indian and South Asian literary language is of course beyond the scope of this essay, and I have undertaken such a discussion in *Enlightenment in the Colony: The Jewish Question and the Crisis of Postcolonial Culture* (Mufti 2007). But it bears repeating here that, since the rise of nationalism in the subcontinent, Urdu has appeared, on the one hand, to be quintessentially a literature of *exile*, by which I mean a corpus of writing practices whose most consistent effect is the displacement of any stable matrix of relations between place, language, and people. In this respect, it has excluded that possibility of "bardic nationalism" (Trumpener 1997), a concept that fits rather well with developments in many Indian literary traditions, including Hindi, but to which the history of Urdu poetics seems not to conform. Throughout its modern history, that is, ever since the bifurcation of the space of vernacular literary practices in North India in the early nineteenth century into distinct

"Hindi" and "Urdu" practices and traditions, it seems never to have managed to generate the *völkisch* mood and atmosphere that has facilitated the restructuration of cultures of writing into the national institution of literature in numerous societies across the world. This is an orientation of Urdu literariness that has somehow survived nationalization of the language itself in Pakistan after the Partition, and even since the liberation of Bangladesh in 1971. In its very constitutive practices, therefore, prior to any polemical or programmatic intent, Urdu literary culture in the post-Partition era calls into question the cultural categories and cultural effects of the nation-state system in the subcontinent, in whose institution through the Partition of British India this very question of Urdu and its relationship to Hindi had, of course, played a significant role.

As I have argued at some length in *Enlightenment in the Colony*, Faiz's verse exploits fully this potential inherent to Urdu literariness. The central drama of his poetry is the dialectic of a collective selfhood at the disjunctures of language, culture, nation, and community. The foremost preoccupation of Faiz's poetry, which defines it as a body of writing, is the suffering of a divided or (we might say) "Partitioned" subject, caught between the desire for union with the beloved (or *viṣāl*) and a recognition that this distance from it (or *hijr*) is the very condition of its selfhood and its movement through life. While it desires unification with or subsumption into the beloved, it cannot quite let go of its condition of distance and alienation from the object of desire, since this is its very condition of being. And it is precisely in those of his poems that are closest to being "lyric" in structure and sensibility, that is, those in which the inward or subjective turn is most sustained, rather than in such explicitly Partition-themed poems as "Freedom's Dawn" ("Ṣubḥ-e a āzādī"), that we may glimpse these social meanings in their fullest crystallization. In a historical register, therefore, the overall effect is that the supposedly autonomous national selves that emerged from Partition are revealed to be what they are—moments or elements within the dialectic of Indian modernity. Thus, within the traditional language of the separation of lover and beloved, self and other, which is instantly legible to readers and listeners of Urdu poetry, Faiz manages to insert and hide a critique of the Partition. In more abstract terms, we might say that in Faiz's poetry both the degradation of human life in colonial and postcolonial capitalism—namely, expropriation—and the failure to achieve a collective selfhood at peace with itself—the larger cultural logic of Partition—find common expression in the suffering of the lyric subject. Faiz thus manages to reconcile, at the level of poetic image, what theory, and Marxism in particular, has struggled to reconcile at the level of concept, namely, exploitation and exclusion.

Let us now look at the poem in question in some detail. Through what means, exactly, is it able to reach out from its linguistic, literary, and historical contexts and engage a wider civilizational and historical space? It was written in 1979 during the repressive military and Islamic fundamentalist regime of General Zia ul-Haq and while the poet, living in self-imposed exile in Beirut, was visiting the United States. It was made famous when the singer Iqbal Bano performed it at a live event in 1985 in Pakistan with a reported audience of around fifty thousand, the audio recording of which began to circulate widely on cassettes underground. The actual title of the poem is a phrase from Arabic—to be precise, a line from the Quran, verse 27 of the fifty-fifth *sūra*, or chapter, called "al-Raḥmān" ("The Merciful"): "Wa yabqā wajhu rabbik" (in Marmaduke Pickthall's [1930] translation: "There remaineth but the Countenance of thy Lord"). In full, verses 26 and 27 of chapter 55 read as follows: "Kullu man 'alaihā fānin. Wa yabqā wajhu rabbik ẓū al-jalāli wa al-ikrām" (All that is thereon will pass away. There remaineth but the Countenance of thy Lord of Might and Glory.) The chapter has a uniquely poetical structure even for the Quran, with a refrain repeated after every verse: "fa bi 'ayyi a'lā'i rabbikumā tukaẓẓibān" (Which is it, of the favors of your Lord, that ye deny?).

Ham dēkhēñgē	We shall see,	1
Lāzim hai kih ham bhī dēkhēñgē	it is inevitable that we too shall see	2
Voh din kih jis kā va'da hai	that promised day	3
Jō lauḥ-e azal mēñ likkhā hai	written on the tablet of eternity	4
Jab ẓulm o sitam kē kōh-e garāñ	when tyranny's steep mountains	5
Rū'ī kī ṭaraḥ uṛ jā'ēñgē	will be like cotton wool, tossed in the wind	6
Ham maḥkūmōñ kē pā'ūñ talē	and beneath us, the governed	7
Jab dhartī dhar dhar dharkēgī	the earth's heart will beat loudly	8
Aur ahl-e ḥakam kē sar ūpar	when over the heads of the rulers	9
Jab bijlī kaṛ kaṛ kaṛkēgī	will be thunder and lightning	10
Jab 'arź-e khudā kē ka'bē sē	when the sanctuary of God's earth	11
Sab but uṭhvā'ē jā'ēñgē	will be cleared of all false gods	12
Ham ahl-e ṣafā mardūd-e ḥaram	we, the righteous and rejected	13
Masnad pē biṭhā'ē jā'ēñgē	will be seated on high	14

Sab tāj učhālē jā'ēñgē	all crowns will be tossed in the air	15
Sab takht girāē jā'ēñgē	all thrones brought crashing down	16
Bas nām rahēgā allāh kā	only the name of God will remain	17
Jō ğā'ib bhī hai ḥāżir bhī	both seen and unseen	18
Jō manẓar bhī hai nāẓir bhī	both spectacle and beholder	19
Uṭhēgā anā al-ḥaq kā na'ra	and a cry will rise—"I am the Truth"	20
Jō maiñ bhī hūñ aur tum bhī hō	it is I, it is you	21
Aur rāj karēgī khalq-e khudā	God's creation will then rule	22
Jō maiñ bhī hūñ aur tum bhī hō	it is I, it is you	23
(Faiz 1979)		

The poem begins with a promise made and remade, in lines 1 and 2—"We shall see / it is inevitable that we too shall see." But the very next line (3) makes clear that the promise is about another promise, already made, "on the tablet of eternity," the promise of a day of some sort of reckoning. In a series of cascading images framed in the future tense (in lines 5–12), the poem then lists the signs of this promised day: the seemingly immovable mountains of tyranny will become light as cotton wool, flying away in the wind; the earth will "beat" loudly beneath "us," those who are the subjects of some power; and over the heads of those in power, there will be deafening thunder; finally, the "sanctuary of God's Earth" will be cleared of all "idols," all false Gods. These apocalyptic images evoke specific Quranic passages, in particular from chapter 99, "al-Zalzala" ("The Earthquake"), but the Quranic elements might themselves have Biblical sources, for instance, Isaiah 24. From line 13 on, we get some sense of what sort of reckoning exactly is being promised here. It is, above all, a *this*-worldly reckoning: crowns and thrones, that is, the *symbols of sovereign power*, will be upturned and removed from their customary place of authority, and "we," the "righteous and rejected" of the world, will take our rightful place. The first-person plural of course marks the place of a subject, first of all simply in grammatical terms, but also more broadly in discursive terms—in the poem, the place of an emergent subject with a key role to play in the apocalyptic drama that unfolds. It appears four times in the poem (once each in lines 1, 2, 7, and 13), and in lines 21 and 23, it appears, we might say, in concealed form, concealed by virtue of being split in two: "main . . . aur . . . tum" (me . . . and . . . you). In other words, here the scene of emergence and self-expression of the collective subject marked by the first-person plural pronoun is replaced with a negotiational interaction of the self and an other, an intimate other marked by the second-person singular-familiar pronoun.

Finally, "masnad" (line 14) is a prop or seat of some sort, but not unequivocally a "throne," which is indicated by "takht" (line 16). It carries the sense of a seat of honor, and here that honor is reserved for the meek and rejected. To be more precise, it appears as the sign of *a form of authority to come* that bypasses the discourse of sovereignty—which is evident in "throne" and "crown"—and in fact comes to replace it. What the poem offers overall, therefore, is *a critique and rejection of the discourse of sovereignty.* Coming after this apocalyptic vision, these lines in Faiz's poem (that is, 13–16) offer, broadly speaking, a "world turned upside down" vision in which the downtrodden, those crushed routinely and seemingly with no recourse against their oppression, come to take their rightful place of dignity and authority. What it seems to foreground is the *historicality* and thus transience of every social order, every social artifact, however primordial or permanent it may appear or claim to be. Every exclusive and abusive social order sees its own end, its day of reckoning—this is the "promise" that the poem elaborates.

In the final seven lines (17–23), the poem takes a more fully philosophical turn. This final segment begins with an invocation of the name of God as that which ultimately remains—this is a translation and paraphrasing of the Quranic phrase of the title—and then offers (in lines 18 and 19) a nondualistic conception of the divine Absolute, which is both absent and present (that is, both unseen and seen), both the viewer and the spectacle. The source of this nondualism is first of all the metaphysics of *taṣawwuf* (Sufism), to be more precise, the philosophy of *waḥdat al-wujūd* ("the oneness of existence" in Arabic), one of the preeminent philosophical traditions in Sufism in India and, according to the influential critic of the mid-twentieth century, Muhammad Hasan Askari, the philosophical ground of the ghazal's lyric tradition in Urdu and of Indo-Islamic civilization more broadly. But it cannot not at the same time also invoke the philosophy of *advaita* ("not two" in Sanskrit) or Vedantic nondualism, because the parallels between these two philosophical systems—the one of Near Eastern, North African, and Andalusian origin in the Middle Ages; the other emerging out of post-Vedic culture in Ancient India—themselves constitute a theme in Indo-Muslim religion and culture, from the early Sufi thinkers of the Chishtiya order to the scholar and statesman Abulkalam Azad, a leading critic of Muslim separatism who wrote in the first half of the twentieth century, in the decades before the Partition of India (Rizvi 1978; and Mufti 2007).

In line 20, this theosophical nondualism is given a specific content, namely, "ana al-ḥaq" (I am the Truth), but because "al-ḥaq" is also, in Sunni orthodoxy, one of the so-called ninety-nine attributes of God, the expression verges on the blasphemous, tending to reduce, if not cancel out entirely, the distance between God and his (human) creation. This ecstatic Sufi utterance, or šaṭḥ, associated with the mystic and martyr Mansur al-Hallaj, executed by Abbasid authorities in 922 CE on charges of blasphemy and political treachery, is turned here into a rallying cry. The execution of al-Hallaj, who is known more commonly as Mansur in the languages of the region, is the subject of numerous ghazals and other poetic compositions in many languages, including, beside Urdu, Persian, Kashmiri, Punjabi, Sindhi, and so on, and numerous other works of art throughout the Persianate world over centuries. This phrase is thus arguably the most famous expression, in capsular form, of Sufi antinomianism, expressing the constitutive tension within Sunni Islam traditionally between piety and devotion, the muftī and the mystic. Faiz's invocation of al-Hallaj caused controversy in Pakistan on the poem's first appearance, seen by the upholders of religious orthodoxy in the era of General Zia's violent and repressive Islamization of the country as a heterodox and even blasphemous gesture. But the reception of the poem in India in recent years makes clear that Faiz manages to somehow translate this imagery of Sufi antinomianism into a secular language of resistance and rebellion.

Having invoked the Hallajian expostulation, which seeks to overcome the polarity of the immanent and the transcendent—"I," finite and immanent, am "Truth," that is, simultaneously transcendent—the poem ends by leaving us with the work of the constitution of the "we," the collective subject, as an exchange between a self and an other, each marked grammatically as singular and familiar, the first introduction of a second-person addressee in the poem. In this form of address, in which the subject speaks to an intimate other—the word in lines 21 and 23 is "tum," Hindi-Urdu equivalent, we might say, of the "thou and thee" form no longer operative in English—the intimacy of the other keeps it from being permanently frozen in the position of other, as object of the subject's desire. As in so many of Faiz's poems, this exchange between self and other takes the form of a dialectic, and one of the semantic valences of this form of appearance of self and other in Faiz's writing points to the problematic of a self-in-partition, an unresolved and dialectical entanglement as the very scene of the emergence of the self.

Writing in self-imposed exile from a Pakistan undergoing a violent so-called Islamization under military rule in the late 1970s, Faiz, who was vilified by many in the country as anti-Pakistani and pro-Indian, enters fully into the language of this totalitarian project at the intersections of religion and state in an Islamic setting and shows how it can be turned against the authoritarian state and its instrumentalization of religious belief and practice. In heavily ironic language, the imagery of monotheistic iconoclasm is turned inside out to reveal the iconoclasts themselves as false gods, claiming the authority to stand outside and above, and able to suspend, the normal course of things. It is a remarkable fact that this poem, with such clearly Islamic markings, could also become available to critics of the authoritarian imbrication of politics and religion in contemporary India. The young people in Delhi who first adopted it for their protests against the attempt of the BJP-ruled state to change the nature of their educational institutions, whom we can safely assume are not for the most part trained in Urdu poetics, and for whom Urdu is, furthermore, meant to be a despised alien and antinational language and culture, seem to have instinctively understood and taken up *the poem's invitation across the borders of language, religion, culture, and nation-state.* They understand that the oversize political personae of Modi and Shah are "false gods" demanding unquestioning submission and devotion, and recognize in this little poem and song from across the border the civilizational resources for orienting oneself to stand up to tyranny. It is also remarkable that Hindutva attacks on the poem and attempts to recode its linguistic, cultural, civilizational, and political complexity as simply "anti-Hindu" language have failed to stop the insertion and reanimation of the poem in the scene of dissensus that has emerged around the ruling party's attempt to reinvent the Indian polity. These attacks have if anything strengthened the popular attachment to it, and its singing and recitation in public have almost become ways of trolling and triggering its critics. In a strange twist, the poem has even been appropriated in song form in a controversial recent film, *The Kashmir Files,* which excoriates progressive students and professors as antinational and attempts to upturn emergent (and insurgent) narratives about the Indian military's violent presence in Kashmir.

What I have attempted to describe here is a *struggle,* a scene of "contestation" of power, as Nivedita Menon and Aditya Nigam (2007) have put it, of authoritarian and antidemocratic forms of majoritarian politics that verge on their edges toward recognizably fascistic forms, by prodemocracy mobilizations coalescing around the goal of protecting the Constitution. The unapologetic appearance of the *dādīs* of Shaheen Bagh in public space as Muslim women as well as Indian citizens is experienced in itself as an act of aggression in the dominant discourse of Hindutva. This emergence sought to redistribute the mode of signification of "Muslim women" in postcolonial India, which, as I have briefly noted, has its own distinct history in which, historically speaking, the figure of Muslim woman has been situated as passive object of control in a competition between the discourse of the state and the patriarchy of the Islamic religious establishment. It momentarily produced a "redistribution of the *sensible*," in Rancière's phrase, overturning the political designation and myth of all Muslim women as oppressed victims requiring the protection of the state, recently reiterated by the BJP government itself in the passage of the Muslim divorce bill, which everyone, including its supporters, understood as a political maneuver. The "Islamic veil" itself in all its forms was recoded and refunctionalized in the course of the protests as the participating women openly espoused their goal of protecting the secularist Constitution of India and as they enacted a politics of coalition with the movement for Dalit survival and rights. The *dādīs* of Shaheen Bagh mark a remarkable emergence at the intersections of the politics of emancipation and citizenship, the poetics of protest, and gendered passages from private to public spaces. Their activism offered no final word but drew concrete and urgent attention to the threat that Hindutva poses to democracy and also performed the very possibility of refusal and dissent.

References

Agamben, Giorgio. 2005. *State of Exception*. Chicago: University of Chicago Press.

Al Jazeera English. 2022. "Arundhati Roy: 'India Is Becoming a Hindu Fascist Enterprise.'" June 17. YouTube video, 0:03:39. https://www.youtube.com/watch?v=qJ1pCMLBPzw&t=2s.

ANHAD (Act Now for Harmony and Democracy), ed. 2022. *Hate Grips the Nation: Gujarat Twenty Years*. New Delhi: ANHAD.

Arendt, Hannah. (1951) 1979. *The Origins of Totalitarianism*. New Edition and with added prefaces. New York: Harcourt Brace and Company.

Ayyub, Rana. 2016. *Gujarat Files: Anatomy of a Cover Up*. Scotts Valley, CA: CreateSpace Independent Publishing Platform.

Banaji, Jairus, ed. 2016a. *Fascism: Essays on Europe and India*. Gurgaon: Three Essays Collective.

Banaji, Jairus. 2016b. "The Political Culture of Fascism." In *What the Nation Really Neets to Know: The JNU Nationalism Lectures*, edited by JNUTA, 256–69. Noida: Harper Collins.

Basu, Anustup. 2020. *Hindutva as Political Monotheism*. Durham, NC: Duke University Press.

Basu, Tapan, Pradip Datta, Sumit Sarkar, Tanika Sarkar, and Sambuddha Sen. 1993. *Khaki Shorts, Saffron Flags*. Hyderabad: Orient Longman.

Bhattacharya, Snigdhendu. 2021. "Romila Thapar, Irfan Habib Decry Hindutva Attempts to Distort India's History." *Wire*, August 13. https://thewire.in/rights /romila-thapar-irfan-habib-decry-hindutva-attempts-to-distort-indias-history.

Brecht, Bertolt. (1953) 2003. "The Solution." https://www.poemhunter.com/poem/the -solution/.

Brosius, Christiane. 2010. *India's Middle Class: New Forms of Urban Leisure, Consumption and Prosperity.* Delhi: Routledge India.

Business Standard. 2017. "Babri Masjid Demolition: The Most Comprehensive Video Coverage from 1992." December 5. YouTube video, 2:37:10. https:// youtu.be/k-bhAFsnv2s.

Chakraborty, Abhishek, and Alok Ranjan. 2022. "Ten States, Fifteen Flashpoints, the Week That Was in India." *India Today*, April 18. https://www.indiatoday.in /india/story/communal-violence-over-the-week-ram-navami-hanuman-jayanti -1938761-2022-04-18.

Chatterjee, Partha. 1993. *Nationalist Thought and the Colonial World: A Derivative Discourse.* Minneapolis: University of Minnesota Press.

Chauhan, Chanchal, ed. 2020. "CAA Protesters Celebrate Republic Day All across India in Their Own Unique Way." *India Today,* January 27. https://www.india today.in/india/story/caa-protests-republicday-india-shaheenbagh-kerala -1640391-2020-01-26.

Cola, Elliott. 2011. "The Poetry of Revolt." *Three Quarks Daily*, January 21. https:// www.jadaliyya.com/Details/23638.

Coppola, Carlo. 2017. *Urdu Poetry, 1935–1970: The Progressive Episode.* Karachi: Oxford University Press.

DO Politics. 2022. "Kapil Mishra Explains Current Situation." July 8. YouTube video, 0.35.30. https://youtu.be/UwrmOuxxSlE.

Doniger, Wendy. 2009. *The Hindus: An Alternative History.* New Delhi: Viking.

Faiz, Faiz Ahmed. 1979. "Wa yabqa wajhu rabbik (Ham dēkhēñgē)." Rekhta. https:// www.rekhta.org/nazms/va-yabqaa-vajh-o-rabbik-hum-dekhenge-ham -dekhenge-faiz-ahmad-faiz-nazms?lang=ur (accessed April 15, 2022).

Gopal, Sarvepalli, ed. 1991. *Anatomy of a Confrontation: The Babri Masjid-Ramjanmabhumi Issue.* New Delhi: Penguin Books India.

Guha, Ranajit. 1997. *Dominance without Hegemony.* Cambridge, MA: Harvard University Press.

Hansen, Thomas Blom. 1999. *The Saffron Wave: Democracy and Hindu Nationalism in Modern India.* Princeton, NJ: Princeton University Press.

Harney, Stefano, and Fred Moten. 2013. *The Undercommons: Fugitive Planning and Black Study.* New York: Minor Compositions.

Jaffrelot, Christopher. 1996. *The Hindu Nationalist Movement in Indian Politics.* New York: Columbia University Press.

Kabir, Ananya Jahanara. 2019. "Chandrashekhar's Azadi with Swag: The Fabulous Mystique of the Bhim Army Chief." *Scroll*, December 24. https://scroll.in

/article/947721/chandrashekhars-azadi-with-swag-the-fabulous-mystique
-of-the-bhim-army-chief.

Kaur, Ravinder. 2020. *Brand New Nation*. Stanford, CA: Stanford University Press.

Kidwai, Ayesha. 2020. Introduction to *Displacement and Citizenship: Histories and Memories of Exclusion*, edited by Vijaya Rao, Shambhavi Prakash, Mallarika Sinha Roy, and Papori Bora. New Delhi: Tulika.

Lee, Joel M. 2021. *Deceptive Majority: Dalits, Hinduism, and Underground Religion*. Cambridge: Cambridge University Press.

Lelyveld, David. 1978. *Aligarh's First Generation: Muslim Solidarity in British India*. Princeton, NJ: Princeton University Press.

Ludden, David E., ed. 2005. *Making India Hindu*. 2nd ed. Delhi: Oxford University Press.

Marx, Karl, and Friedrich Engels. (1848) 1978. "The Communist Manifesto." In *The Marx-Engels Reader*, edited by Robert C. Tucker. 2nd ed. New York: W. W. Norton.

Mehring, Reinhard. 2014. *Carl Schmitt: A Biography*. Cambridge: Polity.

Menon, Dilip. 2006. *The Blindness of Insight: Essays on Caste in Modern India*. Pondicherry: Navayana.

Menon, Nivedita. 2020. "Coronacapitalism and Hindu Rashtra in India." *Thesis Eleven*, August 3. https://thesiseleven.com/2020/08/03/coronacapitalism-and
-hindu-rashtra-in-india/.

Menon, Nivedita, and Aditya Nigam. 2007. *Power and Contestation: India since 1989*. London: Zed.

Mohapatra, Bishnu N. 2014. "Minority Question in India." In *Becoming Minority: How Discourses and Policies Produce Minorities in India and Europe*, edited by Jyotirmaya Tripathy and Sudarsan Padmanabhan, 227–52. Delhi: Sage.

Mufti, Aamir R. 2007. *Enlightenment in the Colony: The Jewish Question and the Crisis of Postcolonial Culture*. Princeton, NJ: Princeton University Press.

Mustafa, Seema. 2020. "Timeline of a Protest." In *Shaheen Bagh and the Idea of India: Writings on a Movement for Justice, Liberty, and Equality*, edited by Seema Mustafa, 35–40. New Delhi: Speaking Tiger.

Nair, Janaki. 2016. "Introduction: A Teach-In for a JNU Spring." In *What the Nation Really Needs to Know: The JNU Nationalism Lectures*, edited by JNUTA, ix–xxv. Noida: Harper Collins.

Nehru, Jawaharlal. (1946) 1985. *The Discovery of India*. Delhi: Oxford University Press.

Nigam, Aditya. 2020. "Fascism, the Revolt of the 'Little Man' and Life after Capitalism— Manifesto of Hope 3." *Kafila*, April 23. https://kafila.online/2020/04/23
/fascism-the-revolt-of-the-little-man-and-life-after-capitalism-manifesto-of
-hope-iii/.

Obama, Barack. 2015. "Narendra Modi." *Time*, April 15. https://time.com/3823155
/narendra-modi-2015-time-100/.

Pathak, Zakia, and Rajeswari Sunder Rajan. 1989. "Shahbano." *Signs* 14, no. 3: 558–82.

Patnaik, Prabhat. 2021. "Why Neoliberalism Needs Fascism." *Boston Review*, July 19. https://bostonreview.net/articles/why-neoliberalism-needs-neofascists/.

Paxton, Robert O. 2005. *The Anatomy of Fascism*. New York: Vintage.

Pickthall, Marmaduke. 1930. *The Meaning of the Glorious Qur'an*. https://www.sacred-texts.com/isl/pick/055.htm.

Prakash, Brahma. 2022. "Bulldozer Is a Sign that Hindutva Is Flat." *Indian Cultural Forum*, May 23. https://indianculturalforum.in/2022/05/23/bulldozer-is-a-sign-that-hindutva-is-flat/.

Rabinbach, Anson, and Sander Gilman, eds. 2013. *The Third Reich Sourcebook*. Berkeley: University of California Press.

Rancière, Jacques. (2000) 2013. *The Politics of Aesthetics*. London: Bloomsbury Academic.

Rizvi, Syed Athar Abbas. 1978. *A History of Sufism in India*. Vol. 1. Delhi: Munshiram Manoharlal.

Sarkar, Sumit. 2016. "The Fascism of the Sangh Parivar." In Banaji 2016a: 135–52.

Savarkar, Vinayak Damodar. (1923) 2003. *Hindutva*. Delhi: Hindi Sahitya Sadan.

Schmitt, Carl. (1921) 2014. *Dictatorship: From the Origin of the Modern Concept of Sovereignty to Proletarian Class Struggle*. Cambridge: Polity.

Schmitt, Carl. (1922) 2005. *Political Theology: Four Chapters on the Concept of Sovereignty*. Chicago: Chicago University Press.

Schmitt, Carl. (1927) 1996. *The Concept of the Political*. Chicago: University of Chicago Press.

Schmitt, Carl. 1933. *Staat, Bewegung, Volk: Die Dreigliederung der politischen Einheit*. Hamburg: Hanseatische Verlagsanstalt.

Sengupta, Sudhabrata. 2020. "The Garden of Freedom." *Caravan Magazine*, February 2. https://caravanmagazine.in/politics/lessons-that-shaheen-bagh-teaches-us-about-citizenship.

Shepherd, Kancha Ilaiah. (1993) 2019. *Why I Am Not a Hindu: A Sudra Critique of Hindutva Philosophy, Culture, and Political Economy*. New Delhi: Sage.

Shinde, Vasant, et al. 2019. "An Ancient Harappan Genome Lacks Ancestry from Steppe Pastoralists or Iranian Farmers." *Cell* 179: 729–35.

Simeon, Dilip. 2016. "The Law of Killing: A Brief History of Indian Fascism." In Banaji 2016a: 153–214.

Strong, Tracy B. 1985. Foreword to Schmitt (1922) 1985: vii–xxxv.

Swadeshi Indology. 2019. "The Aryan Invasion Debate—Rajiv Malhotra." November 18. YouTube video, 0:26:09. https://youtu.be/OFn6Rwlhro0.

Thapar, Romila. 1991. "A Historical Perspective on the Story of Rama." In Gopal 1993: 141–63.

Trumpener, Katie. 1997. *Bardic Nationalism: The Romantic Novel and the British Empire*. Princeton, NJ: Princeton University Press.

"UAE Princess Hits Out against Islamophobic Posts by Indian Expats." 2020. *Middle East Monitor*, April 22. https://www.middleeastmonitor.com/20200422-uae -princess-hits-out-against-islamophobic-posts-by-indian-expats/.

Van der Veer, Peter. 1994. *Religious Nationalism: Hindus and Muslims in India.* Los Angeles: University of California Press.

Vardoulakis, Dimitris. 2020. "The Antinomy of Frictionless Sovereignty: Inverse Relations of Authority and Authoritarianism." *b2o*, August 20. https://www .boundary2.org/2020/08/dimitris-vardoulakis-the-antinomy-of-frictionless -sovereignty-inverse-relations-of-authority-and-authoritarianism/.

Varma, Pavan K. 2014. *The New Indian Middle Class: The Challenge of 2014 and Beyond.* Delhi: Harper Collins.

Weber, Max. (1922) 1978. *Economy and Society: An Outline of Interpretive Sociology.* Vol. 1. Berkeley: University of California Press.

Wire. 2020. "Colloquially Speaking, BJP Is Fascist. And More Insidious Than Indira's Emergency." January 20. YouTube video, 0:59:37. https://youtu.be/5hiDcd 2GiDA.

Wire. 2022. "Modi's Strategy Is Rule by Anarchy, Unrest—from Agnipath to CAA, Farm Laws and Demonitisation." June 23. YouTube video, 0:24:57. https:// youtu.be/aNg5BnuDI5o.

Freedom: The Function of Criticism at All Times

Paul A. Bové

Without criticism...no country can succeed—and no republic can survive.
—John F. Kennedy

Let me list a few items each of which threatens not only the priority of criticism in the literary humanities but also its destruction and that of the humanities by its elimination or displacement. I will begin intramurally. We can argue about each of these items and the motives, forces, and consequences of each. My list is by no means complete and has no order of priority.

Since I teach at Pittsburgh, in an English department once chaired for more than a decade by a leading figure in composition and pedagogy studies, I will begin my list of threats to criticism with rhetoric and composition, disciplines that became pedagogy and related studies.[1] In many

---

1. David Bartholomae retired as the Charles Crow Chair of Expository Writing at the University of Pittsburgh. He served as chair of the Department of English from 1995 to 2009.

boundary 2 50:1 (2023)   DOI 10.1215/01903659-10192174   ©2023 by Paul A. Bové

Research 1 universities, composition began in English departments and became its own subfield, in some part in rebellion against the old lit and comp method of teaching writing in relation to literature. Sometimes these composition subgroups left the English departments to become their own programs or Departments of Composition, Rhetoric, Pedagogy, or combination of the same. Job lines in literary history and criticism, once supported by teaching lit and comp, were lost to hirings in a new subfield, which of course predictably shattered into many sub-subfields. We are now left with composition, pedagogy studies, professional writing, and so on. At times, these fragmented fields (re)gather for professional, administrative, and financial reasons in new departments.[2]

Next on my list is the high theory moment, which shattered English departments and the other national language departments as well, especially German and the Romance language departments, often finding a home in comparative literature.[3] Many theory specialists remained committed to literary criticism—we can take the Yale School as an example—although the work of many theoretically minded critics did not remain within the canons of national literatures and languages or language and literature at all.[4] Some theorists and their acolytes displaced criticism altogether

---

In 2013, he was chosen as Pennsylvania Professor of the Year. University of Pittsburgh, "David Bartholomae," CV, https://www.composition.pitt.edu/sites/default/files/Bartholomae%20CV.pdf (accessed August 17, 2020). The twelfth edition of his influential textbook appeared in September 2019 (Bartholomae, Petrosky, and Waite 2019). A JSTOR search for "David Bartholomae" returned 2,013 search results on August 17, 2020.

2. The Department of Writing Studies at the University of Minnesota, for example, opened in 2007. This department resulted from the unification of other units and departments. University of Minnesota, "Department of Writing Studies," https://cla.umn.edu/writing-studies (accessed August 17, 2020).

3. The High Theory movement introduced French and German language materials into English departments, putting stress on the language-specific nature of research in those departments. Also, theory forced change on the dominant research and teaching frameworks that belonged to the traditions of language-specific departments, challenging the national identities of their projects. Eventually, as theory brought nonliterary texts from anthropology, linguistics, and other disciplines into the field as models for study and as themselves objects of study, the national departments lost focus on the national literatures and languages. Comparative literature departments could at times more easily absorb theory's disruptions, but almost always with some contention. For some evidence of these claims as far as they concern comparative literature, see Komar 1995.

4. As an example of such extranational study see Donato 1993. Donato at the time of his death was a professor in French and Italian, a department he chaired, at the University

with changing grand narratives built on categories derivative of discourses and modes of knowledge close to literature and literary study but clearly independent of and assumed to be prior to literature itself. I am thinking of especially post-Lacanian psychoanalysis, post-Althusserian Marxism, and other discourses derived from extraliterary sources. We can take Fredric Jameson's work on postmodernism and late capital as one instance of an officially approved extraliterary theorizing. As time passed from the heyday of grand theory, competition split the field, and academics began to think of their specific ways of talking as doing theory germane to subareas of research. Merriam-Webster calls these ways of talking "jargons."[5] The jargons also expanded their reach. Narrative theory, for example, migrated from the study of the novel and attached itself to the study of other discourses and their expressions (Booth 1961; Scholes and Kellogg 1966).[6] A famous *Critical Inquiry* conference and special issue on narrative enabled and exemplified this movement.[7]

In addition, and rightly so, postcolonial theory, gender theory, race theory, and other theories generated substantial bodies of work founded on crucial principles. For example, following Edward Said's work in both *Orientalism* and *Culture and Imperialism*, scholars of especially modern

---

of California, Irvine. His study of Flaubert began in and rested on a reading of Hegel, crossing languages and disciplines in a way common among literary theorists of the time. On the Yale School's commitment to literary criticism, see Bloom et al. 1979, which gathered a series of essays on Shelley by Paul De Man, Jacques Derrida, Geoffrey Hartmann, and others.

5. Merriam-Webster gives this as the first definition on the word *jargon*: "the technical terminology or characteristic idiom of a special activity or group" (Merriam-Webster Online, s.v. "jargon," https://www.merriam-webster.com/dictionary/jargon [accessed August 10, 2020]). The *OED* does not have such a definition of the word.

6. The two books cited here typify the pre-theory movement attachment of narrative to fictional literature. Scholes and Kellogg (1966: 3) write that "the dominant form of narrative literature in the West has been the novel." They aimed to put the novel in its place, that is, within the context of other literary narrative forms such as stories, folktales, and confessions.

7. *Critical Inquiry* sponsored a conference titled "Narrative: The Illusion of Sequence" at the University of Chicago on October 26–28, 1979. As the then editor of *Critical Inquiry* says, the special issue that followed "is a 'product' of the symposium in a fairly precise sense" (Mitchell 1980). This issue contains the work of major intellectuals in various disciplines, including history, psychoanalysis, philosophy, ethnography, and others. It catches the excitement and allure active in the theoretically informed events that intentionally disrupted and hoped to remake critical studies.

Western literatures had to consider their role not only in representing the non-Western "other" but in constructing Western national cultural traditions inescapably intertwined with colonizing and imperializing practices. The great tradition of the English novel organizes an imperial society at home (Said 1978).[8] We know from the writings of Hortense Spillers (2003: x) that scholars should not study nor critics engage with the worldliness of texts and experiences unless they in part "create" their objects by differentiating them against normative orders and constraints. Against resistance, these principles acquired limited institutional legitimacy precisely because they made claims within fields of oppositional or resistant intellectual practice. As is often the case in mainstream institutional formations, changing the grounds for disciplinary work always slows as the effort comes near established and self-justified positions.

We can see this in several ways and places. Susan Fraiman (1995: 807), for example, says, apropos Said's reading of Jane Austen, that her "own investment in the woman writer that feminist critics have variously and laboriously wrested from the fray" necessitates the claim that Said is "typing" Austen, a fact "symptomatic of a more general gender politics underlying his postcolonial project."[9] Fraiman's recuperation of Austen rests in a certain established consensus of bourgeois liberal feminism, oppositional and establishment at once. In the humanities, vested interests set aside fundamental principles when these require adjustment. The literary humanities seem especially unwilling to accept that the human sciences can make basic discoveries that must be sustained until overthrown by better argument. Special interests' resistance to the idea that the humanities can produce irrefutable moral and methodological claims finds a parallel in institutional absorption of those discoveries into newly normative and iterative patterns of institutional investment. Career paths open in new models that

---

8. Said lays out these basic points in explaining how Orientalism is both a form of knowledge and domination and as such a means for organizing the political entity, the metropole. See Said 1978: 3–5 for a preliminary statement. See also Said 1993, especially his discussion of Jane Austen. Said (1993: 98) concludes his reading of *Mansfield Park* with an apology for reading her work because "its aesthetic intellectual complexity . . . encodes experiences and does not simply repeat them." In other words, the most complex arts of Western culture demand attention for their worldly inscription within global power relations.

9. Fraiman (1995: 809) also writes, "The question I would raise is not whether Austen contributed to English domination abroad but how her doing so was necessarily inflected and partly disrupted by her position as a bourgeois woman."

require invention within the promises that synthetic approaches offer of high productivity within a fragmented field of study.

Distant reading and world literature are examples of such possibilities (Moretti 2013). World literature has achieved a mainstream institutional prominence. Harvard University created the Institute of World Literature, which in turn links to the recently created *Journal of World Literature*. The institute has organized conferences and four-week summer school sessions around the world to advance the mode of conceiving and studying global literature. Indeed, the institute says that it aims to fill a pedagogical gap in the marketplace of ideas and careers: "Many people are now interested in teaching courses in World Literature and in pursuing research within a global framework, but few programs in comparative or even World Literature have yet established ways to train scholars and teachers to do such work on a broad basis."[10]

The Institute and journal take their titles from Goethe's remarks in 1827: "Ich überzeugt sei, es bilde sich eine allgemeine Weltliteratur, worin uns Deutschen eine ehrenvolle Rolle vorbehalten."[11] Scholars have remarked that Goethe did not invent the notion of world literature, but his formulation compelled serious readers to consider possible imaginative constructions it might stimulate. Among others, in the twentieth century Erich Auerbach and Edward Said stand out for their differing developments of Goethe's term. In our context, in discussing the harm to criticism, Said's turn on Goethe matters more than Auerbach's, precisely because his is the trope whose betrayal matters most.

Said turned *Welt* into *weltlich*. As in his reading of Austen's *Mansfield Park*, Said transposed the materiality of circulating systems—the globality of literature and culture traveling through symbolic and commercial regimes—into the materiality of texts, that is, into a sense of books as the textured traces of historicality, intelligent imagination, and lived experience (Bové 2021: 283–332). Texts are *weltlich* in and through the work they do in social, cultural, and political systems. By this principle, Austen's neglect of Caribbean plantations normalizes the novel as an imperial institution. (One

10. Institute of World Literature, "About," https://iwl.fas.harvard.edu/pages/about (accessed August 12, 2020).
11. Johann Wolfgang von Goethe writing in an 1827 issue of *Über Kunst und Altertum* quoted in Pizer 2000: 215. Pizer makes my institutional point: "Certainly, almost all studies of comparative literature's history as a discrete field of scholarly inquiry recognize Goethe's Weltliteratur paradigm as seminal to the discipline's development," 214.

hopes readers concede that the novel of the great tradition can be an imperial institution and other things; that is the essence of worldliness.) In a final
turn on the *weltlich* figure *Welt*, Said produced the constant presence of
exile and humanity in making the world a place to live and love, conditions
dependent on belonging nowhere to belong everywhere.

In *Orientalism*, Said acknowledged the existence of non-Orientalist
scholarship belonging to the *Geisteswissenschaften* of the nineteenth and
twentieth centuries. He emphasized that non-Orientalist modes of doing
les sciences de l'homme were far more adequate to their responsibilities
and far more sensitive and enlisted in a struggle to sustain their role in a
society otherwise tending in yet more awful directions. For Said, Oriental-
ist studies, especially by the twentieth century, were closely allied with the
forces that put Western political society and humanity at risk. Because the
state, the market, and nationalist popular will directed resources toward
the research and teaching that cooperated with established interests, the
more responsible modes of humanistic work struggled to sustain independent scholarly and critical freedom in the service of political liberty. These
responsible scholars "were perforce more immediately responsive to the
threats to humanistic culture of a self-aggrandizing, amoral technical specialization represented, in part at least, by the rise of fascism in Europe"
(Said 1978: 258). Said's study of Orientalism resulted in two important
conclusions essential to the successful function of the humanities in an
authoritarian or proto-authoritarian political formation. The first of the conclusions is simple. Essential to the necessary function of the humanities is
the intellectually independent critically engaged scholar critic. In the 1930s,
for example, as in our own period, the independent scholar critic stood facing fascism and the technical, technological concentrations of power in the
political economic order. Today, the analogies would be with scholars facing
authoritarian illiberalism, in movements such as Fidesz in Hungary, Alternative für Deutschland, and the Tea Party and other partisan and familial
rightist alignments in the United States. For Said, the paradigmatic scholar
critic, among several in the interwar years, was Erich Auerbach. His writing
program while an exile in Turkey was massive, loving, and worldly. Above
all, he understood the real consequences of then current political vectors, and he had the long historical vision to understand the genealogical
development from which that present arrangement emerged. It matters far
less to Said that Auerbach attempted a synthesis of humanistic culture as it
was ending than that Auerbach's was work of a certain kind. "The aim was
a synthesis of Western culture in which the synthesis itself was matched

in importance by the very gesture of doing it" (Said 1978: 258–59). What had Auerbach achieved? He had brought into history, as Hortense Spillers insists critics must do, an object created against the background of ruling consensus. "The discrete particular," Said concluded, "was thus converted into a highly mediated symbol of the world-historical process." Said's echo of Adorno here is purposive.[12] It leads to Said's second conclusion and completes the parallel between his time and ours.

Auerbach became a Romance rather than a German or classical philologist. This moved him away from the careers and funding available along the nationalist intellectual track. He also identified with "the humanistic tradition of involvement in a national culture or literature not one's own" (259). In effect, such independent humanistic scholarship stood against the patriarchy of national language within the politics and propaganda of authoritarian and racialized nationalism. It also stood outside the career paths offered and determined by larger forces in the political economy. The exiled Said sympathized with the Jewish Auerbach, who fled to Turkey and then to the United States. Just as significant, however, is Said's sympathy for the decision Auerbach took to exile himself, as it were, from a regime that would demand cooperation in exchange for employment, status, and funding.

Like Auerbach (1973: 11–78), Said valued Dante's adaptation of the classical and Christian tradition of *figura* to secular history. In turn, Said created a figure of Auerbach as a "discrete particular" of the threatened and dying form of literary humanistic studies, the disappearance of which Said noted and lamented as soon as the early 1980s. What then is the figure of Auerbach? We know the Auerbachian figure takes on the hardest tasks with the longest historical vision and an understanding of shaping forces, the consequences of which he imagines. Against these forces and within the long history, he does work of a kind not easily done and generally unsupported, work that until recently has remained a point of reference for critical scholarship. The Auerbach figure was above all independent of alluring prospects by first refusing the institutional temptations and finally and fundamentally by being a Jew, whose life chances were at risk and deeply circumscribed. Auerbach adapted his circumstances to a profound intellectual exile that began before his move to Turkey and that sustained and reflected his deepest humanistic values. Neither melancholy nor cynicism scarred his work. Auerbach concluded his programmatic essay, "Philology and '*Weltliteratur*,'" with the ethically foundational statement of how

12. For a discussion of Adorno and the particular, see Bové 2021: 4–15, 43–78.

intellectuals should stand in relation to their world and their responsibilities: "Delicatus ille est adhuc cui patria dulcís est, fortis autem cui omne solum patria est, perfectus vero cui mundus totus exilium est" (Hugo of St. Victor, quoted in Auerbach 1969: 1–17). Hugo of St. Victor wrote these lines in his *Didascalion*, and Auerbach chose them to express the severe discipline critical scholarship requires, namely, to separate from one's home and one's inheritance, even though these offer the most precious seeming and enabling resources. Auerbach's ethics are layered but simple. The critical intellectual, the humanist philologist, must self-exile from nation because "our philological home is the earth" (Auerbach 1969: 17). The underlying motives are two: love of the world and its inhabitants and freedom to earn and express that love through creatively intelligent responsible and responsive work. Finding a home in mainstream institutions, disciplines, and practices—belonging communally to select groups of specialists or jargon speakers—these are ethical errors that Auerbach sensed and Said saw belonged to the emergence of technological orders tied to fascism and authoritarianism.

Said disentangled some consequences of Auerbach's situation and work, leaving us the two general conclusions I have mentioned. These consequences, these conclusions, which many may never know or might ignore and set aside, matter because the love for humanity and the struggle to be free of developing authoritarian and technological domination is constant. Like Auerbach, Said opposed nationalism, not only as an ideological position but as part of the ideological apparatus apparent in specialized areas of study. American studies experts, for example, can easily remain in love with their national tradition, even as its critics, because that tradition is an enabling career resource, a necessity for work and productivity. Similarly, narrow field or subfield specialization is a form of "homing" that can deny freedom needed to earn the love for humanity. The worldly complexity of humanity does not exist in nor can it be adequately found in a technologically defined deep well of specialization the borders of which are patrolled by the jargons and institutions that house them. "That's not in my field" emblematizes the willingness not to try to know, to come near, to produce the work that matches in importance the very worldly demands made by the historical moment and tendencies. The development of fields and subfields might appear to be an act of disentangling, generating more experts with deeper but narrower curiosity. Such a model is not, however, that model of the humanities, nor does it preserve the essential quality of the humanities, the responsibility lovingly to nurture the possibility of the human with the most enriched judgment. The standards and goals in this critical intellectual ethic are high and quite precisely not easily adopted by those at home in expert institutions: "The more one is able to leave one's cultural home, the more easily is one able to judge it, and the whole world as well, with the spiritual detachment *and* generosity necessary for true vision" (Said 1978: 259). Said concludes with a consequential postulate we ignore at our peril: "The more easily, too, does one assess oneself and alien cultures with the same combination of intimacy and distance."

In his Auerbach, Said poses the highest goals and most estimable qualities of critical humanism and the secular humanist critic. The university and other institutions that once harbored humanistic scholarship should have done a better job of inculcating the personal and professional qualities required to meet this ethical ideal. Of course, not to be at home in any locality means not to be satisfied with a career in any available subfield, with professional success as a leader in composition, digital humanities, postcolonialism, or other MLA-listed work areas. The university's humanistic pedagogy should require both constant suspicion of established rhetorics and practices of recognized areas, "sites" where conversation goes on easily among those with similar concerns and jargons. Also, the university should have sought and inculcated the qualities needed to assess the personal and institutional practices in which the scholar works while studying the object of investigation. Where there is the most consensus and ease of conversation there should be the gravest ethical concern. Above all, the universities should have realized the continuing social and species value of humanistic ethics of the type figured in this Auerbach. It should always preserve the humanist capacity for judgment outside even the aesthetic sphere of artistic and cultural evaluation. It should above all have inculcated in itself and the members of its departments the need to cultivate persons with just the ethical and intellectual ambitions and standards of such figures as this Auerbach. We should remember that this Auerbach appears as a figure of such value to human and worldly life as it does because it emerged from the study of technologically driven political economies running in parallel with or in direct connection to forms of tyranny and authoritarianism.[13] Not

---

13. We could study the systematic adoption of authorized practices by thinking about meritocracy, especially the effort of some to sustain an essential meritocratic position within a changing reward system, one in which natural language knowledge has less market value than machine language. We could also recall the rarity of leading intellectuals within the meritocracy. For a useful critique of meritocracy, see Rimbert 2020.

to preserve the independent place of critical humanistic work and qualities is to put at risk creativity, imagination, and freedom. Unfortunately, as I have hinted, the universities, often with the agreement of academics within the humanistic departments, abandoned these ethical standards with unfortunate political consequences. The intention of most was not to advance authoritarianism and in some case not even technological domination, although recent applications of data science to the formation of professionals inside what were English and other humanistic departments such as history proves the willingness of many colleagues to advance within the technophilic tracks funded by the state and Silicon Valley.

Digital humanities is not the only development harmful to criticism as such an ethically and intellectually high art. From fairly early on in the construction of "World Literature," colleagues have worried about the institute's place at the metropolitan center of the American empire and what seems to have been its journal's decision to publish in the lingua franca of the global order, English. Jacob Emery (2014) noted that global English, represented in this case by the successful anthology *Norton Anthology of World Literature*, made redundant the founding insight of modern thinking about world literature, namely, the Saidian notion of worldliness as the given material fact: "Even though literature is already in the world by virtue of being written, the redundant modifier 'World Literature' adds value." Rather than accept that literature is always *weltlich*, that is, secular and contrapuntal, carrying always the marks of human struggles for freedom from systemic and cultural constraints, "World Literature" turns to neoliberal adaptation for placement. "World Literature responds to the forces of globalization by identifying with them," Emery concludes. Nothing less is lost than criticism as a secular worldly act. In its place comes the spectacular simulation of criticism formed by the conventional apparatus of mainstream political institutional formations.

"World Literature" studies find themselves at home in the imperial center, in the imperial language, and within the dominant neoliberal technological and political economic structure. "World Literature" always contained the potential to justify such imperial practices and notions. Goethe said that that Germans and the German language were especially apt to conduct the business of world literature.[14] Unlike Auerbach, he did not suggest alienating the study and judgment of world literatures from his home or national lan-

---

14. Damrosch 2014 follows its editor's introduction with Goethe, "Conversations with Eckermann on *Weltliteratur*" (15–22), as the founding theoretical statement in the field.

guage, from his (mistaken) notion of the special ethical position of the modern German. In the conversation with Eckermann, Goethe spoke of how the German could most easily adapt to "foreign idiosyncrasies" and how this and "the great supplement of our language make German translations particularly accurate and satisfying" (Yadav 2009). In other words, Goethe's speculations on world literature blatantly centered the German nation and language in his approach to the world of literary circulation. Today's critics would find this centering completely unsatisfactory, especially since it belongs to the European ethnographic tendency at the heart of Orientalism to map the world in relation to its privileged metropolitan centers. World literature studies replicates this condemned Goethean gesture with its easy centering of English. World literature studies neglects or refuses the difficult critical task of being not at home as an essential condition to love and to be human. The institutionalization of world literature repeated Goethe's program to bring the world's literatures together through the uniqueness of a metropolitan, ethically advanced language, substituting English for German. The Englishing of world literature within the metropole expands the original Weimar program and develops it in good part via the imperial institutions of US university instruction.[15]

The editors of *The Journal of World Literature* hold appointments in the United States, the PRC, Australia, Israel, and Belgium. Among their outstanding credentials are PhDs from Harvard, Yale, and Michigan and professorships in English and comparative literature. The journal's call does not rest on or emerge from the sort of principles engaged critical thinking about world literature has developed over the last century. Rather, the call represents its virtue in a pluralistic and diverse openness that would create a professional community whose identifying characteristics are not critical or "self-reflexive." "The *Journal of World Literature* aspires to bring together scholars interested in developing the concept of World Literature, and to provide the most suitable environment for contributions from all the world's literary traditions. It creates a forum for re-visiting global literary heritages, discovering valuable works that have been undeservedly ignored, and introducing aspects of the transnational global dissemination of literature, with translation as a focus."[16] Emery (2014) notes that "the extraordinary thing"

15. For two definitive treatments of the problematic nature of English-centered humanistic work, see Cleary 2021 and Mufti 2016.
16. *Journal of World Literature*, "Overview," https://brill.com/view/journals/jwl/jwl-overview .xml (accessed August 13, 2020).

about world literature studies "is the ferment of scholarly activity it repre-sents." "Build a field and they will come" might be the best rubric for this truth.

Aamir Mufti has studied the imperial construction that is world litera-ture and its persistent ramifications common even in oppositional tropes meant to break the metropolitan grasp inherent especially in the Englishing of world literature. Notions such as diversity or the local inhere within the world literature construct that not only fantasizes a seductive one world of literature but, as an extension of European politics, the plurality of national languages and literatures meant as the content of the world literature dream. Developing Said's insistence that the critic must be of the world but of no nation, Mufti explains how to consider seriously the critical secular force of "*weltlich.*" Mufti (2016) calls this force the "radicalization of philol-ogy." He describes the proper subject for literary study resting on the basic principles necessary to guide work aiming to meet its humanistic responsi-bilities, which he explains:

> What we have to teach when we teach World Literature is precisely the history (and the contemporary workings) of these relations of force and powers of assimilation and the ways in which writers and texts respond to such pressures from a variety of locations in the world. The universalism that is inherent in the task of rethinking the concepts of World Literature thus has to be confronted with linguistic heterogeneity and the concept itself uncoupled from the effects of standardization both within and across languages and cultures that come masked as diversity. (Mufti 2016: 280)

Many literary humanists in their practice and in their institutional decisions have forgotten these responsibilities essential to the humanities, and so they move away from any identity with humanism if not the literary. They adopt the model of social and natural science, the pose of neutrality, of openness to the development of thinking about a field, without the judg-ment about the project that must constantly accompany work freighted, as in world literature, with consequences inherent in the modes by which our work replicates metropolitan modalities, themselves part of the long history of empire, technologization, and authoritarianism.

Of course, some will say that contemporary world literature studies rest upon continuing efforts at struggle in worldly terms—postcolonial stud-ies, antiracialist movements, and gender studies. In several moments of great intellectual and cultural importance, and most often against considerable resistance, women and those whom the ruling classes call minorities gained vital positions in the academy, often successfully breaking open the established fields of study, introducing entire cultures, the archives of multiple intertwined histories and literatures, into institutions often ill-prepared and unwilling to welcome them. Sometimes, after long struggle, many excellent things have happened. The work done by Farah Jasmine Griffin is exemplary. She brought African American music and the spoken word together in particularly important books that played a role in the creation of the new Department of African American and Diaspora Studies at Columbia. Her work also influenced the Pulitzer decision to award the Music Prize for 2018 to Kendrick Lamar.[17] So, with imaginative critical struggle within fragmentation and against resistance comes vital new work of social consequence and reconsolidation in important new institutions for research and criticism.

Along the way, some forces defined by other critical and creative ambitions damaged the authority of criticism in the literary humanities. The creation of women's studies programs, for example, in large public research universities such as Wisconsin, brought the social sciences into contest with the humanities. Academic critique of misogynistic politics requires bringing all possible methods to bear to reveal the workings of transactional oppression. A special issue of *Signs*, for example, titled "Gender and the Rise of the Global Right," suggests how the humanities have marginalized themselves at times in this effort (Graff, Kapur, and Walters 2019). This special issue has a plurality of contributors from the social sciences. The few contributors with literary humanities backgrounds, that is, with advanced degrees in the study of language and literature or an academic appointment in such a field, more or less leave behind their literary critical knowledge and methods in their accounts of organizations, ideas, and memes that contribute to social injustice, such as the suppression of abortion rights (Mason 2019).[18] Social science models entered into what had been literature departments, and with the end of the theory movement, social science methods escaped the reach of critical judgment once associated with the humanities.

17. Kendrick Lamar won the Pulitzer Prize for music in 2018 for his rap album *DAMN.* See Pulitzer Prizes, "The 2018 Pulitzer Prize Winner in Music," https://www.pulitzer.org /winners/kendrick-lamar (accessed August 18, 2020).
18. Professor Mason took a PhD in English from the University of Minnesota and holds a professorship in English at the University of Kentucky. She is also affiliated faculty with the Center for Right Wing Studies at Berkeley. University of Kentucky, "Carol Mason," https://gws.as.uky.edu/users/cama239 (accessed August 13, 2020).

What in English we call the humanities and in French *les sciences humaines* were in German the *Geisteswissenschaften*. These are not identical notions. In French, the human sciences would include all those disciplines that study the human—what in American universities we would often call social sciences, such as anthropology. However, the German research university, on which founders modeled the great American research universities, assigned the *Geisteswissenschaften* two tasks that American literary humanities especially have, or risk having, abandoned. The *Geisteswissenschaften* had two authorized tasks: to balance the research university's commitments to the natural sciences and to evaluate the nature, place, and function of all knowledge and knowledge production, including that of science. In other words, the originary function and long-standing aim of the humanities was to be both an alternative to the growth of science in the universities and a legitimate source for evaluating the scientific technological project. Scholars have studied the long history of natural, medical, and now technical or data sciences' rise to dominance in the university (Rossiter 1992). Scientific dominance is so normal that critics no longer lament the fact but study science for its (only sometimes forced) sell out to capitalism (Day 2018). As in the case of *Signs*, methods and values have traveled from the social sciences toward the humanities rather than from the literary fields, with their traditional expertise in language, cultural forms, and historical human experience. The traditional ideal of studying art in language to develop humanistic sensibilities as well as technical capacities to read the culture and its politics has lost considerable hold, even when, as in the case of the essay on abortion rights in this special issue of *Signs*, an important aspect of the avowed topic is rhetoric. Moreover, the role Dilthey imagined for the humanities as the agent to examine and criticize the function of scientific and other methods of knowledge production and formation has given way before the apparent utility and profitability of natural, data, and social science (Bové 2014). All these disciplines have an at least implicit reason to defend their established interests by disregarding or repressing the critical humanities.

Two other developments threaten not only the priority but also the existence of criticism. One is Distant Reading, associated with Franco Moretti but now developed far beyond his original ideas, about which skeptics and defenders have said perhaps too much.[19] Let us disentangle some

19. See Schiff 2014 and Arac 2002. For the linkages between Distant Reading and world literature, see Moretti 2000.

of Distant Reading's goals and consequences. Perhaps its most fundamental aim is to replace the research and pedagogical methods that relied upon the immanent (or intimate) study of particular writings (now called texts) with models of apprehension that gather writings into large categorizable bodies of study beyond the reach of immanent reading. The result should be knowledge of a kind not available to close reading or theory. Knowledge, not experience, not *Bildung*, is aim and result. Forming the human in the experience with and of literary and artistic creations is not a goal; indeed, Distant Reading considers such a goal as impossible as the survival of humanistic culture after modernity. To legitimate this end of Europe account, Moretti's *Distant Reading* tells an antithetical, even Gnostic version of Said's story in *Orientalism*. Moretti admits that the great twentieth-century philologists such as Auerbach and his model, Han Robert Curtius, saw humanistic culture dissipating into paradoxically ever richer and more threatening fragments. We could tell a story over this of the crisis of European empires inducing the colloquial effect, the center will not hold. In Moretti's account, modernity destroyed the meaning and comfort provided by the totality of humanistic culture when it existed and could be known as such. Moretti imagines that Distant Reading could supplement that experience and by its technological and conceptual innovations—essentially the end of intimate reading—could regather the knowledge of and in that culture, but differently. Distant Reading could take on the fragmenting pluralities that were other to Western humanistic culture and reorganize the field as world literature in a globalized era. The results would replace the collapsed European unity with the richness of non-European worlds; the process and product would displace and supplement the end of Europe. In this way, Moretti belongs to a long tradition of European intellectuals who have used the crisis of Europe to rethink the world, often recentering the metropole in new ways (Bové 2021: 31). In other words again, Distant Reading would rework the ambitions and seek the satisfactions of empire.

What techniques would produce this knowledge and this new formation? First, concepts resting on world theory and then modes of divested reading that distribute what once would have been experience into outsourcing, the means to produce the data needed to give a new formation to Goethe's charge to do world literature. All efforts to meet Goethe's charge rest on a privileged subject, identity, and language. The available technology mediates the intent and result. Distant Reading, tied to world literature, would provide all the steps paralleling German in Goethe's command (Moretti 2013: 5–9, 41–45).

When Distant Reading meets its logical bedfellow, Silicon Valley technologies of data science, then it can become "Digital Humanities," where the avowed new knowledge has to do with quantity and speed, with processing a larger number of texts (data) more quickly than humans unassisted can do, and often making the material visible, mapping it graphically or as in a game. The end results are many, we are told:

> This shift from reading a single book "on paper" to the possibility of browsing many digital texts is one of the origins and principal pillars of the Digital Humanities domain, which helps to develop solutions to handle vast amounts of cultural heritage data—text being the main data type. In contrast to the traditional methods, the Digital Humanities allow to pose new research questions on cultural heritage datasets. Thereby, existent algorithms and tools provided by the computer science domain are used, but for various research questions in the humanities, scholars need to invent new methods in collaboration with computer scientists. . . . A major impulse for this trend was given by Franco Moretti. (Jänicke et al. 2015)

The union of digital humanities and Distant Reading stands out in Moretti's plan, and scholars should stress this in evaluating its consequences.[20] Phenomena such as the world literature initiative, Distant Reading, and their intersections with digital humanities provide new career possibilities when the state no longer invests in the literary humanities as it did during the Cold War (Kosar 2011).[21] These new careers fill places in faculties not in addition to but as replacements for scholars formed in the practice of learning natural languages and reading books on paper. Furthermore, this displacement not only removes from society the specially trained scholars formed in relation to paper but also, by pedagogical and institutional adjustment, removes from the social world human beings whose lives, experience, and formation rest on the worldliness of history, traces of which disappear as these new constellations replace them with data and archives.

20. Arac turns to this point in his essay, Arac 2002.
21. Title III of the National Defense Education Act of 1958 funded not only science and math but modern foreign language programs; title VI funded area studies programs and their attendant foreign language studies. The legislation stated its purpose succinctly: "To strength the national defense and to encourage and assist in the expansion and improvement of educational programs to meet critical national needs; and for other purposes." National Defense Education Program, 20 U.S.C. §§ 401–589 (1958).

Critics should examine the origins of and sentiments in similar phrases used by world literature persons and digital humanists as terms of self-legitimation. Each is concerned with "heritage," world literature with literary heritage and digital humanities with "cultural heritage," especially as made into data sets. In 1972, UNESCO adopted, and most nation-states have signed, the Convention concerning the Protection of World Cultural and Natural Heritage (Haw 2013). Inherently, heritage is a matter of property in economy, tradition, practice, and law.[22] A long history of the term is beyond the reach of this paper. A shorter examination of its use and effects within international neoliberal regimes could be modeled on Sarah Brouillette's disentanglement of UNESCO's involvement with literary culture. Her study exposes how "the critical discourses of World Literature" ground themselves "in the political economy of global literary institutions and markets" (Brouillette 2019: 2). She demystifies claims that UNESCO preserves unique treasures of human creativity or supports the creation and distribution of new literatures circulating among hungry readers. The cultural heritage model applied to books results in profitable "literary tourism and festival programming" while meeting at best the sentimental needs of liberal culture or the globalizing regulation of neoliberal control and distribution methods. The result, she argues, is not a story of triumph but "a story of decline."

Digital humanists claim they produce new knowledge and study vastly more material than any reader can do. They can produce data sets where they are needed, and they can visualize or gamify objects and processes not previously available for knowledge in any but Cartesian and fragmentary ways.[23] That these claims appear virtuous is a consequence of money flowing in some directions and not others; this is an effect of competitive state policy and neoliberal assertions of the priority of data imitating the intelligence of the market.[24] We have seen that Said noticed a similar pat-

22. Oxford English Dictionary Online, s.v. "heritage," https://www-oed-com.pitt.idm.oclc .org/view/Entry/86230?result=1&rskey=gCa7sX& (accessed August 18, 2020).

23. For a list of projects funded by the National Endowment of the Humanities, see "Funded Projects Query Form," https://securegrants.neh.gov/publicquery/main.aspx?q=1 &a=0&n=0&o=0&ot=0&k=0&f=0&s=0&cd=0&p=0&d=1&dv=12&y=0&prd=0&cov=0&prz =0&wp=0&ob=year&or=DESC (accessed August 20, 2020). I cannot establish that this sample is representative of all work done in digital humanities, but it illustrates the kind of work the state funds.

24. The National Endowment for the Humanities (NEH) created the Office of Digital Humanities in 2008. The NEH support for digital humanities projects intensified at that

tern in the interwar years of the twentieth century, namely the development of a nationally supported technocentric cultural economy parallel or linked to the development of an authoritarian politics (Simms 2019).[25] In choosing romance philology, Auerbach loosened his relation to this complex before fleeing to Turkey to protect his life from Nazi genocide. Said's reading of Auerbach establishes a figure for the humanities expressing and living the ethics required to judge and be other than the kinds of subject promoted by such a techno-statist project. Perhaps Hannah Arendt's (1963) influence acted on Said in this work on Auerbach. This philologist always stands against the banality of evil so normalized as to be invisible to many in the intelligentsia, those who sustained professional and bureaucratic careers up to and even past the moment when the disaster of Nazism glared up from its ground (Haffner 2002).

The new digital sciences dissolve not only the notion but the fact or possibility that the humanities might be the place for the critical judgment of knowledge production. As a dominant pedagogical model, they will also replace the education needed to form the humanists capable of exercising such judgment. The data scientists transform "books" or "art works" into things suitable for the machine. Digitalists identify the object of their processing as "cultural heritage data," a gesture that adapts materials to the machine and platform. The gesture has provoked resistance from those who defend libraries (Darnton 2010). However, more important is the digi-

---

time: "Endowment created an office devoted to fostering the marriage between technology and the humanities. All it took was the Internet" (Hindley 2018). The NEH tells the story of its intensifying investment in digital humanities as a result, in part, of its consultation with digital humanities "pioneers" who "regularly encountered skepticism about the value of their work." The NEH decided to reject the judgment of the humanists whose work it had supported for decades "to concentrate its support for the Digital Humanities." Digital humanities pioneers benefited not only from the NEH's funding but from the symbolic force of its policy shift: "NEH's recognition of the field and its imprimatur helped scholars signal to their institutions, donors, and tenure and promotion committees the significance of their work." This article does not explain how the NEH funded this initiative at a time of declining appropriations from the US Congress. Nor does it explain if the shift in funding resulted in fewer resources available for those who were skeptical of digital humanities or doing more traditional humanistic work.

25. Simms (2019: 1–23) examines how Hitler developed an anticapitalist, anti-Anglo-Saxon political anxiety after World War I and explains how this played a part in Hitler's later violent policies. As part of his study, Simms makes clear that Hitler was not alone in Germany worrying the national need to compete with Anglo-Saxons across the range of intellectual, material, and political frontiers.

talists' not so silent aggression against ways of speaking that exclude their methods or would, at best, reduce their methods to the service of humanists. The tool must have priority over the hand for the instrumentalists of history. In its final form, this technophilic constellation of Distant Reading, world literature, and digital humanities will remove the human subject from the encounter with what society used to call literature, which figure, lest we forget, embodies a long-lasting originary institution of human life and experience that has, until recently, been cultivated and nurtured as such because, as in the case of Dante, it could assign to proper hellish places those who offend against the human.[26] A final way to see this constellation would be as an aggression against memory, against the shared experiences of the work humans do upon themselves, as its results, means, and records rest in writing, reading, and criticizing. This is true even as the adaptation to the digital humanities alters the human relation to the question of the human. As Walter Benjamin (1999: 217) alerted us during the technophilic authoritarian interwar years, the human itself is at risk in such formations: "the *physis* that is being organized for it in technology can, through all its political and factual reality, be produced only in that image space to which profane illumination initiates us." First, representatives of this constellation admit they would displace the basic and perhaps permanent discoveries of the humanities (Smithies 2014). If, as Benjamin suggests, technology mediates not only the relation between the human and the natural, it also mediates the relations among humans, the relation of the human to itself, and life itself to the question of the human, the necessity and possibility of thinking the human. Then, second, in so doing, this constellation, in canceling the intimate encounter between book and reader, removes from the experience of forming a humanist the insight into the record of human self-making of the kind that gives us an Auerbach or *Mimesis*. Losing that intimacy distanced by love obscures the central fact that humans have made themselves historical beings. Nurturing that fact offers freedom to the human as the species aspires to think and make itself. Freedom comes from a deep sense

26. See, for example, Auerbach 1953: 174–202. For an elaboration of the importance of this text to the human as well as the humanities, see Bové 2008: 40–56. For those who remember Raymond Williams's keyword entry on "literature," an objection will come to mind: "literature," in the sense I am using it, is a modern category whose history we trace from the eighteenth century. However, we should not commit the nominalist's error and believe that something does not exist until we have a term to name it. Also, keep in mind that from the thirteenth century, according to Williams ([1976] 1983: 184), literature would nicely elide with literacy, that is, individual reading and the book or manuscript.

of historicality. The humanist knows that the world presented as reality has about it no necessity. Its contingency means it can yield to alternatives imagined by art and critics (Bové 2021).

Digitized Distant Reading accelerates the death of the reader. Roland Barthes's spectacular essay, "La mort de l'auteur," often lazily lamented for killing off the writer, meditated profoundly on the temporal and economic relations between the person of the writer and the text, especially as these affect the act of reading. Barthes's (1968: 61–67) analysis changed the conception of literature and the function of the critical humanist by decentering the figure of the established causal subject-identity represented as the outside origin of writing. Barthes's (1968: 66) conclusion placed the reader at the core of literature: "Le vrai lieu de l'écriture, c'est la lecture." Since Barthes's demonstration that experimental writing shifted the center of writing from the author to the reader, we can better situate Hortense Spiller's claim that readers must in part create their object. In the study of problems and texts excluded from the regular business of normalized academic humanities, Spillers insists that theorizing of race, gender, and writing requires the partial creation of an object against a censoring and resisting background. Such intense counter-reading devoted to the liberatory potential of critical creativity as Spillers displays it develops and legitimates the principal Barthes discovered. Spillers's work assumed the worldliness of texts as well as their sheer facticity. As Barthes would have put it, Spillers untangled the complicated interweavings of experience produced and recorded in language—all as part of the effort to free language in relation to the political project of freeing persons and traditions against the overwhelming resistance of exclusionary pressures (68).[27]

The death of the author hypothesis had proven its value when Spillers, in the arduous task of criticism, disentangled the realities of a Black studies movement that had migrated to the academy. Spillers solidified a principle in work far from the scene of its original articulation. The reader became for Spillers (2003: xvi) the problem of "the speaking subject," the figure that must be studied to understand the "dilemma" of Black intellectuals whose relation to the academy—as destination or not—threatened to mire "the African-American Studies ensemble" in "a retrogressive, male-centered, uncritical synthesis." Because of Spillers's work, a new principle with ethical political force imposed a responsibility on humanists: the critical

---

27. "Dans l'écriture multiple; en effet, tout est à démêler, mais rien n'est à déchiffrer" (Barthes 1968: 66).

reader must engage with the culturally, politically, and racially important forms of human life in our society and literature. Criticism, now so much under attack, had to become and remain a space for antiracism and human freedom to nurture the question, What is the human?

Not long after the death of the author, however, a countermovement began, one that would displace Barthes's and Spillers's principles for criticism as essential elements of humanistic literary education. For digital humanities, Distant Reading, and their nexus in world literature, the reader became a superfluous obstruction to a new science that would map or graph measurable results from the massed archives of "cultural heritage," a capacity beyond the limits imposed by individual finitude. To put it briefly, Distant Reading would eliminate the subject from literary study as how the knowledge of literature would be gained in a culture; consequently, it would eliminate the training that produced humanists and so would eliminate literary humanists themselves as a category of human potentiality, resigning them to the ash heap of history. In other words yet again, distance learning deskills literary scholars; its pedagogies displace the training required to create literary humanists; and computer language learning or coding replaces the acquisition and mastery of natural languages. As I have suggested, the goals of Distant Reading are of a kind like the aims of digital humanities. Each would reduce the trained judgment of the literary humanist to irrelevance and thereby establish the impunity of science and pseudo-scientific technical practices and theories to regulate the value and production of knowledge, indeed, to redefine the function of the humanities as a matter only of knowledge, wherein lies the traditional sign of positivism (Long and So 2019).[28] As a result, literary humanists would disappear

28. The authors judge that Nan Da, in her critique of computational science, has no right to speak from outside what they consider to be the needed expertise: "The errors reflect a basic lack of understanding of fundamental statistical concepts and are akin to an outsider to literary studies calling George Eliot a 'famous male author.' Even more concerning, Da fails to understand statistical method as a contextual, historical, and interpretive project. The essay's greatest error, to be blunt, is a humanist one" (Long and So 2019). It would not matter to a critical judgment that *Middlemarch* fails in its claims to representational realism if the author's gender were "properly" known. Indeed, one might say it is the height of antihumanist arrogance to pass over with such a sense of self-evidence the gender-bending of that name, George Eliot. More important, however, Hoyt and So demonstrate my contention that digital humanities would remove the function of judgment long associated with the humanities from the university, thereby allowing computational and other sciences their impunity in the service of forces that no critic would be allowed to disentangle. I thank Hoyt and So for providing such simple evidence. I also thank Aamir Mufti for reminding me to read this forum.

from the university and so from the society. Have we considered the consequences of this canceling?

At least since Aristotle and then again since the passage from Renaissance humanism in the West to the Baroque crisis of allegoresis, the now often deconstructed human subject has been the mechanism for possessing, experiencing, valuing, and legitimating research into and sustaining the pedagogies of literature. The post-humanist technical modes for breaking down criticism, if we take Moretti's displacement of the subject into a technological field, come up against and would erase the significance of diverse artists whose difference from value of the digital constellation stands out in figures such as James Baldwin and Paul Preciado. These artists present their own subjectivities in various forms of creative struggle against repressive regimes. Literature itself, in these exemplary instances, embodies values antagonistic to those advanced by the anti-humanist constellation within the technophilic academy. Preciado's (2013: 11–12) remarkable *Testo Junkie* introduces itself as outside categories of writing, all of which it uses to make itself at once familiar and alien, intimate and distant. Read the book to imagine the violence of transforming its experimental and fictional record of a body transgressed by what it is not and then reimagine it reduced to data of cultural heritage. The second image sterilizes human existence, degrades its value, denies the free uniqueness of vision and experiment. Ironically, it would hide the evident, in this case, of the power and contradictory potentials of pharmacology in a biopolitics specific to neoliberalism and the complexities of willed gendering it constructs. In the simplest terms, the work of art asserts values other than and opposite to those that mock the humanist. This might well be because the pharmacological and technological cultures, while not the same, overlap considerably.

James Baldwin is one of the most important artists thinking the experience of race in America. The ruling qualities in his art, in his poetics, and in his politics are gravely at odds with the technophilic, professional, and American nationalist projects that are shifting critical humanism, the vehicle for imaginative and effective reception of his work from the American social world. Is the shift of those poetic possibilities not then a form of racism? Baldwin made "a moving point of the general unknowability of the artist, of the inescapable and perhaps inexplicable function of the artist active in a society or set of social groups" (Bové 2021: 254). He willingly accepted the term *artist* to describe his life and work. He embraced the term to assert the necessity of freedom, ethical integrity, and the identity of art "as essential to the universal human project." Baldwin made as explicit as possible the values and responsibilities inherent in the humanistic projects that define the species' best efforts: "The artist's struggle for his integrity," Baldwin ([1963] 2011: 50–51) writes, "must be considered as a kind of metaphor for the struggle, which is universal and daily, of all human beings on the face of this globe to get to become human beings." Baldwin's aspirational ethics require the working out of life as a process of nurturing and advancing the human. Moreover, not the technologist or meritocrat but the poet and the critic house the aspiration most fully. "Poets (by which I mean all artists) are finally the only people who know the truth about us. Soldiers don't. Statesmen don't. Priests don't. Union leaders don't. Only poets." Baldwin warned a racist, technophilic, and war making America of the dystopia that needlessly waited on its path: "when it ceases to produce poets, and, what is even more crucial, when it ceases in any way whatever to believe in the report that only poets can make" (51). Critical humanists are the kinds of persons who can hear, amplify, and disentangle those reports—in all their contradictory complexity. Technical devices for disrupting the humanities have an inherent problem in dealing with race, gender, and other locations of violent discrimination and criminal oppression, of cultural silencing, of an absence from the archives.[29] They replace the human relations of love, the movements of intimacy and distance, hindering the task Spillers lays out as essential, the responsibility to create the loved object against the dangerous processes of normalization (Hepworth and Church 2018).

Academic schools, departments, and disciplines in numerous ways make visible the disruption of traditional humanistic modes and their developments. Schools, doing the bidding of their administrative leaders, often "nudge" faculty toward the new forms of practice. Just as the National

29. The Internet finance site Investopedia lists *disruptive* among the dictionary of financial and commercial terms it defines. It points out that *disruptive* has become a buzzword since Christensen (1997) 2013. Investopedia points out that disruption aims to replace "an older process, product, or habit" with a process that "usually has superior attributes that are immediately obvious." The disruptive is a "threat" to established practice that can allow new profit opportunities. Investopedia, "Terms," https://www.investopedia.com /terms/d/disruptive-technology.asp (accessed August 20, 2020). I note how this characterization of disruption applies to several technologies, such as distant learning and digital humanities as well as to the procedures followed by the NEH to advance digital humanities with funds and legitimacy in established institutions. This definition also suggests how and why the disruptive attracts as a source of opportunity for early adopters who can then guide others to normalize behavior in line with new machines. The cell phone stands out, of course, as does "platforming" and "gaming" in education as well as social exchange systems like Twitter and Facebook.

Endowment for the Humanities offers money for desired disruptive new fields, so academic leaders guide faculty with funds and other privileges toward the leaders' goals for the discipline. In this, the leaders embrace and follow the technology of neoliberal management theorists and behavioral economics (Spiliakos 2017). In keeping with neoliberal control of the workplace comes control of the work done, of its objects and purposes. Departments dissolve as much from this motive as from enrollment challenges and the pluralization of concern. The word *studies* in departmental names is an example of such disruption. It is a noun titling many departments and fields. Columbia University proudly advertises the Department of French and Romance Philology as "one of the oldest and most distinguished French Departments in the United States."[30] Other prestigious universities also have French departments—Yale for example. Yet others—Harvard, Princeton, Pittsburgh, and Michigan—have departments of French and Italian or locate the study of these languages in departments of Romance languages. However, several other universities and colleges have some variation of departments of French studies—UCLA, Bryn Mawr, Smith, Brown, Penn State, Rice, and many others. Almost all major universities and college still have English departments, but "English Studies" has begun to appear in renaming those units, suggesting the felt need to accommodate the fact that English departments now do many things—to solidify the truth that English is no longer the one or (few) more things it used to be. In the UK, English studies seems a bit more common than in the United States. Durham University though finds a parallel in Miami University; both have English studies departments. A brief look at faculty listings, course offerings, degree programs, and methods taught suggests that in many cases "studies" represents the disruption of a field into many subfields, preparing the way for sub-subfields.

Of course, these choices were not necessary but made with the consent of the governed in many cases who felt the pressure and allure of administrative and statist policies and promises as well as the felt need to get beyond the inherited limits of whatever had seemed natural for so long. Nonetheless, departments had some choices. They might have remained French departments, for example, or, by contrast, become Francophonie departments, redefining French away from the nation-state. Given the *Oxford English Dictionary*'s decision to bring Indian words into the diction-

---

30. Columbia University, "French," https://french.columbia.edu/content/welcome-department -chair (accessed August 20, 2020).

ary, others might have remade themselves as departments of Englishes rather than English studies (Salazar 2017). Why might this matter?[31]

The National Council of Teachers of English published a book called *English Studies: An Introduction to the Discipline(s)*. In it, they speak of "the important qualities and functions of English studies' constituent disciplines" and advertise it this way: "Faculty and students in both undergraduate and graduate courses will find the volume an invaluable overview of an increasingly fragmented field, as will department administrators who are responsible for evaluating the contributions of diverse faculty members but whose academic training may be specific to one discipline."[32] English is no longer a discipline. It is an institutional home for several constituent disciplines. My own department offers undergraduate degrees in literature, composition, writing, and film and media studies. Each of these offers various tracks with highly credentialed distinguished colleagues teaching in each. The graduate program offers PhDs in cultural and critical studies, which might include work in digital humanities or pedagogy or archive or public humanities specializations. Another PhD in film and media studies could also include similar elements as well as other tracks leading to a dissertation. We also offer an MA in various areas and one of the oldest MFA programs in poetry writing, creative nonfiction, fiction, life writing, journalism, and so on. Several theories divide study in any one of these subfields. Even the constituent units have constituents in part because of the proliferation of subfields within the larger institutional frame. These subfields are sometimes specific to subject matters, which remain available to methods recognized by the traditional departments. None of what I describe describes only one department but characterizes the active professional life of any number of distinguished departments in Research 1 universities. Fragmentation and renewal can lead to needed advances on lines of basic humanistic principles.

As Spillers told us in *Black and White in Color*, studying Black literature within English departments has achieved a hard-won place, and in some schools has acquired its own separate department or program; recognized need for institutional identity coordinates with uniqueness of subject and method. Moreover, of course, in this case, political reasons of a national

31. For some sense of the history of English as a national and transnational value and struggle with profound institutional and political consequences, see Cleary 2021.
32. National Council of Teachers of English, "Store," https://secure.ncte.org/store/english -studies (accessed January 11, 2021).

kind press hard upon the university. Nevertheless, just as Columbia made an advance, Yale faced the mass resignation of faculty from its programs in ethnic studies to protest a failure of administrative support (Valentin 2019; Brown 2019).

The emergence of "studies" as an appendage eases the proliferation of subfields and their specific ways of speaking—often called "theories"—that separate participant speakers within the same department. As I said earlier, dictionaries call these local ways of speaking jargons. There can be no unified English department once colleagues stop speaking enough of the same language to understand or care about what happens among speakers in other subspecialties. In the extreme, departments house colleagues who do criticism and others who disbelieve in the very idea of doing so. Institutionally, academics speak of fragmentation in terms of hyperspecialization, of experts living and working in deep wells, uninformed by developments or traditions elsewhere. Moreover, institutional *ethoi* require tolerance of all the different subpractices, if, for example, there are such things as MLA sessions on the subfields. Anecdotally, many people would like to prove the dire fact of this situation by noting colleagues do not attend lectures and seminars from outside their subareas. Institutional thinkers about these questions differentiate between what they call strong and weak disciplines. Neuroscience is a strong discipline. English and comp lit are weak ones. The material consequences of that judgment are obvious. Conceptually, the difference is also clear. Some scholars worried about the political consequence of their fields' weakness want to ameliorate the problem but first need to understand it.

The Center for African American Research and Policy (CAARP) promotes examination of the characteristics and political consequences of strong versus weak fields. In the biological sciences, they argue, the hard/soft divide is the classic difference between pure and applied. Importantly, however, this apparent division is a consequence of the adaptability of research areas to the markets, which itself follows from the degree to which a given field of biology studies human life. The market determines strong versus weak in this case but only because the life sciences already meet the most fundamental criterion. CAARP's research discovered that strong disciplines are not necessarily any more applied than they are necessarily pure, that is, they are unmotivated by market forces. Rather, strong disciplines, those with the highest level of efficacy and value, are "based on the level of paradigmatic development within a field" (Jones 2011). What does this mean? First, it means a field with a clear memory of agreed-upon bases for future work derived from basic principles established by previous researchers and theorists. Second, it means these bases are shared and cannot be abandoned without substantial research not only correcting them but also replacing them with other shared foundations. Third, it means that whatever happens in any subfield can and often does matter to all others practicing elsewhere, requiring shared understanding of the consequences for each subfield of the learning in other fields. No subarea is or should be immune to work in other areas, that is, no subfield should feel itself at home in a jargon of self-reflection or conversation. Finally, it means practitioners understand that the work of the field has consequences outside itself because it is as a unified intellectual project more likely to alter the forms and ideas of social institutions and interests.

This little description suggests the humanities and cultural studies fields are weak disciplines, whose current crises result in part from their own behavior and from the distaste of their enemies inside and outside the university. Of course, a full takeover of former humanities departments by digitalists would give those departments the sort of unity normal in stronger disciplines. I have tried to suggest the cost of such a disruptive takeover and the need for humanists to evaluate its consequences for society, the species, and the planet before embracing the seemingly more secure and seductive paths on offer. Strong and weak in this institutional sense give no points to intellectual projects of a cultural-political sort attached to the experience and social existence of persons whose interests reside in the recognition provided by the institutionalized writing done in relation to their experience. It does, however, suggest that if the field were stronger it would better achieve whatever unified goals it might desire, even as subfields' specialists developed forms of research. (Colleagues might recover some strength if, rather than speaking into deep wells, their writing always included a clear statement of its *cui bono*: why does this work matter, to whom, and for what reason? Escaping the resonant tunnels not only shares knowledge but allows judgment to resonate. Each writer should state why the writing does indeed matter to its readers, even those outside the echoing conversations.) As I have already said, the history of literary humanism's highest achievements and ambitions show that criticism should be the customary practice and archive for a stronger field. But not everyone would agree, and disagreement comes from scholars who appear closer to the literary humanists that digital or distant studies persons might be.

Rita Felski's recent work, for example, is an attempt to unify literary studies into a single work area under slogans such as *how to do things with texts* or *stop being suspicious.* Felski's book, *The Limits of Critique*, appeared in 2015, and a coedited collection, *Critique and Postcritique*, appeared in 2017 (Felski 2015; Felski and Anker 2017). *The Limits of Critique* proposed various forms of affect—"attunement, identification, and affiliation"—as unifying sentiments, whose processes not only should be investigated across all subfields but should be taken as unifying the social subject in relation to which literary and other cultural consumables stand (Felski 2020). Once upon a time, one could make arguments believing, in good faith, they might have corrective value. Of course, the desire to have such arguments rested on the critical ethic, at times on suspicion, and often on the belief that errors exist for correction. In the crisis of 2008, Felski began her anticritical pedagogy by degrading art into the ordinariness of commodity consumption (Felski 2008). She argued that turning away from literature as an archive of "superiority" and toward the affective relations of people with books would relegitimate the humanities. I want to emphasize this moment as crucial in the harming of criticism. Were there time, this threshold would lead us into the age of fiscal crisis and austerity.

For now, we should address argument and error. The first chapter of Felski's 2008 book is called "Recognition," which, given the long paradigmatic history of literary studies, should rest on Aristotle's work. In a strong discipline, new work claims its relation to established principles and discoveries. The risk otherwise is mere projection. For Felski, recognition means nothing more than a reader seeing herself reflected in a book. She offers as an example the trans author Stephen Gordon, who, on reading Kraft-Ebbing, reports his pleasure and surprise in learning that others had felt confounded in their identity. Felski's story has to do with only a presumably innocent Gordon recording directly and frankly a mirrorlike moment. Gordon's delight and pleasure becomes one of a set of "vignettes of recognition," which together enable an aesthetics of self-discovery. She quotes Gadamer to legitimate clichés of experience such as Gordon's: "something that exists outside of me inspires a revised or altered sense of who I am" (Felski 2008: 24–25). The intellectual problems with this way of speaking are many. With the elimination of literature's specialness Felski also eliminates the critic, replacing the critic with the manipulator of texts, the figure who gives liberal commodity status to the poem or novel as nothing different from any other commodity any person might encounter in such a way as to feel. Felski licenses the seductive commodity's effect on the subject, making the "study of literature" as much part of commodity capitalism as advertising. Walter Benjamin had, of course, provided the definitive analysis of the seductive pleasure felt by consumers of mass-produced offerings. Writing of Benjamin's essay, "Paris, the Capital of the Nineteenth Century," Margaret Cohen (1989: 88) put the status of the commodity's control of desire in this way:

> Benjamin associates the phantasmagoria with commodity culture's experience of its material and intellectual products, echoing Marx's use of the term in *Capital*. . . . Benjamin extends Marx's statement on the phantasmagorical powers of the commodity to cover the entire domain of Parisian cultural products, a use of phantasmagoria that Marx himself initiates in *The Eighteenth Brumaire*. If the commodities displayed within the Universal Exhibitions manifest themselves as a phantasmagoria—"the phantasmagoria of capitalist culture reaches its most brilliant display in the Universal Exhibition of 1867"—intellectual reflection in the 19th century also takes on a phantasmagorical cast.

To replace criticism with willing submission to the commodity's control of affect and intellect is to sustain its phantasmagoria. The commodity as vampire lurks behind the unspoken seduction by narcissistic recognition in Felski's story of liberal self-development and liberation (Muschamp 2000).[33] She recommends we adopt this way of working in the humanities—or perhaps not, because with this way of work, they are no longer the humanities. Is this the intent?

The critic might be suspicious of this story, of this way of consuming art and literature like any other jewel box. The point of Felski's anticritical departure is simple: artworks are no different than other consumable objects or experiences that give pleasure. (The not incidental consequence is to eliminate the critic as gatekeeper in judging value.) Art joins all other objects and practices as helping devices along the way toward "self-fashioning"—a term popularized by the New Historicism and presumed to settle the aesthetic experience question (Alpers 1988). If English or literary

---

33. Muschamp (2000) gave a basic description of one inescapable conclusion to Benjamin's great study of Paris and modernity, which should have prevented Felski's work: "The arcade itself was a visual device: a spatial frame around the shop windows that inspired passersby with the desire to purchase la vie en rose. Behind the windows, novelties continuously appear. Parisians regard themselves in the reflective glass. Benjamin uses the word 'phantasmagoria' to describe the dream state in which the social contract is rewritten. 'The Arcades Project' is an Enlightenment project. By bringing awareness to its readers, the book will release them from the hold of manufactured states of mind."

study in general were a strong discipline—for example, as strong as economics in the age of Hayek—it would remember not only Benjamin but that recognition translates *anagnorisis*, which means the opposite of what Felski claims recognition means. The humanities do discover things that are reasonably certain and inheritable conclusions of thought. Aristotle's (1984: 2323, para. 1452a) *Poetics* has established that recognition is "a change from ignorance to knowledge, producing love or hate between the persons destined by the poet for good or bad fortune." Anagnorisis is the obverse of immediate familiarity. Gordon, Felski would have readers believe, recognizes himself in what she first read. The mechanism is self-seeing, a coming to the already known. Recognition in this sense is repetition, as the *ana* in anagnorisis means "again." The ruling affect is empathy, the basis for commonality or continuity. Anagnorisis is about other things and rests on other qualities.

In Aristotle, in the moment of anagnorisis, there is a trope, a turning in experience from this to that. There is a shift from one concept or belief to another. The shift is an intellectual act aiming toward an identification with either good or evil, an act itself resting on the critical faculty of judgment. Aristotle did not assume that poetry was not special, because theater was a socially crucial and definitive political fact in Athens. While it might purge pity and fear among the born citizen men in the audience, criticism—that is, the work Aristotle himself did—was far different from taking a lead from or granting priority to the audience's nonanalytic responses to the particular materials before them. The work of specific tragedies—not "the tragic"—purged pity and fear (Hays 2020). There was something important about the art form, which itself required careful intellectual analysis because it was itself the highest example of intelligent imagination at work. Aristotle had analyzed tragedy and poetics with a theory of imitation as an anthropological quality of the human species' being. Aristotle began from the observation of children learning by imitation, from delight in imitation, and in viewing successful imitation. Yet, in 2008—nearly twenty-five hundred years later!—Felski (2008: 24) proposes as the basis of an anticritical orientation this liberal claim about Wilde's *The Picture of Dorian Gray*: "if we, as readers, are made aware of a more general impressionability and susceptibility to imitation through Dorian's response, has an act of recognition not nevertheless taken place?" Aristotle was a serious thinker. Imitation provided pleasure to children who saw imitation, but imitation done properly, which is to say in the highest forms that became art, such as the Greek tragedy, would provide the species with important experience and formation. Aristotle stresses that not all persons can take the same gifts away from art's offerings. Philosophers, Aristotle's name for the most curious and capable people, would benefit from and delight most in the best imitative arts. They would learn the most, find places where thought could expand, where demands for discrimination were required, and where the qualities that made a being human could be best developed. We should recall that among those qualities were the principal goals of justice, freedom, and ecological responsibility—this last most important for a biologist of the nonhuman.

At the foundation of the study of literature, then, there is criticism (Bové 2021: 135–85). Although I am not happy at Aristotle's attempt to bring poetry within the critical purview of philosophy, I recognize, with some discomfort, how effectively and almost inescapably he set a basis for criticism as an essential human quality, secondary only to the primary capacity to imitate, to become human in *mimesis*. "Imitation is natural...from childhood....It is also natural for all to delight in works of imitation" (Aristotle 1984: 2318, para. 1448b). The proof of these claims "is shown by experience: though the objects themselves may be painful to see, we delight to view the most realistic representations of them in art." There is yet more and stronger evidence for our delight: "to be learning something is the greatest of pleasures not only to the philosopher but also to the rest of humankind." Needless to say, Felski does not discuss Aristotle on the question of recognition, raising his name only once to cite Paul Ricoeur's important but obvious point that for Aristotle mimesis is creative, not iterative.

Felski and her ephebes move on from discussing the uses of literature to the critique of critique, to a sometimes more general objection to criticism, to sometimes preserving of the word *criticism* for the new modes of doing things with texts. In 2015, the political Right took control of the Danish Government and made draconian cuts to the country's national system of tertiary and graduate education, especially in the humanities.[34] In 2016, that government appointed Felski a Bohr Fellow for five years with funding of over US $4 million. Let me stress that I am not making a personal remark here. Rather I find it interesting that a government made up of neoliberal right-of-center and far-right parties, intent on cutting tertiary education in the humanities, chooses to fund such research agendas as "how to do

34. Wikipedia, "2015 Danish General Election," last edited on July 26, 2022, https://en.wikipedia.org/wiki/2015_Danish_general_election#Aftermath_and_government_formation. See also Myklebust 2017.

things with texts." Let us say the government did not find this work threatening to its own desires. Of course, possibly the award flew in the face of the government.

A general question underlies my references to Felski. Do academic projects replicate or extend modes of cultural and economic motives in the general society, even when the academic workers think of themselves as oppositional or resistant? Does the academy too easily adopt and reiterate new products offered internally that help publication and careers? Does it iterate and normalize those products without sufficient worry, that is, without critical review of the sources and consequences of these new modes? Does the profession proceed as if internal work has no extramural relevance or allegiances? Is it indifferent to the possible extramural origins, such as Silicon Valley or state conflict with geopolitical competitors, that enable and motivate internal rebranding and reconfigurations?

Jill Lepore's (2020) *If Then: How the Simulmatics Corporation Invented the Future* led the author to caution the public about universities' embrace of "data science." She has two primary concerns. First is the waste of resources associated with intellectual faddism. "On a lot of campuses, the word 'data' mashed together with the word 'science' has a sort of alchemical magic. It mints gold! . . . But there is a lot of dross, and it's where you'd go if you were, not to put too fine a point on it, a huckster. Meanwhile, other parts of colleges and university are starving, and the culture as a whole is in a state of seemingly bottomless anguish" (Goldstein 2020). Second "data science" has close family connections, especially through funding sources, with distressingly damaging people, corporations, and technologies that have harmed persons and society. Simulmatics Corporation developed and implemented predictive analytics that "lurks behind the screen of every device." The corporation failed but, as Lepore (2020: 5) shows, it "helped invent the data-mad and near-totalitarian twenty-first century," in which machines and social forces "obsessed with the future" leave us in a state where we are "unable to improve it." Lepore laments that universities have not done the moral critical work necessary to understand and judge the effects of money and its sources on the wave of data science. She gives the wonderful example of Harvard University awarding an honorary degree to Mark Zuckerberg. "This is the person," she says, "whose company has all but destroyed journalism and utterly undermined our system of political representation. In whose name are we endorsing this stuff?" (Goldstein 2020)

Lepore gives us some context for what has happened to the critical fields. The movement toward digital humanities exemplifies the problem. It would displace the critical judgment necessary for the moral review of data science, its sources, and its effects. The recent book *Distant Horizons* is a microexample of the larger crisis. Ted Underwood set out to distinguish fiction from nonfiction, using only internal evidence, by delegating the task to an algorithm. "This is where," he writes, "the technical innovations of the last forty years start to matter" (Underwood 2019: 18). The word *innovation* appears several times throughout the book, when the author identifies digital capacities to answer new questions or when defending machine mining of language and literature from more traditional critics. Underwood took a PhD in English at Cornell, taught at Colby College, rose to become professor of English at the University of Illinois in 2014, and in 2016 moved his tenure to become professor of information sciences at the same university. Underwood rhetorizes his concern for the traditional forms of literary study, explains his affection for literature and respect for his former colleagues, and moves to solve problems against many of their objections. "It is true," he writes, "that numbers tend to become more useful at large scales of inquiry. But this book's emphasis on the very largest historical patterns has been shaped by the temporary rhetorical obstacles that confront a controversial innovation" (167). He also builds his work on Moretti's theory of Distant Reading. What do we have here? A technical solution to a motif legitimated in the language of innovation. The book does not contain an evaluative reflection on what it means to adapt powerfully normative technologies and memes of the ruling class. It does not concern itself with the place of these elements in an unjust society or their desire to displace humanists from the academy and society. The book does not speculate on the consequences of disruptive innovation for the field of literary studies the author left behind or on the broader implications for the social order of the delegitimation and displacement of those work forms replaced by the new technologists' followers.[35] I looked for theoretical and historical reflection on the deeper consequences of this work, and I found none.

This book would legitimate its innovatory successes in terms of knowledge. *Knowledge* is a particularly important and problematic term. I do not mean obvious and tiring things about the perspectival nature of knowledge but the idea that knowledge is an inherent good over and against, for

---

35. "Disruptive technology significantly alters the way businesses or entire industries operate. It often forces companies to change the way they approach their business for fear of losing market share or becoming irrelevant. Recent examples of disruptive technologies include e-commerce and ride-sharing" (Smith 2022).

example, experience, confusion, truth, or imagination. The author tells us that numbers are no more objective than words and that statistical models are just tentative interpretations of evidence (Underwood 2019: xviii). His rhetoric aims to convince his readers that his machine works in the same terms he believes traditional scholars think and work. The utter absurdity of this parallelism never appears in the discussion.

Consider the ancient opposition between knowledge and experience, which we began to touch in Aristotle. Were we speaking in classical Greek or modern German we would have an easier time of this, but in English, we must explain the issue. Let me begin at the end, as it were. Forming a critical humanist through the studies traditionally associated with languages, literature, and history depends on the experiential qualities of education. "Knowledge" lies in a textbook or at the end of a bibliographical search. For example, we can know what Derrida says of Plato, but we do not experience Derrida's encounter with Plato without our own encounters with both, each independently and the two together, with whatever other knowledges and forms of experience we come to understand are necessary to come close to their encounter to judge it or to enable an interested imaginative effort to transport their work to another place of our own making. We cannot become humanists without these critical encounters with other poems and their actions that form us as humanists. Underwood tells us that we can judge the value of his knowledge by examining the code underlying his work. If we find a coding error, then we can reject the knowledge he produces. Of course, we can always argue about what the results "mean," which tells us, presumably, that the knowledge has no meaning. We have a term for believing in such knowledge/meaning dichotomies, which mimic the truth/value dichotomy, and that term is *positivism.*

At least for some time in the nineteenth and twentieth centuries in the world Mr. Putin calls the home of obsolete Western liberalism, universities struggled to defend and promote humanistic forms of educated judgment to exercise some critical control over the power of authorized knowledge formations (Marcus 2019). The Germans theorized the *Geisteswissenschaften* for this reason, and the French what they call *les sciences humaines.* Recent discussions of the Anthropocene, which were preceded by important postcolonial and gender questionings of the anthropos, cast shadows over the ideological human subject at the center of some of these German and French forms. Nonetheless, those shadows only intensify the question, What is the human? which especially technophilic theorists seem to occlude except in technophoric utopianism. Underwood's Moretti-derived title, *Distant Horizons*, belongs to an age that believes in the singularity and expresses itself as snark and trolling; it is an age beyond irony and satire. Digital humanities makes a claim to broad horizons and long historical views, time made space to be covered quickly. Yet, nowhere in the book does the word *colonial* appear (Earhart 2016).[36] I searched the digital copy for *empire*, and the only results—proving the trustworthiness of algorithms—were for the word *empirical*. Gender appears a lot because the algorithm reads grammatical gender. This book serves the interests of a right-wing politics. It removes the various experiences of historical humanistic inquiry from our fields of knowledge and, more important, hides our species' onto-logical capacities to aspire. No discussion of the colonial, of imperialism, or lived gender matters; no discussion of freedom, ethics, and imagination; only knowledge produced in a way that the machine determines, as distant horizons, matter or appear, and these because they supposedly are beyond the vision of a mere human eye.

At one beginning of Western literary criticism and theory in the East-ern Mediterranean millennia ago—and this is the only horizon within which I speak now—Aristotle, in *The Poetics*, lays out a theory of mimesis, which is also a theory of *poiesis*, of poetic creation in art and the social world. He adds to this complex theory, which is already something of a philosophical anthropology, a theory of curiosity, of a desire for creative investigation into the products of *poiesis*. These investigations involve analysis, careful study, and above all judgment. Moreover, in and through all of this, Aristotle asks the basic question, What is the human? He draws upon observation. Fol-lowing his usual method of regression to a source, he observes that children learn by and take delight in imitation. The latter is not copying but inventive replication and variation, the beginning of transport and tradition.[37] The pro-cess evolves into ritual, religion, and most importantly art and the making of political society. For our purposes, the most important Aristotelian contribu-tion to the study of literature lies in the discovery that the impulse to art and politics is both creative and critical (Bové 2021: 135–85). Moreover, and this is vital to the largest argument and is a claim essential to the literary human-ities since at least the fifteenth century in the West, the human is not itself

36. Rather than interrogate the actual historical relations along lines of political economy, the author reflects on her own positionality as a white woman writing on African American culture and on the need for the best tools. The author is a recognized historian of digital humanities and its disruption of established forms. Also see Earhart 2015.

37. I borrow the word *transport* from the poetry of Wallace Stevens (Bové 2021: 116–34).

without these mimetic, poetic, and critical capacities, to which we owe the obligations of nurture and renewal (Bové 2008: 48–50). We understand that the tactics of power in forms of biopolitics, technophilia, the concentration of capital, and denial of education can substantially alter the very being of the anthropos so that whatever consciousness it might have had of its own creative and critical capacities can disappear from its socialized species being. This is one of the conditions for populations to support and desire death-dealing. However, does not the recovery or cultivation of such consciousness hinge upon a repudiation of the anticriticism position? Does it not require an interrogation of the technophilics, whose use of the biosphere as a free commons for the generation and consumption of electricity and rare earth resources is highly irresponsible and dystopic (Pearce 2018)?[38] Does it not also rest upon an experiential and value-laden sense of the relational destruction inherent in the human/nonhuman deception? In other words, does Aristotle's investigation into the work of intellectual curiosity, with its aims in judgment as well as knowledge, give a critical foundation to forms of self-formation that might find themselves productively, actively, and creatively at home in various of *les sciences humaines*? Another way to put this might be to ask how the human mind should best work even in a project aspiring to post-human notions and outcomes. Is the experience of human production for critical as well as pleasurable purposes not essential to the formations of judgment around such new knowledges as statistical biology, active space poetics, and so on? In addition, does the embodied mind not train itself in the relations it exposes and alters, through actions or passions it judges most fit to its responsibilities, even if those are speciescidal, that is, the self-murdering of the species and much of the planet (Friedman 2019)?

All of this is to say that the movement against the critical humanities within the university has been a long-intended rightist political ambition, one that has led the many into serving the politicians of austerity with the models they demand—such as making the humanities entrepreneurial. Curiously, now that neoliberal stress on the entrepreneur has lost cache under authoritarian nationalist politics, a politics that, as in Russia and the PRC, lease out wealth from the state, humanist bureaucrats are attempting to catch up

---

38. See also, MIT, "The Future of Strategic Natural Resources: Environmental Damage," https://web.mit.edu/12.000/www/m2016/finalwebsite/problems/environment.html (accessed August 23, 2020), for an account of the destructive effects of mining the rare earths essential to digital culture and its economic titans' profitability. In an era of concentrated power and gross inequality, see Nicas 2020.

to a neoliberal phase no longer central to political economy (Condee 2019). Propaganda and power are not the same thing of course. In the strongest sense, the Right's relation to wealth and populations requires domination to the exclusion of competing centers of power and prefers amnesia to historical memory. The authoritarian Right destroys independent institutions to concentrate political power in the hands of tyrants. The neoliberal Right gathers wealth and so power within the hands of a few gigantic corporations and unimaginatively and unimaginably rich billionaires. These groups and persons control and dispose immense resources outside democratic control. Policy follows money that sets the infrastructure to control work. Denying independence of action to public and political institutions is the antidemocratic aim of this right. Neoliberal management styles, with their concentration of power in deciding groups, self-buttressed by a belief in data, reclaim resources that once were dispersed to persons, groups, and small institutions to allow for freedom of action and decision. The growth of university bureaucracy during austerity accompanies the loss of faculty power in decision making. Decisionism obliges proletarians to accept direction or welcome nudges (Wallace-Wells 2010; Sunstein 2014).

These systems prefer above all the elimination of critical intelligence, of the values of experience and encounter, of adversarial creation. They have also sadly found within the academy agents of their own purposes, and the politics of austerity has helped divide an intellectual cadre, especially along generational lines, in ways that serve its own interest. We could talk more of hyperspecialization, of the career anxiety and speed up in educational formation that makes earlier career scholars especially unable to spend time in the more expansive work of becoming in the broadest sense a humanist critic rather than a mere local specialist. But for now, we can note the extramural pressures that force change or provide opportunities for change upon the university and the humanists that it once sheltered and nurtured.

References

Alpers, Svetlana. 1988. *Rembrandt's Enterprise: The Studio and the Market*. Chicago: University of Chicago Press.

Arac, Jonathan. 2002. "Anglo-Globalism?" *New Left Review*, July/August. https://new leftreview-org.pitt.idm.oclc.org/issues/II16/articles/jonathan-arac-anglo -globalism.

Arendt, Hannah. 1963. *Eichmann in Jerusalem: A Report on the Banality of Evil*. New York: Viking.

Aristotle. 1984. "Poetics." In *The Complete Works of Aristotle: The Revised Oxford Translation*, vol. 2, edited by Jonathan Barnes, 2316–40. Princeton, NJ: Princeton University Press.

Auerbach, Erich. 1953. "Farinata and Cavalcante." In *Mimesis*, translated by Willard Trask, 174–202. Princeton, NJ: Princeton University Press.

Auerbach, Erich. 1969. "Philology and '*Weltliteratur.*'" Translated by Maire Said and Edward Said, 1–17. *Centennial Review* 13, no. 1: 1–17.

Auerbach, Erich. 1973. "Figura." In *Scenes from the Drama of European Literature,* translated by Ralph Manheim, 11–78. Gloucester, MA: Peter Smith.

Baldwin, James. (1963) 2011. "The Artist's Struggle for Integrity." In *The Cross of Redemption*, edited by Randall Kenan, 50–58. New York: Vintage.

Barthes, Roland. 1968. "La mort de l'auteur." *Manteia*, no. 5: 61–67.

Bartholomae, David, Anthony Petrosky, and Stacey Waite. 2019. *Ways of Reading.* Boston: Bedford/St. Martin's.

Benjamin, Walter. 1999. "Surrealism: The Last Snapshot of the European Intelligentsia." In *Walter Benjamin: Selected Writings,* vol. 2, translated by Edmund Jephcott, edited by Marcus P. Bullock, Howard Eiland, and Gary Smith, 207–21. Cambridge, MA: Belknap Press of Harvard University Press.

Bloom, Harold, Paul de Man, Jacques Derrida, Geoffrey Hartman, and J. Hillis Miller. 1979. *Deconstruction and Criticism.* New York: Seabury Press.

Booth, Wayne. 1961. *The Rhetoric of Fiction.* Chicago: University of Chicago Press.

Bové, Paul A. 2008. *Poetry against Torture: Criticism, History, and the Human.* Hong Kong: Hong Kong University Press.

Bové, Paul A. 2014. "The Human in University Education." *Los Angeles Review of Books*, November 13. https://lareviewofbooks.org/article/human-university-education/.

Bové, Paul A. 2021. *Love's Shadow.* Cambridge, MA: Harvard University Press.

Brouillette, Sarah. 2019. *UNESCO and the Fate of the Literary.* Stanford: Stanford University Press.

Brown, Sarah. 2019. "13 Yale Professors Threatened to Resign From Ethnic Studies. The University Listened." *Chronicle of Higher Education*, May 3. https://www.chronicle.com/article/13-yale-professors-threatened-to-resign-from-ethnic-studies-the-university-listened/.

Christensen, Clayton. (1997) 2013. *The Innovator's Dilemma.* New York: Harper Business.

Cleary, Joseph. 2021. "The English Department as Imperial Commonwealth; or, The Global Past and Global Future of English Studies." *boundary 2* 48, no. 1: 139–76.

Cohen, Margaret. 1989. "Walter Benjamin's Phantasmagoria." *New German Critique*, no. 48: 87–107.

Condee, Nancy. 2019. "Wishful Thinking: The End of Sovereignty in Postcommunism's Third Decade." Presentation, *boundary 2* conference "*b2@Pitt*,"

April 5, Pittsburgh, PA. Posted by *boundary 2* on June 7. YouTube video, 0:34:00. https://www.youtube.com/watch?v=v7o6OLc6mEA.

Damrosch, David, ed. 2014. *World Literature in Theory*. Malden, MA: John Wiley & Sons.

Darnton, Robert. 2010. "Google and the Future of Books: An Exchange." *New York Review of Books*, January 14. https://www.nybooks.com/articles/2010/01/14 /google-the-future-of-books-an-exchange/.

Day, Meagan. 2018. "Capitalism is Ruining Science." *Jacobin*, July 9. https:// www.jacobinmag.com/2018/07/capitalism-science-research-academia -funding-publishing.

Donato, Eugenio. 1993. *The Script of Decadence: Essays on the Fictions of Flaubert and the Poetics of Romanticism*. New York: Oxford University Press.

Earhart, Amy E. 2015. *Traces of the Old, Uses of the New: The Emergence of Digital Literary Studies*. Ann Arbor: University of Michigan Press.

Earhart, Amy E. 2016. "Digital Humanities Futures: Conflict, Power, and Public Knowledge." *Digital Studies/le Champ Numérique* 9. https://doi.org/10.16995 /dscn.1.

Emery, Jacob. 2014. "Jacob Emery Reviews David Damrosch's *World Literature in Theory*." *Asymptote*. https://www.asymptotejournal.com/criticism/david-damrosch -world-literature-in-theory/.

Felski, Rita. 2008. *Uses of Literature*. Malden, MA: Blackwell.

Felski, Rita. 2015. *The Limits of Critique*. Chicago: University of Chicago Press.

Felski, Rita. 2020. *Hooked: Art and Attachment*. Chicago: University of Chicago Press.

Felski, Rita, and Elizabeth S. Anker, eds. 2017. *Critique and Postcritique*. Durham, NC: Duke University Press.

Fraiman, Susan. 1995. "Jane Austen and Edward Said: Gender, Culture, and Imperialism." *Critical Inquiry* 21, no. 4: 805–21.

Friedman, Lisa. 2019. "U.S. Weakens Law Protecting Species at Risk." *New York Times*, August 12.

Goldstein, Evan. 2020. "Higher Ed Has a Silicon Valley Problem: Jill Lepore on How Algorithms Came to Supersede Art, and the Distorting Effect of Money in Academe." *Chronicle of Higher Education*, September 23. https://www .chronicle.com/article/higher-ed-has-a-silicon-valley-problem.

Graff, Agnieszka, Ratna Kapur, and Suzanna Danuta Walters, eds. 2019. "Gender and the Rise of the Global Right." Special issue, *Signs* 44, no. 3. https:// www.journals.uchicago.edu/toc/signs/2019/44/3.

Haffner, Sebastian. 2002. *Defying Hitler: A Memoir*. Translated by Oliver Pretzel. New York: Farrar, Straus and Giroux.

Haw, Jim. 2013. "The UNESCO World Heritage Site Selection Process." *Scientific American*, June 10. https://blogs.scientificamerican.com/expeditions/the -unesco-world-heritage-site-selection-process/.

Hays, Michael. 2020. "Notes Toward a History of Tragedy and the 'Tragic.'" *boundary 2* 47, no. 2: 19–27.

Hepworth, Katherine, and Christopher Church. 2018. "Racism in the Machine: Visualization Ethics in Digital Humanities Projects." *Digital Humanities Quarterly* 12, no. 4. https://www.digitalhumanities.org/dhq/vol/12/4/000408/000408 .html.

Hindley, Meredith. 2018. "The Office of Digital Humanities Turns Ten." *Humanities: The Magazine of the National Endowment for the Humanities* 39, no. 2. https://www.neh.gov/humanities/2018/spring/feature/the-office-digital -humanities-turns-ten.

Jänicke, Stefan, Greta Franzini, Muhammad Faisal Cheema, and Gerik Scheuermann. 2015. "On Close and Distant Reading in Digital Humanities: A Survey and Future Challenges." *STAR*. https://doi.org/10.2312/eurovisstar.20151113.

Jones, Willis A. 2011. "Variation among Academic Disciplines: An Update on Analytical Frameworks and Research." *Journal of the Professoriate* 6, no. 1: 9–27.

Komar, Kathleen L. 1995. "The State of Comparative Literature: Theory and Practice, 1994." *World Literature Today* 69, no. 2: 287–92.

Kosar, Kevin R. 2011. "National Defense Education Act of 1958." Federal Education Policy History, June 3. https://federaleducationpolicy.wordpress.com /2011/06/03/national-defense-education-act-of-1958-2/.

Lepore, Jill. 2020. *If Then: How the Simulmatics Corporation Invented the Future.* New York: Liveright.

Long, Hoyt, and Richard So. 2019. "Trust in Numbers." *Critical Inquiry Online Forum*, April 1. https://critinq.wordpress.com/2019/04/01/computational-literary -studies-participant-forum-responses-6/.

Marcus, Jonathan. 2019. "Putin: Russian President Says Liberalism 'Obsolete.'" *BBC*, June 28. https://www.bbc.com/news/world-europe-48795764.

Mason, Carol. 2019. "Opposing Abortion to Protect Women: Transnational Strategy since the 1990s." *Signs* 44, no. 3: 665–92.

Mitchell, W. J. T. 1980. "On Narrative." *Critical Inquiry* 7, no. 1: 1–4.

Moretti, Franco. 2000. "Conjectures on World Literature." *New Left Review* 1, January/ February. https://newleftreview.org/issues/II1/articles/franco-moretti-conjec tures-on-world-literature.

Moretti, Franco. 2013. *Distant Reading*. London: Verso.

Mufti, Aamir. 2016. *Forget English*. Cambridge, MA: Harvard University Press.

Muschamp, Herbert. 2000. "The Passages of Paris and of Benjamin's Mind." *New York Times*, January 16.

Myklebust, Jan Petter. 2017. "Students to Mobilise against University Budget Cuts." *University World News*, September 16. https://www.universityworldnews .com/post.php?story=20170916055558222.

Nicas, Jack. 2020. "Apple Reaches $2 Trillion, Punctuating Big Tech's Grip." *New York Times*, August 19.

Pearce, Fred. 2018. "Energy Hogs: Can the World's Huge Data Centers Be Made More Efficient." *Yale Environment 360*, April 3. https://e360.yale.edu/features /energy-hogs-can-huge-data-centers-be-made-more-efficient.

Pizer, John. 2000. "'World Literature' Paradigm and Contemporary Cultural Globalization." *Comparative Literature* 52, no. 3: 213–27.

Preciado, Paul B. 2013. Introduction to *Testo Junkie: Sex, Drugs, and Politics in the Pharmacopornographic Era*, 11–12. Translated by Bruce Benderson. New York: Feminist Press.

Rimbert, Pierre. 2020. "La bourgeoisie intellectuelle, une élite héréditaire." *Le Monde diplomatique*, August. https://www.monde-diplomatique.fr/2020/08 /RIMBERT/62101.

Rossiter, Margaret W. 1992. "Philanthropy, Structure, and Personality; or, The Interplay of Outside Money and Inside Influence." In *Science at Harvard University: Historical Perspectives*, edited by Clark A. Elliott and Margaret W. Rossiter, 13–27. London: Associated University Presses.

Said, Edward W. 1978. *Orientalism*. New York: Pantheon.

Said, Edward W. 1993. *Culture and Imperialism*. New York: Alfred A. Knopf.

Salazar, Danica. 2017. "Release Notes: Indian English." *OED Blog*, September 28. https://public.oed.com/blog/september-2017-update-release-notes-indian -english/.

Schiff, Randy P. 2014. "Resisting Surfaces: Description, Distant Reading, and Textual Entanglement." *Exemplaria: Surface, Symptom, and the Future of Critique* 26, nos. 2–3: 273–90.

Scholes, Robert, and Robert Kellogg. 1966. *The Nature of Narrative*. New York: Oxford University Press.

Simms, Brendan. 2019. *Hitler: Only the World Was Enough*. New York: Penguin.

Smith, Tim. 2022. "Disruptive Technology." Investopedia. Updated April 2, 2022. https://www.investopedia.com/terms/d/disruptive-technology.asp (accessed March 11, 2019).

Smithies, James. 2014. "Digital Humanities, Postfoundationalism, Postindustrial Culture." *Digital Humanities Quarterly* 8, no. 1. https://www.digitalhumanities .org/dhq/vol/8/1/000172/000172.html.

Spiliakos, Alexandra. 2017. "Nudging Change: Why We Do What We Do." *Business Insights* (blog), October 13. https://online.hbs.edu/blog/post/nudging-change -why-we-do-what-we-do.

Spillers, Hortense. 2003. *Black and White in Color*. Chicago: University of Chicago Press.

Sunstein, Cass R. 2014. "Nudging: A Very Short Guide." *Journal of Consumer Policy* 37, no. 4: 583–88.

Underwood, Ted. 2019. *Distant Horizons: Digital Evidence and Literary Change*. Chicago: University of Chicago Press.

Valentin, Wilson. 2019. "Farah Jasmine Griffin Chairs New African American and

African Diaspora Studies Department." *Columbia News*, January 3. https://news.columbia.edu/africanamericanstudies.

Wallace-Wells, Benjamin. 2010. "Cass Sunstein Wants to Nudge Us." *New York Times*, May 13.

Williams, Raymond. (1976) 1983. *Keywords: A Vocabulary of Culture and Society*. New York: Oxford University Press.

Yadav, Alok. 2009. "Johann Wolfgang von Goethe (1749–1832) on Weltliteratur." Archived course material. George Mason University. https://www.coursehero.com/file/71530017/Goethe-on-World-Literature-compiled-by-Alok-Yadav-2009pdf/.

Contributors

April Anson is an assistant professor of public humanities at San Diego State University, core faculty for the Institute for Ethics and Public Affairs, and affiliate faculty in American Indian studies. Anson was a Mellon postdoctoral fellow at the University of Pennsylvania, and her work has appeared in *Resilience*, *Environmental History*, *Western American Literature*, and others.

Anindita Banerjee is an associate professor of comparative literature at Cornell University. She chairs the humanities division of the Environment and Sustainability Program in the Colleges of Arts and Sciences and Agriculture and Life Sciences and serves on the advisory board of the Atkinson Center for Sustainability at Cornell.

Paul A. Bové is the author of *Love's Shadow* and edited *boundary 2* from 1988 to 2023.

Leah Feldman is associate professor of comparative literature at the University of Chicago. Her work explores the aesthetics and politics of literary and cultural entanglements that traverse the Caucasus and Central Asia—from the formation of the Soviet empire to its collapse. She is the author of *On the Threshold of Eurasia: Orientalism and Revolutionary Aesthetics in the Caucasus* (2018).

Olivia C. Harrison is associate professor of French and comparative literature at the University of Southern California. Her publications include *Transcolonial Maghreb: Imagining Palestine in the Era of Decolonization* (2016), *Souffles-Anfas: A Critical Anthology from the Moroccan Journal of Culture and Politics* (2016), and essays on North African literature, Beur and banlieue cultural production, and postcolonial theory.

boundary 2 50:1 (2023)   DOI 10.1215/01903659-10192188   ©2023 by Duke University Press

Aamir R. Mufti was born and raised in Karachi and is professor of comparative literature at UCLA. Trained in literature and anthropology, he worked at Columbia University with Edward Said. His major works include *Enlightenment in the Colony: The Jewish Question and the Crisis of Postcolonial Culture* and *Forget English! Orientalisms and World Literatures*.

Donald E. Pease is the Ted and Helen Geisel Third Century Professor in the Humanities and founding director of the Futures of American Studies Institute at Dartmouth. Pease is the author of *Visionary Compacts: American Renaissance Writing in Cultural Context*, *The New American Exceptionalism*, and *Theodor SEUSS Geisel*, and the editor or coeditor of twelve volumes, including *The American Renaissance Reconsidered*, *Cultures of US Imperialism*, *The Futures of American Studies*, *American Studies as Transnational Practice: Turning toward the Transpacific*, and, most recently, *Democratic Cultures and Populist Imaginaries*.

Keep up to date on new scholarship

Issue alerts are a great way to stay current on all the cutting-edge scholarship from your favorite Duke University Press journals. This free service delivers tables of contents directly to your inbox, informing you of the latest groundbreaking work as soon as it is published.

To sign up for issue alerts:

1. Visit **dukeu.press/register** and register for an account. You do not need to provide a customer number.

2. After registering, visit **dukeu.press/alerts**.

3. Go to "Latest Issue Alerts" and click on "Add Alerts."

4. Select as many publications as you would like from the pop-up window and click "Add Alerts."

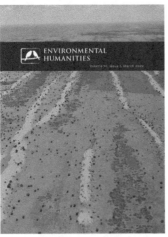